Born in Indonesia of Dutch heritage, Berend experienced his first plane flight at six weeks old and grew up around the world in countries such as England, Holland, the Netherland Antilles and Singapore before settling in South Africa. After completing High School he studied Medicine at the University of Stellenbosch where he met his wife, Ulane.

Specializing in Anesthetics in England and South Africa, Dr. Mets holds Fellowships of the Faculty of Anaesthetists from both the Royal College of Surgeons in England and the College of Medicine in South Africa.

Embarking on an academic career he completed a PhD in Pharmacology at the University of Cape Town, before moving to New York City to become an Assistant Professor of Anesthesiology at Columbia University. Here he continued his research career, was in charge of residency training, and Ulane gave birth to their only son, Elbert.

A Diplomat of the American Board of Anesthesiology, Professor Mets moved to the Pennsylvania State University College of Medicine where he is now Chair of Anesthesiology and Perioperative Medicine.

In pursuit of teaching anesthesia, as well as to experience the remarkable world we live in, Berend has travelled to more than eighty countries, believing that there is one universal language – respect.

A prolific author of academic texts on Anesthesia, Leadership and Education, *Waking Up Safer?* is Dr. Mets' first book.

Visit Dr. Mets' website: www.berendmets.com. You can also follow him on Twitter @Dr_B_Mets.

D0874521

WAKING UP SAFER?

Waking Up Safer?

An Anesthesiologist's Record

BEREND METS

SilverWood

Published in 2018 by SilverWood Books

SilverWood Books Ltd
14 Small Street, Bristol, BS1 1DE, United Kingdom
www.silverwoodbooks.co.uk

ISBN 978-1-78132-749-4 (paperback)
ISBN 978-1-78132-801-9 (ebook)

British Library Cataloguing in Publication Data
A CIP catalogue record for this book is available from
the British Library

Page design and typesetting by SilverWood Books
Printed on responsibly sourced paper

For Ulane

Work Harder
Hope for Luck
Never Give Up

– Vietnamese Proverb

Contents

Acknowledgements

First and foremost, I thank my colleagues and patients for all they have taught me. Wittingly or unconsciously, their stories told in these pages have schooled me to be a safer Anesthesiologist.

Special thanks go to my wife, Ulane. Meeting at medical school, we embarked on life's adventure together and never looked back.

The Rolling Stones too played their part. Re-energizing me with the best rock and roll music a gentleman can hope for – "Gimme Shelter" – the all-time favorite.

My brother-in-law, deserves specific mention. A Submariner and Rear Admiral (Ret) in the South African Navy, Derek Christian read every page, offering comment and advice on the book's writing.

And a disclaimer. A great deal that I have written about my personal and professional medical history is of course from memory and a few notes and records stretching back over thirty years or more. Many of my colleagues appear in these pages, and the words and actions ascribed to them may not be exact, but are included to give a sense of how the conversations or stories flowed. The factual content of the book is as precise as I can establish from the literature reviewed. Where errors occur, they are mine and mine only.

I hope and trust that I have done the rich history of anesthesia justice in these pages.

– Berend Mets, 2018

An Anesthesiologist's Record

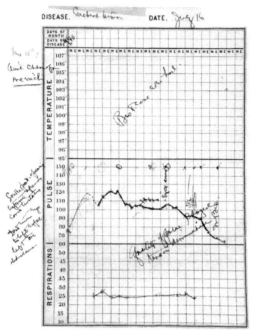

One of the first chloroform anesthesia records: Dr. Harvey Cushing, July 16, 1895.[1]

Great knowledge comes from the humblest of origins.
– *John Littlewood*

I gave my first anesthetic on January 4, 1982.

Three days previously, I woke up in a hospital bed – an intravenous drip in my arm – to the sound of nurses singing in the New Year at Edendale Hospital, South Africa.

My inaugural anesthetic was as terrifying to administer as the first recorded nitrous oxide anesthetic on December 11, 1844. At that time, sitting in the operating chair, Horace Wells inhaled deeply from a silk bag filled with nitrous oxide "till insensibility relaxed the muscles of his arms – his hands fell on his breast – his head dropped on the head-rest," allowing Dr. John Riggs to painlessly extract an offending tooth. Wells and Riggs had agreed that they would "push the administration of nitrous oxide to a point hitherto unknown."

This resulted in Wells becoming completely unconscious and Riggs commenting, "we knew not whether death or success confronted us."[2]

Fortunately, general anesthesia, the administration of drugs to induce reversible coma – not death – was the happy outcome of this historic event.

This balance between life and death – induced to avoid the memory or pain of surgery – is the practicing anesthesiologist's daily concern.

Before anesthesia, very few surgeries were performed. When done at all, operations were limited in scope and often only a last resort, with death as a common outcome. With the evolution of anesthetic practice, surgery has become essentially safer. Death associated with anesthesia improving ninety-fold from one per 1,560 administrations in 1954[3] to one per 142,857 administrations in 2014.[4]

The author, a professor of anesthesiology, had the good fortune of learning, practicing and teaching anesthesia in the midst of this trajectory. Starting anesthetic practice with just a finger on the pulse – as the monitor of patient well-being – and progressing to providing the most sophisticated cardiac anesthetics in environments that resemble the inside of a Boeing cockpit in complexity.

This anesthesiologist's record tells the story of the evolution of anesthetic practice; allowing operations to be performed on ever sicker patients, with increasing safety.

1

Beginnings

How the author came to specialize in anesthetics

Edendale Hospital, Kwazulu, Natal, 1982.

You are never more alive than when you are scared to death.
– *Anonymous*

In the early morning of New Year's Day 1982, I found myself, barely conscious, lying on a cold operating room floor. I was trying to get up but I could not. An anaesthetist roused from his semi-somnolent state by my collapse was poking my outstretched arm, trying to start an intravenous line. He was not succeeding.

Earlier, the last day of my surgical internship had started off reasonably normally in the surgical out patient department of Edendale Hospital.

The massive hospital, an imposing red-brick building, lay on the slopes of a hill overlooking the Mzunduzi River in the lovely green pastoral landscape of Kwazulu, Natal. Created as a Bantustan, Kwazulu* was intended by the apartheid government to serve as a semi-independent homeland for the Zulu nation. Built in Edendale Township, on land settled by a hundred families a century earlier, the hospital had grown to over 1,600 beds. The surrounding verdant area, from where many patients came, was crisscrossed by dusty roads, winding foot paths, Zulu huts and make shift lean-tos. Sturdily built brick houses dotted nearby Plessislaer, a spot with a tragic history.

In January 1839 a group of Voortrekkers led by Jan du Plessis, harboring fresh memories of recent Zulu battles at Blood River, arrived in the area and set up their laager. A laager is an encampment – established by circling wagons – to defend against Zulu attack. One cold winter's night, a fire broke out from an unguarded candle, igniting stores of gunpowder with the loss of ten lives. Two children lay buried in Plessislaer; their grave stones standing close to Edendale Hospital's doctors' quarters, where we would see in the New Year.[1]

Apartheid South Africa was at full throttle in 1982. The Nationalist government in power ran a police state with segregated schools, transportation, townships and hospital facilities. All blacks, be they Xhosa, or Zulu, were classified "non-white." Only "non-white" patients were seen at Edendale hospital while all "white" patients were seen at Grey's Hospital in neighboring Pietermaritzburg. Nine kilometers away, a long winding road meandered through the country-side from Pietermaritzburg, on to Henley Dam, bussing Zulu patients to the

---

* Place of the Zulus in the Zulu language.

hospital gate and beyond; creating a hub of activity around its entrance.

Zulu patients were not always sure about the value of the country's fourth largest hospital in their midst, believing that it was the place you went to die. Frequenting the village Sangoma first to find a cure – the diviner would incorrectly identify their source of illness. Then, with incantations and the throwing of bones, ineffective, sometimes toxic remedies were prescribed, sickening the patient further and delaying treatment. Arriving at the hospital with advanced disease, the epithet, "the place you go to die," became a self-fulfilling prophecy.

The other reason many patients died in Edendale Hospital was because of the Zulus proud tradition as a warrior nation. On weekends and especially on New Year's Eve – fueled by copious amounts of sorghum beer – coupled with a penchant for armed conflict with pangas* and knob kieries,† Zulu tribes would attack each other with violent vengeance.

If not always popular with the locals, Edendale Hospital was a very popular training site for graduating medical students to complete the required intern year as a house officer. There were around thirty highly sought after house officer positions a year. Consequently, many applications from South Africa's five traditionally "white" and two traditionally "black" medical schools crossed the superintendent, Dr. J. G. Walker's, desk. Especially popular because Edendale had full-time specialist appointments for all of the departments, despite being somewhat under-resourced by university teaching hospital standards. Accordingly, interns had enormous consultant-level experience to gain, while still having a great deal of autonomy.

So too on New Year's Eve, 1982.

The surgical team that day comprised four interns, one surgical registrar, and one surgical consultant. All had drawn the short straws; no one volunteered for this last day of the year. Everyone was planning to celebrate in the doctors' pub, Easy Riders, close to the graves of Plessislaer. We also knew that we were in for a very hectic night. The surgical out patient department (SOPD) would soon look like a war zone from the drunken brawling that was common in Kwazulu. We knew too that we would be lucky to see the surgical consultant at all, until the next morning's intensive care rounds. At

* Pangas are very long and sharp knives.
† Knob kieries, are wooden clubs with a hard knob at one end, very effective skull splitters.

these rounds, having completed our year's training, we would meet up with next year's interns – about to face their first day – starting the whole year's process all over again.*

Nonetheless, we were ready and willing, and prepared to manage SOPD without our surgical consultant. After all, we four interns were now veterans of a year of internship experience. We had learnt many things about patient care – not found in medical textbooks – that would serve us well on this last, busiest, surgical day of the year.

For example, we were now masters of resuscitation with intravenous fluids and blood products – experience gained through many nights on call in SOPD that frequently played out like this:

Two or three vehicles of various description would arrive with horns blaring or sirens shrieking, disgorging the victims from a Zulu tribal clash at the front door of the hospital and into SOPD. Blood from recently opened stab wounds leaking on stretchers and floors, leaving a trail into the examination rooms. The stench of alcohol and vomit permeating the department as the drunken victims, shouting abuse, were manhandled on to stretchers so that we doctors could evaluate, treat and establish surgical necessity. Quickly placing two or three intravenous lines, we ran wide-open intravenous fluids until the first recordable blood pressure could be found. The ever present nurses restraining, mollifying and assisting the bellicose patients, while the hospital guards assigned to SOPD made sure that no one still carried a panga or knob kierie with them. Selected for their fearsome height, weight and fighting spirit, the hospital guards strictly enforced the "No Weapons" signs posted at the entrance. Any patient found by the guards to have a weapon was unceremoniously picked up and literally dumped outside the hospital gates, no matter the extent of their injury, never to be allowed access again.†

Given the chaotic violence we contended with, we interns had learned how to rapidly ascertain whether patients were dead or alive or just blind drunk.‡

This was critically important, but not always easy as it was usually in the dark. A police van arriving outside the hospital entrance, blue light flashing –

---

* Edendale Hospital was one of the first hospitals in the country to have a specialized intensive care unit, which was rudimentary at best, by today's standards, having a few ventilators and beds.

† This extreme measure had been found necessary as there were multiple instances of assaults, some leading to murder, through stabbings on the hospital wards.

‡ The ability to determine life or death became very important for me as an anesthesiologist, but that's in the future.

a doctor would be summoned by a constable to climb in the back to certify another victim of the tribal warfare; dead or alive. Inevitably occurring at the same time that the mayhem of the live victims was unfolding in SOPD, this left our colleagues one doctor down, trying to sort out this critical situation in the back of a dimly lit police van with a failing flashlight.

The ability to ascertain life or death speedily was also important in responding to emergencies within the vast hospital. As an intern, if you did ever get the chance to sleep in the doctors' quarters, you left your room telephone number with the switchboard so that you could be called urgently to render care, from anywhere in the depths of the hospital.* An emergency telephone call from a ward could go like this: "Doctor, the patient is gasping." "Gasping" was a term commonly used by nursing staff to communicate that the patient was having breathing problems. Medically speaking, when patients are near death, they breathe with what is known as agonal breathing, which resembles gasping. The new intern, on hearing this, would run – literally – to the far-flung ward to attempt to save this life, usually to arrive, unfortunately, at a long-dead patient. But now, after a year, we were experienced interns in the matter of determining life or death. If faced with the call, "Doctor, the patient is gasping," we would not run immediately but ask, "Sister, has the patient *stopped* gasping (i.e. are they dead) or is the patient *still* gasping (i.e. are they alive)?" If the latter, then, we must run – and quickly.

Veteran interns like ourselves were also adept at identifying the "stabbed heart." Given the Zulu fondness for hand to hand combat with sharp knives, a common presentation was a patient with a small stab wound in the chest, extremely low blood pressure – not amenable to intravenous fluids – with engorged veins in the neck. The dagger had penetrated through the pericardium – a thick fibrous sack encasing the heart – and on into the blood-filled chambers below. Blood leaking into the pericardial sack – which was unyielding – constraining the heart-pump function with deadly effect; if not treated quickly.

Life-saving chest tube drain placement was also an important skill developed as an intern – expeditiously placed to relieve the built-up gas or blood from a knife puncture to the chest causing lung collapse. On some particularly heavy days, three doctors at a time were deployed to place these drains to

---

* In those days there were no beepers or cell phones and the only communication was directly by telephone.

21

clear the backlog of patients. A risky procedure at best. Misplacement of the chest tube into the heart resulting in immediate death from exsanguination – catastrophic blood loss.

So, in short, we were ready for New Year's Eve. But let me recount how it all began.

My mother, Thea Pleijsier, detested the smell of oil refinery fumes in Indonesia. Especially when she was pregnant. She disliked even more the fear induced by the screeching sound of German V2 rockets launched from occupied Holland to attack London in late 1944. Many were launched from The Hague, where she grew up. The fear was not the rocket launch itself, but a possible launch failure. Rockets could explode or fall back on to the families below, killing and maiming. Consequently, each screeching launch was closely listened to for sounds of falter, and its dissipation met with a sigh of relief. Thirteen is a young age to be in a war; such memories, as well as the privation that her baker's family had to endure during the occupation, contributed to Thea's wishes to become a nurse and leave Holland if that opportunity arose. As a nurse, Thea knew she would be able to alleviate others' suffering and so after the war she enrolled in nursing school at the Zuidwal Hospital. There, serving as a student nurse in the operating theatres, she met my father, a young doctor, perfecting his surgical skills.

Johann Mets was born in Bandung on the island of Java, a part of the Indonesian archipelago. His father served as a captain in the Dutch Army in charge of a large ammunitions factory supporting the war effort against the Japanese. Munitions were in great demand to supply the Dutch and Indonesian soldiers fighting the invading Japanese militia and so Captain Mets was soon promoted to serve as a major. After Pearl Harbor and the fall of Singapore, the fall of Java occurred in 1942 – the Japanese army occupying Indonesia. Johann being only seventeen, could not volunteer for the flying corps, as he had wanted to, but he was an experienced boy scout. Thus, together with a group of his scout friends, he enlisted in a volunteer training corps. His unit secretly tasked with pulling together arms, ammunitions and provisions, to set up a concealed camp for Indonesian and Dutch resistance fighters in the surrounding jungle. Under the watchful eyes of Japanese soldiers and secret police, the feared Kempetai, this was a perilous undertaking.

Smuggling individual carbines, revolvers, pistols and grenades by bicycle, to hidden locations for safekeeping, Johann and his three friends set about the task at hand. Using trail experience and knowledge of the surrounding area gained on scouting trips, they planned to hide the armaments in a secret spot cut into the jungle alongside a well-known path outside Bandung. The plan duly executed – the arms and provisions carefully buried at the specified location – the friends spent a cold night huddled together in the jungle. Rising before dawn, they cut their way back through the jungle, misjudging the exit point on to the adjacent road. Spotted by local farmers, the alarm was raised. Returning down the jungle path they were ambushed by local Indonesian field police at gun point. Problematic at best as three of the four friends still had revolvers hidden in their pockets. If these guns were found by the Japanese, execution for gun running was their certain fate. The Indonesian policemen had been charged by the Japanese to apprehend and imprison suspicious individuals. Grasping what Johann and his friends were up to, the Indonesian police, no friends of the Japanese invaders, were probably secretly on the boys side. Recognizing that the boy scouts had concealed weapons that needed to be jettisoned, the police didn't search them. Instead they walked well in front of the friends down the jungle path – loudly talking to each other – with never a glance backwards and with no one bringing up the rear. The three revolvers and an incriminating military map were quietly returned to the jungle forever. Hence, when the boys were imprisoned by the Kempetai, they were completely clean. Their lives had been saved by the Indonesian police and they could stick to their agreed to story that they were boy-scouting in the area when spotted coming out of the jungle. The boys were separated and incarcerated, interrogated and suffered multiple beatings, but never revealed their true role as gun runners. For his troubles, my father was put in solitary confinement and spent the next three years in various Japanese concentration camps in Indonesia, many times serving as a nursing assistant, which confirmed his wish to pursue medicine as a career. Following the dropping of the atomic bombs on Hiroshima and Nagasaki in early August 1945, the Japanese Emperor capitulated and Johann Mets was freed on August 17 – three years to the day after he was picked up in the jungle by the Indonesian police. In fact, all of my father's family were interned in separate Japanese concentration camps around Indonesia. Nonetheless they were of one mind – the dropping of the atomic bombs saved their lives – sure in the belief that they would have died in the concentration camps otherwise. Major Mets, my grandfather, served most of the war in the excruciating Death Camps of Burma, building the planned railroad over the river Kwai. He was freed too, at the end of the war, eventually to return to civilian life in Holland and an early death – aged only sixty-one.

In turn, Johann was also evacuated by ship and returned to Holland to study medicine at Leiden University.

In 1952, the now Doctor Johann Mets was assisting an operation in the theatres of the Zuidwal Hospital in The Hague. As now, so too then, all surgeries are performed with everyone in the room hatted, masked and gowned, so that only the upper face and eyes are visible. He looked up from the surgical field to see the surgical nurse, meeting her eyes...and, "Her eyes responded." Dr. Mets took this as a hopeful sign and courtship followed, leading to marriage.

The KLM* McDonald Douglas DC-3 aircraft could not land on the airstrip until the goats had been cleared from the runway. The plane had to circle twice before a safe landing could be assured. The trip had been a long one stretching over two days, starting at Schiphol in Amsterdam, with refueling in Rome, and then an overnight stay in Bangkok, before flying through Jakarta, with a final flight to Plaju in Sumatra.

My father had joined Shell International as a medical officer, serving as a doctor for staff and families stationed to manage an oil refinery in Palembang, Indonesia. He wanted to return to the country of his birth to practice medicine. My mother had been easily persuaded to leave Holland and by now was heavily pregnant. She was not quite so sure, though, when she arrived in their new home in Plaju. No matter how conveniently it was stationed next to the hospital where I was to be born: she suffered mightily from the overbearing heat and ever present smell of refinery fumes.

Medical officers in training at base hospitals like this one in Plaju, in 1956, were expected to develop the necessary skills to be able to serve patients in jungle hospitals around Indonesia. By themselves as the only practicing doctor for miles around, they needed to learn to perform anesthetics and surgeries, perfect pediatric and obstetric practice, and be able to manage patients without

---

* KLM the Koninklijke Luchtvaart Maatschappij ("Royal Aviation Society") was established in 1919. The first international flights were from Schiphol to Batavia, now known as Jakarta, the capital of Indonesia.

physician colleagues to back them up. If they planned to have their own children, while serving in such single-doctor hospitals, they would need to learn how to deliver their wives by themselves under such circumstances. Hence, on a very hot August day, at one o'clock in the morning – my mother well recalls the clock on the wall – my father delivered me by himself. A colleague doctor standing behind a white screen just in case he needed help.

From there, following his career as a refinery doctor for Shell, we lived all over the world, travelling throughout Indonesia, Singapore, England, Holland, the West Indies and eventually settled in South Africa, where I in turn pursued medical training.

As a medical student at Stellenbosch University in 1980, I was not particularly impressed with Anesthetics.* We had received a few lectures on the subject during medical school, but the professor had said it was too dangerous to know too much about.† So instead of lectures on anaesthesia, we were shown movies about other subjects. We did however have to shadow a number of specialist anaesthetists in the operating theatre – and they seemed clever enough – but the practice just seemed boring. This impression was reinforced by the fact that, at the time, one often saw an anesthetist sitting in the operating room reading the daily newspaper, while semi-observing the surgery from a distance. This did not look like the dynamic doctor I wanted to be. So I never really planned to specialize in anesthetics. However, in order to be registered as a medical practitioner in South Africa, interns had to complete twenty documented anaesthetic administrations and complete a full year as a medical officer before they were allowed to enter specialist training. I had intended to either become a general practitioner or specialize in internal medicine after this medical officer year so I enrolled for three months of anesthetics and orthopedics and six months of obstetrics to fulfill this medical officer year requirement. Some experience in anesthesia was thought useful as many general practitioners at that time provided anaesthetics in South Africa. All I had to do to get started on my medical officer year was complete my internship.

*

<hr>

* This is the English spelling for the name of the specialty. In United States English, this is spelt as anesthetics, and interchangeably used with anesthesiology as the word to describe the specialty. Confusingly, in the U.S.A. an anesthetist describes a nurse anesthetist. An anesthesiologist describes a doctor who has completed specialist residency training in anesthesia. I will use the English spelling in the chapters referring to training in South Africa and England, and the American spelling at all other times.

† Lest we try administering anesthetics without further training.

The afternoon in SOPD was hotting up. The double front door of the Edendale Hospital was wide open to receive patients. Dusty cars and ambulances were arriving, ferrying patients from the surrounding area. A huge guard stood sentry to ensure that no weapons were brought in and that general order was maintained. The hospital doors opened on to a large hallway with an immaculately polished terracotta floor allowing access to the bank of three elevators, leading upstairs to the second floor, where the operating rooms were already in action. Off to the left, the stairway reached the six stories above. Patients with chest drains, draining into water-sealed bottles – bubbling with each exhalation – could be seen walking up and down these stairs, dangling the bottles on a string by their sides.* If you turned to the right, as you entered the hospital, a wide brick passageway opened on to a large patient waiting area already crammed with a number of stretchers holding patients in various stages of distress. Intravenous fluid bottles were hanging overhead. Some patients already had chest drains in place, others were being readied to go to a surgical room where new chest drains could be placed and other minor operations performed. Others still were being prepared for surgery on the second floor above. Meanwhile, in the four examination bays to the right of this overcrowded waiting area, patients were being evaluated and treated. These bays opened on to a common corridor. Each had a bed, a blood pressure cuff mounted on the wall, as well as a plastic curtain allowing privacy, when needed, and a place to hang the multiple intravenous fluid bags or bottles that were needed for resuscitation. Empty intravenous bottles already littered the floor, left there in the need for haste in resuscitation. A few patients had been seen earlier for regular complaints, an acute appendicitis or minor surgical concerns, but by late afternoon, on New Year's Eve, the bays were filled with patients, usually drunk, stabbed, or assaulted, and bleeding. With many more to come.

Tonight, I was assigned as the surgical intern who would assist the surgical registrar, Dr. Norman Dubazane in the operating theatres. Already four patients were being readied for surgery, so I knew that I would spend the rest of the night assisting, rather than triaging and resuscitating the wounded, with my three colleagues, Drs. Steff Schlagintweit, Mark Slack and Norman Miller in SOPD. We had agreed however, that if at all possible, the whole surgical

---

* The physiotherapists advised patients to walk up and down these stairs to re-expand their lungs, because the vigorous breathing this required, forced deep inhalations and exhalations, the trapped pleural air escaping as bubbles through the underwater drains.

team would down tools just before midnight, so we too could join our thirty graduating intern colleagues at the Easy Riders doctors' pub, to see in the New Year together. The culmination of the internship year is a momentous occasion for any young doctor. Having celebrated the New Year together we would then get on with the rest of the evening's work in theatre and SOPD afterwards.

This is exactly what happened:

Norman led the operating surgical team and we worked non-stop until 11:45p.m. We checked that all patients had been attended to in SOPD, let the nurses know where we would be, and joined our colleagues to see in the new year at Easy Riders.

We were back in the OR operating at around thirty minutes after midnight with a full slate of surgical patients till the morning. The second case after midnight required surgical exploration of the belly for "stabbed abdomen." An abdominal X-ray had shown free air under the patient's diaphragm. Having examined the patient in SOPD, my colleagues had established "rebound pain," so there was a concern that bowel might have been perforated by the stab wound, with dire consequences. Peritonitis could develop if the hole was not found and sutured closed. The patient had been anaesthetized and intubated and the abdominal wall incised and opened by Dr. Dubazana. Norman was operating from the patient's left while I was assisting from the right. The usual procedure was that the surgeon placed sutures and the assistant would use scissors, at the surgeon's request, to cut off the tied sutures. The surgeon announcing, "Cut, cut," to indicate when to do so. We were well into the operation, and had both been standing for about an hour and a half. Norman again said, "Cut," and then louder, "Cut! …CUT!" when I failed to respond. I was trying to, but couldn't. I was feeling hot, my brain fuzzy – I could not see clearly. I said, "I can't," and fell to the ground.

I found myself, barely conscious, lying on my back, on the cold operating theatre floor. I was trying to get up, but I could not. I knew that this was hypoglycemia – low blood sugar – at the end of a very long day. But I could not move. I was trying to speak to the anaesthetist who had bent down to see what was wrong, trying to tell him that all I need is some glucose. But I could not get up and I could not really say anything. The cold floor, did feel good, though. After multiple painful attempts, the anaesthetist eventually succeeded in placing an intravenous catheter in my arm and started the administration of glucose. I was picked up and transferred out of the theatre across the corridor and onto a hospital bed. This was the "call" bed in what passed for the doctors' lounge. Really, just a small room. Across the hallway from the theatre, the room looked out over the Edendale hills beyond and was situated on the second floor over the entrance hallway of the hospital. I remember little else.

But I do remember that I woke up on New Year's Day, the sun starting to stream in through the window, with a reassuring intravenous drip in my arm, to the sound of the nurses downstairs at the hospital entrance singing in the new year. They were singing, Nkosi Sikelel iAfrika,* and using the customary discarded wet tea leaves to sweep up the blood from the terracotta floor below. Then they would polish it back to its former immaculate red sheen – a good start to the first day of 1982.

On January 4, I gave my first anaesthetic in the same operating theatre, where I so recently had spent time on the floor. Dr. Colin Kirkpatrick, who had just retired from the National Health Service in England, was to be my proctor for this first case. He was there to assist and instruct whenever I needed help. There were seven operating theatres in Edendale hospital at that time, staffed by three specialist anaesthetists, one or two registrars in training, and a number of medical officers like myself. We had all signed up for a three- to six-month rotation. This was a scary business to those who understood what was going on. We had little to no training and were soon left on our own to fend for our patients.

The reason that patients generally did well was that we administered basic anaesthetics to usually healthy adult patients for relatively simple orthopedic, gynecological and surgical procedures. Also, we had simple anaesthetic devices, minimal anaesthetic drugs and little to no monitoring equipment, so there really was not much that could distract us from watching the patient very closely with a finger continuously on the pulse.

Here is how it went, as I recall now thirty-five years on. The young man was deposited outside of the operating theatre on a stretcher by a nursing aide. He was to have an orthopedic procedure on his leg for which a general anaesthetic was indicated. I did not speak much Zulu but, "Kunjane," How are you?, was

---

* Nkosi Sikelel, already widely sung, would become the National Anthem, when the National Party lost power to the African National Congress in 1994, and the country was freed of the apartheid system.

always met with a smile and the reply, "Longile," I am well. I was nervous, my heart beating in my chest, just under the throat, my palms slightly sweaty; I was about to administer drugs that in any other setting would be lethal. I placed an intravenous (IV) line in my patient's arm vein and an infusion of Plasmalyte B fluid was started to administer IV anaesthetic drugs. Previously, I had checked the anaesthetic machine, tested what little equipment we had, and aspirated and mixed anaesthetic drugs from their vials into readied syringes.

The only monitoring device, a cuff to manually measure blood pressure, was attached to the patient's arm. I felt the patient's radial pulse, on the thumb-side of his wrist, to determine its strength and how fast it was going. (Mine was going faster.) Then intravenous sodium pentothal was administered through the fast-running IV until the patient was unconscious – euphemistically called "falling asleep." This was quickly followed by a drug, Alloferine, to paralyze the patient's muscles, so that I could intubate (place a red rubber tube) via the mouth using a laryngoscope with a light to view the opening (glottis) to the trachea. Having listened to the patient's lungs to ensure that the endotracheal tube was in the correct location, I then added in halothane, an anaesthetic gas, to continue the anaesthetic throughout the operation. The endotracheal tube was connected to the anaesthesia hoses and the Bird ventilator[*] was started to ensure mechanical ventilation of the lungs. Halothane was used to keep my patient unconscious, morphine was given IV to decrease the anaesthetic requirement and provide pain relief after the operation. During the course of the operation I sat with my finger on the patient's pulse to measure the heart rate and intermittently measure blood pressure, jotting these findings down on a paper anaesthetic record. Adjusting the anaesthetic depth by dialing in more or less halothane concentration as required. I gave Plasmalyte B, an intravenous fluid provided in glass bottles, as necessary, to counter drops in blood pressure or blood loss. When the operation was almost completed, I started to relax a little and administered a paralytic reversal agent called neostigmine mixed with a little atropine – to counteract the heart rate slowing that occurs with this drug. I switched off the halothane and squeezed the anaesthetic bag to continue ventilation of the lungs, having switched off the Bird ventilator. This

---

[*] Forrest Morton Bird (1921-2015), an American aviator, inventor and biomedical engineer, created one of the first reliable mass produced mechanical ventilators. Noisy, complicated to use, and surrounded by a see-through green plastic capsule about the size of a shoe box, the Bird Mark 7 Respirator was widely adopted and fondly just called the Bird ventilator.

would serve to allow the halothane to be exhaled from his body and would eventually result in him "waking up" from anaesthesia. He started coughing on the endotracheal tube, and when fully awake, trying to pull the endotracheal tube out himself. I took it out, with a last squeeze on the anaesthesia bag to fill his lungs with oxygen. This I did, just in case he had laryngospasm (closure of the airway). Filling the lungs with oxygen first would buy me precious time to treat this complication before he started going blue from lack of oxygen going to his brain. Fortunately, my first anaesthetic went off uneventfully to my great relief. I was pleased and surprised. I had just administered deadly drugs to a totally alive patient, inducing reversible coma and total paralysis of his muscles, which if not supported, would result in certain death from asphyxia. I had then sustained and monitored him, keeping him unconscious so that he had no memory or pain during the surgery and then – reversing the situation – had brought him back to life afterwards.

I was hooked. It was a mysterious and magical process, affording almost complete control over the patient's life. It was inherently scary, but immensely satisfying and fun to do.

"You are never more alive than when you are scared to death."

I resolved to become an anesthesiologist.

2

A Brief History of Anesthesia

From 1842 to 1956

A replica of Morton's first ether inhaler, with two original books by Joseph Priestley.

We knew not whether death or success confronted us.

– Dr. John Riggs (1845)

Napoleon's surgeon in chief, Baron Dominique Lorey, relied on a sharp blow to the colonel's head to remove a bullet from his foot. A blow to the side of the face was a well accepted technique to induce anesthesia used by Professor Weinlecher of Vienna and others until the end of the nineteenth century.[1] This was not, however, universally well received by the patient. The colonel in question stating, "Sir, you have taken cowardly advantage of my condition." The surgeon replying, "The operation is over, here is the bullet, please give me your hand."

The scope of surgery possible with such crude anesthetic techniques was obviously limited.

Hence the history of surgery and anesthesia are closely intertwined. As anesthetic techniques developed, so more extensive surgery could be performed.[2] Today hearts, lungs or livers can be surgically replaced while the patient is anesthetized and medically managed by anesthesiologists.

Recognizing the importance of the invention of surgical anesthesia to the development of surgery, 'Doctor's Day' in the U.S.A. annually commemorates the first anesthetic provided by Dr. Crawford Long – using sulphuric ether – on March 30, 1842.

While general anesthesia is thus a relatively new invention, surgery is not. Surgery has been with us for centuries, described as far back as ten thousand years Before the Common Era (BCE). However, it was very limited in scope.

Archaeologists have found evidence of Inca human skulls which had been trephined – holes drilled in the skull – thought to allow evil humors to escape. Many of these exhumed skulls show that healing had taken place before death, indicating that this brutal practice occurred while the patients were alive and likely, fully conscious.

As early as 1700 BCE, Egyptian surgeons removed tumors and aneurysms, literally burning the breast tumors off of the patients. So common was limited surgery at this time that the Babylonian Code of Hammurabi listed the costs of different surgeries, including incision of tumors. Uncommon however – in fact almost non-existent – was a mention of pain relief for such surgical interventions.[3]

Claudius Galen (129-199 BCE) a Greek philosopher, who served the Roman empire as a surgeon to gladiators, performed amputations, cataract extractions, and Cesarean sections. He was considered very effective. Only five gladiators under his care died, while sixty had died during the previous surgeon's tenure. To perfect his knowledge of surgical anatomy – and so to advance surgical techniques – he vivisected monkeys and pigs because human dissection was prohibited by the Romans. Galen published extensively in Greek, reputedly as many as five hundred treatises, which perpetuated for centuries the many errors of extrapolation from these live animal dissections to human anatomy. Nevertheless, his fame and writings informed surgical procedures until the Renaissance.

During the Middle Ages and beyond, Church edicts further restricted the use of surgery. In 1163 monks were forbidden to shed blood, and thus operate, so surgery was performed by barbers instead. Having a natural proclivity with knives – cutting hair and shaving – barbers also extracted teeth, repaired hernias, removed bladder stones and cataracts, earning the name, "barber surgeons." The red and white "barber pole," still used today, signifying the bandages and the bloodletting which was an added mainstay of a barber's practice.

Pain management during this long era of surgical procedures has been poorly described – often finding a basis in the use of alcohol, opium, cannabis or mandragora,* an extract from plants.[4] Perhaps the earliest description hails from China, where in 500 BCE Hua Tuo combined wine and some herbs in a mixture named "mafeisin" – better known as "cannabis boil powder." During 40-90 CE another Greek, Pedanius Dioscorides, used opium and mandragora to minimize pain from surgery. He was later credited with coining the word "anesthesia" that described the insensate state so produced. It is however unlikely that the anesthetic state was reliably achieved using these drugs. And, in addition to being ineffective, would often be the death of the patient.

Alcohol would seem to be a natural anesthetic and has been used throughout the ages. It is unreliable in its effect. Overdosing can kill and any amount causing inebriation can result in belligerence, lack of co-operation and vomiting. Vomiting in turn precludes further administration (except per rectum, which is even more unreliable). The inebriated surgical patient needing to be tied down to provide the desired immobility to perform the operation.

Opium in overdose could also kill by stopping breathing, while mandragora

---

* Hyoscine, an amnestic sedative which unreliably minimizes recall of the surgery.

was not without problems either, causing extreme confusion, overheating of the body and so, death.

In the Middle Ages, a soporific sponge was used. "Take…opium, juice of hyoscyamine, juice of hemlock, poppy, mandragora, Ivy…and put these altogether in a vessel and plunge there in a new sea-sponge just as it comes from the sea. And put this in the sun during the dog-days until all the liquid is consumed." When the dried sponge was needed for a planned surgery, it was wetted first, placed under the nose of the patient and deep breathing encouraged until sleep ensued. After the operation, the patient was revived with a new sponge soaked in vinegar.[5]

One of the reasons why the practice of anesthesia did not progress was because none of these approaches were standardized. Nor were there attempts to purify or regulate doses for administration, with the adherent problem that in many instances death rather than pain relief was the result.

So, as an alternative, physical measures to relieve the pain from surgery were tried. An approach was to apply local pressure to nerves supplying the body part where surgery was contemplated or to administer ice to deaden the pain. Alternatively a tourniquet was wound tightly around a limb, cutting off all blood supply, in an attempt to mitigate the excruciating pain from amputation. Yet another approach was used for circumcision or castration by the gelders of India. A rope was tightened around the neck or finger pressure applied to the carotid arteries leading to the brain. Resulting in temporary unconsciousness, this allowed the operation to be performed – quickly.

In 1275, a seminal event occurred in the history of anesthesia which would bear fruit only centuries later. The well-known Spanish alchemist Raymond Lully mixed vitriol (sulphuric acid) with wine. After distillation, this left a whitish liquid – sulphuric ether – which he called sweet vitriol. Lully had no use for this at the time. Six centuries were to pass before William T. Morton would administer this compound in the first public demonstration of a surgical ether anesthetic, in 1846.

During the Renaissance, with the waning influence of the Church and the prohibition of human dissection lifted, surgical techniques advanced. Publication of the classic book *On the Fabric of the Human Body* by Andreas Vesalius in 1543 rectified many of the errors in human anatomy perpetuated by Galen's writings. A new era of discovery in surgery dawned, fueled by the increasing tension between barber surgeons and the French academic surgeons who were being trained in academic institutions. While barber surgeons were more accessible to patients, the academic surgeons were becoming more learned as Latin texts were translated to French, advancing new operative techniques.

In 1540, Valerius Cordis, a German botanist, once again produced ether. Paracelsus, a famous chemist, noting that ether "has associated with it such sweetness that it is taken even by chickens, they fall asleep from it for a while, but awaken later without harm." However, Paracelsus was not a surgeon and so the leap to using this as an anesthetic was not realized.

Further constraining progress was the taboo against pain relief. Church teachings of the time regarding the pain of childbirth as a just and necessary punishment by God. As an example, in 1591, a young mother from Edinburgh, Eufane MacAyane, was dragged from her home after giving birth to twins for the sin of crying out repeatedly for pain relief during the difficult labor. Her pleas for mercy were ignored and the Church ordained that she be thrown into a pit and buried alive.[5]

By the late eighteenth century, William Hunter, a respected British surgeon, declared to his students, "Anatomy is the basis of cutting."[6] He had by then performed and described a remarkable variety of surgical techniques. Nonetheless, surgery remained a very limited profession. The potential for infection and the overbearing pain associated with the procedures curbed the surgeons' reach and contributed to one in two patients dying after surgery. Breaching the abdomen or thoracic cage to perform surgery was anathema and frowned upon as almost universally fatal. So surgeons were severely restricted, performing only external operations such as amputations.[2] Because of the excruciating pain, a measure of a surgeon's skill was the speed with which he could perform an operation. Consequently, they were regularly timed. Leg amputations could be performed in under sixty seconds as the skin, muscle and bone were quickly severed. However, the need to close the remaining stump would require another fifteen to twenty minutes of agonizingly painful surgery. Hence, surgical operations were considered a last resort.

Consider a leg amputation performed at the London Hospital built in 1871. Its only operating theatre was on the top floor of the hospital and had a glass skylight. Tiers of staged gallery seats flanked the operating floor in a U-shaped configuration allowing spectators to view the surgical proceedings. The skylight allowing ambient light rather than just candlelight for the operation. The top floor location was doubly important as it also insulated fellow patients in the hospital below from the screams of pain emanating from the operating theatre. When a surgical patient entered, a bell was wrung in warning, summoning attendants to close all the heavy wooden doors, further dampening the inevitable screams.

Central to the theatre was a sturdy wooden table. Around it gathered at least five strong men to pin the patient down. The patient would be walked in – usually somewhat inebriated – and helped unsteadily to lie down. One strong man sat at the head of the table on a chair grasping the patient around the chest while two others held down his arms. Still two more held him down at the waist and pinned down his good leg. A tourniquet was tightened around his thigh above the planned amputation site. A surgeon's walking stick thrust in to the patient's mouth, completed the preparation (having something to bite down on would stem the patient's yelling). The surgical assistant steadied the leg, ready for amputation. The spectators hushed and pulled out their pocket watches ready to time the amputation. The surgeon proceeded, stabbing through the skin and bone at lightning speed, completing the procedure as quickly as possible. Nevertheless, the patient would start screaming and thrashing around in such agony that surgeons who administered this cruelty would regularly be sick themselves; before or after the operation.

Few have been willing to write about the suffering that was endured. However, two did, both writing to Professor James Young Simpson of Edinburgh. A young surgeon noting:

Before the days of anaesthetics, a patient preparing for an operation was like a condemned criminal preparing for execution. He counted the days before the appointed day came. He counted the hours of that day till the appointed hour came. He listened for the echo in the street for the surgeon's carriage. He watched for his pull at the doorbell: for the foot on the stair; for his step in the room; for the production of his dreaded instruments; for his few grave words, and his last preparations before beginning. And then he surrendered his liberty and, revolting at the necessity, submitted to be held or bound, and helplessly gave himself up to the 'cruel knife'.[7]

A patient, Professor George Wilson, underwent ankle surgery performed by Professor Symes. Penning in support of the use of anesthetics, he wrote:

> Of the agony it occasioned I will say nothing. Suffering so great as I underwent cannot be expressed in words, and thus fortunately cannot be recalled, but the black whirlwind of emotion, the horror of great darkness, and the sense of desertion by God and man, bordering close on despair, which swept through my mind and overwhelmed my heart, I can never forget however gladly I would do so. During the operation in spite of the pain it occasioned, my senses were preternaturally acute, as I have been told they generally are in such circumstances. I still recall with unwelcome vividness the spreading out of the instruments: the twisting of the tourniquet: the first incision: the fingering of the sawed bone: the sponge pressed on the flap: the tying of the blood-vessels: the stitching of the skin: the bloody dismembered limb lying on the floor.[8]

One would have thought that with such recorded suffering and the associated limitations on the practice of surgery, surgeons would be clamoring for a method of relieving pain. They were! Hence it was no surprise that the first publication heralding a possible solution to the problem, "Insensibility during surgical operations produced by inhalation," was received with great excitement.[9] Written by Dr. Henry Jacob Bigelow, one of the surgeons at the Massachusetts General Hospital, its description of general anesthesia provided the transformational spark necessary to the wide application of surgery – making it the life-saving medical discipline it is today.

That story, of the discovery of general anesthesia, starts in Leeds, England and criss-crosses the Atlantic Ocean.

Joseph Priestley (1733-1804), the son of a hand-loom worker, was brought up a strict Calvinist by his aunt, Mrs. Keighley. He was hard-working, dedicated and of scholarly disposition. Having been trained as a dissenting minister, he took over Mill Hill Chapel in Leeds in the north of England in 1773 and served as a schoolmaster and experimenter in physics, science, chemistry and electricity. Priestley was prolific, authoring more than 128 titles, on religion, politics and science.[10]

In August of 1774, conducting one of many experiments, Priestley focused the sun's rays, using a large burning lens, to heat mercuric oxide, so creating the future anesthetic gas, nitrous oxide. He called this "dephlogisticated nitrous air," but was at a loss as to what to do with it. It killed his mice and so he declared it poisonous and dangerous. In later experiments, he identified oxygen, which is used as a component of every general anesthetic administered today, noting that candles burned brighter in oxygen and that mice lived twice as long as in common air. He published these discoveries in 1775 in three books entitled: *Experiments and Observations on Different Types of Air.*[11] While Priestley's experimental publications were highly regarded, his religious teachings were not consistently well received – his house and laboratory burnt down by dissenters during the "Priestley Riots" of 1791. Forcibly evicted at the age of sixty-one, Dr. Priestley and his family emigrated to the New World. Settling in tranquil Pennsylvania, he again established a laboratory on the bend of the Susquehanna river to continue his work. At his death in 1804, he could not have known that his discovery of nitrous oxide would follow him to the New World. He paved the way for the first nitrous oxide anesthetic demonstration by Horace Wells at the Massachusetts General Hospital in 1844. The evolution of anesthetic practice migrating from the Old to the New World and back again, just as the development of surgical practice had done before it.

Henry Hill Hickman (1800-30) made a singular contribution to the anesthetic story. He proposed that an anesthetic could be a gas. Henry was born in Shropshire, England in 1800. By 1825 he was familiar with the writings of Joseph Priestley. Knowing that animals like Priestley's mice need oxygen to live,[*] Hickman studied suspended animation by placing a puppy under an inverted air-tight glass flask. Panting avidly as its oxygen supply dwindled, the air-tight glass flask filled with exhaled carbon dioxide and the puppy's respiration inevitably slowed, as it slipped into a coma. Quickly lifting the flask, Hickman cut off the puppy's ear, carbon dioxide narcosis providing the anesthetic. The puppy recovering fully afterwards – minus an ear. In spite of these successful experiments, multiple claims that Hickman had demonstrated painless surgery were rejected by the Royal Society in London and the French Académie Royale de Médecine. Depressed, Hickman committed suicide at the

---

[*] At the cellular level, in a process known as oxidative phosphorylation, oxygen is instrumental in generating an energy bundle known as adenosine triphosphatase (ATP). ATP, in turn, provides the energy for cellular life while oxygen is converted to carbon dioxide. Asphyxiation causes cell death through insufficient ATP. Carbon dioxide is eliminated through frequent exhalations as a buildup in the body leads to coma and death.

age of thirty, the fate of far too many in this brief history. However, before his death he probably tried nitrous oxide on his puppies, writing to Cornish chemist Humphry Davy of its success.[1]

Thomas Beddoes (1760-1808), a prominent physician in Bristol, launched an effort to use gases in medicine. Tuberculosis and other chronic lung diseases were the great killers of the time in the crowded and polluted cities of England. Having read Priestley's discourses on The Different Types of Air, he established a new style laboratory-clinic in 1798; the Pneumatic Institute. With funding from renowned potter Josiah Wedgewood, Beddoes hoped to conduct experiments, using different gases, to find treatments for patients with lung problems. A busy man, he needed a superintendent to run the new Pneumatic Institute. Fortunately, he received a letter recommending a penniless but rakishly popular chemist named Humphry Davy. Despite knowing that Priestly had considered it poisonous, Beddoes charged Davy with finding a use for nitrous oxide.[*][12]

Humphrey Davy (1778-1829) was twenty-one and fearless. Convinced that nitrous oxide might be used for anesthesia, he could not experiment on the Pneumatic Institute's chickens[†] for fear of killing them. Instead, in the tried and trusted tradition of experimental medicine, he secretly practiced on himself. First, Humphrey prepared nitrous oxide in the lab and stored it in glass flasks. He planned to conduct an experiment to capture his personal experiences and document the effects of nitrous oxide inhalation. Then, he sat himself down on a stool and gulped nitrous oxide from the gas-filled flasks. After a few gulps he experienced "a delightful feeling of lightness and a faint feeling of numbing which gave way to an acute sense of hearing." And then he started to laugh, his body shaking with mirth. Dropping the flask, it shattered to the floor, ending the experiment abruptly. Davy had intended to document these effects by writing them down as the experiment unfolded, however instead of a scientific analysis, he wrote a poem.[7] Charged with a demonstration of nitrous oxide by his boss, Davy experimented avidly over the next days – learning that unbearable pain from his wisdom teeth erupting, was greatly relieved by three large inhaled doses.

---

[*] Nitrous oxide is commonly represented as N_2O, signifying its structure of two nitrogen molecules bound to one oxygen molecule. This oxygen molecule might give one a false sense of security, but it is tightly bound and not useable by the body to counter asphyxiation. If 100% N_2O is inhaled, it can indeed kill, (and has) through cellular asphyxia in displacing all useable oxygen and air in the lungs.

[†] Like Paracelsus five hundred years earlier.

On January 11, 1799, Humphry Davy feeling sufficiently prepared, demonstrated the use of nitrous oxide inhalation to Dr. Beddoes and Dr. Kinglake. He had purified quantities of nitrous oxide storing this in a silk bag. Davy took four large inhalations from the bag and became stuporous, slumping back in his seat. Beddoes removed the bag from Davy's mouth, much alarmed by events. Upon recovering, Davy started giggling and laughingly declaimed, "The universe is composed of impressions, ideas, pleasures and pains."

While no therapeutic use for nitrous oxide had been discovered, "Laughing Gas" had so been invented and was greatly popularized through the Pneumatic Institute. The Adelphi Theatre in London, as late as 1824, advertising, "Laughing Gas will continue to be administered to any of the audience as first experienced by Sir Humphry Davy." Laughing gas parties becoming all the rage, while experimental inhalation in medical schools by pupils was roundly condemned as being foolish.[10]

Notwithstanding that Davy wrote in his book *Medical Vapors*, "As nitrous oxide in its intensive operation appears capable of destroying physical pain, it may be used with advantage during surgical operation..." this avenue of experimentation was never developed by Humphrey nor picked up by anyone else until much later. Instead, Humphrey went on to invent the Davy Lamp for miners and describe the making of gunpowder – earning himself a knighthood for his service to science.

For the next step in the story of anesthesia we must follow Priestley to the New World.

Gardner Colton (1814-1898) was an impecunious medical student at the College of Physicians and Surgeons of Columbia University in New York City. He found it hard to pay his medical school fees, but as a nominal chemist he earned a little money by giving chemistry lectures to a Young Ladies Club in the city. In one of these lectures Colton demonstrated how to make and use nitrous oxide. Hearing of the frivolity that ensued, his fellow medical students entreated him to hold another laughing gas demonstration for their benefit. They had so much fun that a friend suggested Colton should hold a lecture-demonstration on a larger scale – perhaps a Grand Exhibition at the nearby Broadway Tabernacle. Colton was intrigued, but had no money. In fact, he was contemplating leaving medicine for the lack of it. But as he said, "I was determined to carry [the demonstration] out." He was also motivated by the fact that lecture-demonstrations were becoming increasingly popular and a good money-making proposition as audiences sought educational entertainment. So inspired, Gardner, having considerable charm, was able to convince Mr. Hale, the owner of the Broadway Tabernacle, to allow a one-night rental for fifty dollars. Crucially, to be paid after the event. Over the next three weeks Colton busied himself, advertising widely. The Grand Exhibition would comprise a lecture and a demonstration – highlighting the making of laughing gas, at least seventy-four gallons of it. Colton would deploy two separate bags for the administration of nitrous oxide, so that the thirty young men who had volunteered to partake would not have to wait for very long. Twelve stout men would be engaged on stage to ensure that participants under the influence did not fall and injure themselves. The day arrived, tickets were priced steeply at twenty-five cents, nonetheless there was a crush at the door and the Tabernacle was filled to capacity – causing a delayed start to the proceedings. Gardner leapt on to the stage and started with a lecture recounting Priestley's findings seventy years earlier – it was 1844. Demonstrating the making of nitrous oxide, he poured a mixture of two parts water and one part nitric acid over copper filings in a large container. Bubbles formed and were collected into readied gas bags. Taking some himself, Colton then offered the gas bags to all comers, one at a time. It was a laughing success – Colton made $535.00 and decided to forsake his medical studies and go into business. That summer he held exhibitions in all the major towns and cities of New England including Hartford, Connecticut.

Horace Wells (1815-1848) was a disturbed man. He grew up well enough; his parents were intelligent and considered wealthy for the region of Vermont. At nineteen, after his father's death, instead of the ministry he decided on dentistry, travelling to Boston to apprentice in his chosen field.[13] In 1836 Wells moved to Hartford to establish his practice and soon took rank among the first in the city, well known for his skillful dentistry. Writing in medical journals he supplemented his considerable income inventing devices as varied as coal sifters and gold solders for teeth.* A sought after tutor, Wells apprenticed many dental students including William T. Morton, with whom he briefly practiced

---

* The latter patent was certified by Dr. Charles T. Jackson, a prominent chemist, who would later claim primacy for the invention of ether anesthesia.

in Boston, and John M. Riggs, who became a well regarded dentist and surgeon. Ever mindful of the harrowing pain associated with teeth-pulling, Wells sought opportunities to further his knowledge in science. Reading in the *Hartford Courant* that there was to be a Grand Exhibition on December 10 demonstrating inhaled nitrous oxide, "laughing gas," by Mr. G. Q. Colton, he endeavored to go. Elizabeth, his wife, joining him at the exhibition. On paying the twenty-five-cent admission, they sat down to view the spectacle together. Although this was to be just a scientific entertainment, Elizabeth would later recount that this was the beginning of, "an unspeakable evil."

Reprising his performance at the Tabernacle, Colton delivered his lecture and demonstrated the use of nitrous oxide. He had stored nitrous oxide in a big bladder bag, fitted with a wooden spigot, similar to that found on country cider barrels. Inhaling nitrous oxide deeply a number of times, he demonstrated no ill effect. Then he asked for volunteers. Horace was the first of ten, together with his dental assistant, Sam Cooley. Duly taking his turn at the bag he made a fool of himself on the stage, climbing down to rejoin his wife later. Witnessing from his seat how Sam Cooley, upon taking a few deep inhalations, thrashed and danced about, crashing into a wooden stool on the stage, and spurted blood from a gashed wound. Coming too from the fall and back in his seat, Horace turned to Sam and asked, "Did you feel any pain?" "No!"...was Cooley's reply. This got Wells thinking. After the show, he asked Colton whether nitrous oxide might be used to relieve the pain from tooth pulling. Colton wasn't sure but endeavored to give him some to try it out. He agreed to join Wells in his dental practice the next day with a bag of nitrous oxide.

The next day, December 11, 1844, was to be auspicious. Gardner Colton and Sam Cooley, joined Horace at his home together with John Riggs the dentist. The plan: Wells would be the patient and John Riggs would endeavor to extract a painful wisdom tooth that had been troubling for some time. Horace sat down in a comfortable arm-chair whilst Colton prepared the bag with nitrous oxide and John Riggs readied himself to extract the tooth. Riggs' own accounting of the historic event – some call the first general anesthetic – does it the most justice:

Wells took the bag in his lap – held the tube to his mouth and inhaled till insensibility relaxed the muscles of his arms – his hands fell on his breast – his head dropped on the head-rest and I instantly passed the forceps into his mouth on to the tooth and extracted it. Mr. Colton, Cooley and the two there stood by the open door ready to run out if Wells jumped up from the chair and made any hostile demonstrations. You may ask, why did he not get up? Simply because he could not. Our agreement, the night previous was, to push the administration to a point hitherto unknown.

We knew not whether death or success confronted us. It was terra incognito we were bound to explore – the result is known to the world. No one but Wells and myself knew to what point the inhalation was to be carried – the result was painfully problematical to us but the great law of Nature, hitherto unknown, was kind to us and a grand discovery was born into the world.[13]

Within minutes after the extraction, Wells awoke. Feeling the gap in his mouth where the offending wisdom teeth had been, he declared, "It is the greatest discovery ever made. I didn't feel as much as the prick of a pin." He was so excited about this discovery that soon most of Hartford new about the "new era in teeth pulling." Together with John Riggs, Wells continued practicing with nitrous oxide performing at least fifteen further operations. Morton, his former Boston colleague, hearing of this success helped arrange an invitation to demonstrate the technique before the senior medical students of Dr. John C. Warren. The demonstration was planned for January 20, 1845, at the Medical School of Harvard University.

John Collins Warren (1778-1856) was the pre-eminent Boston surgeon of his time. He was short of stature, but his neat hair, angular jaw, and erect commanding posture made him look taller than he really was. In manners, he was brusque and severe. As a European medical student, he had resolved to never waste a minute of the day and so by 1845 he had everything that the medical profession could offer in terms of respect and reputation. But as a surgeon there remained an abiding concern: the pain he caused practicing surgery. He wrote, "What surgeon has not at these times been inspired with a wish to find some means of lessening the sufferings he was obliged to inflict?"[12] When word reached Boston that a dentist might have found a solution to the problem, he instructed his assistant Dr. Hayward to send an invitation to Horace Wells. Wells was requested to lecture on nitrous oxide and demonstrate its administration for a planned surgical operation in the single operating theater at the Massachusetts General Hospital where Dr. Warren was surgeon in chief. This operating theater was modeled on the first operating room in London, with a sky-lit dome providing ambient light and galleried semi-circular tiered seating, allowing spectators to view the surgical proceedings. The Americans had added some further refinements: there were hooks, rings and pulleys set in the wall, which could be used to keep the patients in place during surgery. On the day of the planned demonstration, medical students, a few faculty and Wells's erstwhile colleague, Dr. William Morton – who brought dental instruments for his use – sat in anticipation in the galleries. Word was soon received that the scheduled patient had absconded, being too fearful of the planned amputation. A substitute needed to be found and so a medical student with a painful tooth volunteered. Wells was justly nervous in front of this audience, not having the same pure supply of nitrous oxide that Sam Cooley usually provided. He tentatively administered the nitrous oxide to the medical student, but later said he withdrew the bladder too soon. Wells nevertheless set about pulling the tooth with some confidence, having prac-ticed this fifteen times back home. All seemed to go well until the patient cried out, writhing in pain. The audience hissed and booed this poor demonstration and jeered Horace Wells out of the operating theater calling it a "humbug affair." Wells never recovered from this ignominious failed performance with nitrous oxide. He slunk back to Hartford the next day and closed his dental practice in a state of depression.

William T. G. Morton (1819-1868) was a strikingly attractive man, always in a rush, often a rush to make money. He was also a swindler and trickster wanted in three states for embezzlement and bad debts. Although he had studied dentistry and medicine, he was regarded as a man of limited medical knowledge and could not write grammatically nor legibly. Some might charac-terize him as a psychopath.

Charles T. Jackson (1805-1888) was brought up as a gentleman. After completing Harvard Medical School, he travelled to Paris to immerse himself in his true love, the new field of chemistry. He liked explaining, holding forth at length on subjects as varied as telegraphy, gun cotton, the stomach – all subjects around which controversy later arose in priority conflicts. It was to be the same with ether. Protesting that he could not make ends meet as a doctor, Jackson built the most advanced private laboratory in Boston, publishing extensively and creating a hub for scientists to meet and greet and just hang around the lab. On October 25, 1843, in walked Horace Wells and William Morton, seeking a certificate of chemical verification for a newly designed dental plate. Jackson wrote later, "This is when I first saw them and unfortunately made their acquaintance."[12]

These brief characterizations are crucial to understanding the primacy of the idea of using sulphuric ether* as a general anesthetic for surgical anesthesia.

Morton claimed that the idea came to him spontaneously in the summer of 1846 when a friend was telling him about ether frolics at a recent party. This propelled him to purchase sulphuric ether in a demijohn from Messers Brewer & Co of Boston, so that he could practice on his farm animals. In subsequent affidavits contesting Morton's version of events, Jackson's attorney's demonstrated that no such demijohn was ever sold to Morton.[15]

The more likely version of events is that Morton got the idea of using sulphuric ether from Jackson during a visit to his Boston Laboratory on Sept 30, 1846. He learned there that ether was in fact not a gas, as he had previously thought, but a liquid. It is likely that he never experimented on anyone except for a few brief self-inhalations that day. This impulsiveness was typical of the man. On hearing this information, Morton then rushed back to his dental office, offering five dollars to any passerby who would have a tooth extracted using the ether fumes. Nobody was interested. That evening, Eben Frost, a wood sawyer by profession and a good friend, showed up at Morton's office with a painful tooth. This could have been serendipity, but was probably staged by Morton, as Albert Tenney a newspaperman was already at the office to record the event. Jackson, who lived nearby, was not. Frost sat down and Morton encouraged him to take four deep inhalations from a handkerchief, doused with ether liquid, that he had poured out of a flask. The sawyer became unconscious, Morton pulled the tooth, then sprinkled water on Frost's face to awaken him. "Are you ready to have the tooth out?" Morton asked. "I am ready," Frost mumbled with some apparent slurring. "Well, it is out now!" Morton said, with mounting excitement. "There it is on the floor."

"A New and Valuable Discovery," the *Boston Transcript* reported on October 2.

That it was indeed.

---

* Diethyl ether with the structure H_5C_2-O-C_2H_5 was synthetized by distilling sulphuric acid with ethyl alcohol. The so formed ether, is indeed an anesthetic, which if given in sufficient dose can produce unconsciousness and in overdose can kill. It is highly flammable, pungent, and extremely nauseating to patients.

Dr. Henry J Bigelow (1818-1880) at twenty-eight years, a junior member of the Surgical House staff, at the Massachusetts General Hospital, read the *Boston Transcript* article. Henry, who was present at the failed nitrous oxide demonstration by Horace Wells the previous year, realized that his boss, John C. Warren, was still interested in alleviating the pain from surgery. Having observed thirty-seven trials of ether administration for dental patients by Morton in his offices, Bigelow invited him to conduct a demonstration in the same operating theatre, at the Harvard Medical School.

The added responsibility of providing a general anesthetic for a surgical operation, rather than just for the relatively quick tooth-pulling, must have weighed heavily on Morton's mind. Not sufficiently however, to stop him from collaborating with Jackson to take out a patent for the discovery of anesthesia with sulphuric ether. Their problem was that sulphuric ether was easily recognized by its distinctive smell. To disguise this, Morton added oil of orange and called the new mixture Letheon. Patenting a medical discovery by a self-respecting doctor was unheard of at the time, but Morton took no heed, consistent with his self-serving nature. Restricting the free availability of a breakthrough that would decrease human suffering was an egregiously cold-blooded thing to do. But Morton did not care, hiring R. H. Reddy Esq, on October 1, the day immediately after the first successful ether administration, to establish a patent. Morton knowing full well that if such a discovery were patentable, the financial possibilities would be staggering.

Accordingly, just to be sure, upon receiving an invitation from Dr. Henry Bigelow to anesthetize a patient the next day, Morton rushed to fashion a new apparatus – rather than a handkerchief – for ether administration. He hoped in this way to turn the discovery of anesthesia with ether into a patentable *invention*. For help he turned to a well-known physician scientist, conchologist and equipment maker, Augustus Gould. Together they hastily finalized the construction: a glass globe, known as a retort, containing a sea sponge. On one side – at ten o'clock – protruded a glass tube and on the other – at two o'clock – a wooden spigot. Ether would need to be poured into the glass tube to partially fill the retort and wet the sponge, so increasing the surface area for evaporation, and the concentration of ether available. For the device to work, the patient would need to inhale deeply from the opened spigot to draw air into the retort and over the etherized sponge. An advanced device, by any account, when compared to the soporific sponges of the Middle Ages.

Edward Gilbert Abbott (1825-55) had suffered from a jaw tumor from birth. A printer by trade, his early life was a constant struggle against poverty. Admitted to the Harvard Medical School for surgery on Sept 25, 1846, his admission notes documented his age as twenty years, and the extent of the jaw tumor as one to two inches in diameter. Slovenly in appearance, he was unfashionably dressed, tall, thin, weak and probably tubercular – the cause of his parents' deaths.[16] Surgery was scheduled for 10 o'clock, October 16 in the Massachusetts General Hospital's only operating theater.

John C. Warren, chief surgeon, stood ready in the theater surveying the gallery where medical students, surgeons and a few others sat waiting with anticipation. Word had spread that a surgical pain killer had been found and so eminent physicians sat in the gallery and crowded round the operating table. Just in case, Abbott had been strapped down as usual in the seated position. Warren looked at his pocket watch. It was past ten; Morton was late. Surgeon Heywood, his assistant, prepared to start. "Stop," said Warren. "We have promised Mr. Morton a chance. We will give him a few more minutes." He looked around at the gathered audience and announced, "There is a gentleman who claims that he has discovered that the inhalation of a certain agent will produce insensibility to pain during surgical operations, with safety to the patient. I have decided to permit him to try the experiment"[12]*

Morton burst into the operating theater, he knew he was late but he had to finalize the construction of his apparatus, which he now carried under his arm, never fully tested. It was 10:25a.m. October 16, 1846. Warren with some irritation turned to Morton and said, "Your patient is ready."

As he stepped up to administer the anesthetic, Morton must have remembered his wife Elizabeth's admonishments, "Either you will fail or you will kill the patient and be tried for manslaughter." His hands were shaking. He was not so sure about the inhaler that he had in his hands nor the purity of the ether he poured onto the sponge nestling in the globe. He was especially nervous, having not practiced the administration with the hastily assembled device.

Speaking quietly to Gilbert Abbott, to encourage him, Morton took him by the hand and pointed out Mr. Eben Frost in the gallery who he had invited for added reassurance (probably for both of them), who could testify

---

* It is believed that a photographer was present to take a daguerreotype, but he took no pictures, because the sight of blood made him nauseated. Hence there are only paintings illustrating this famous even. One depicted on the front cover. (Etherday 1846) used as a background for the front cover.

to the ether's success. Then he asked, "Are you afraid?" "No, I feel confident and will do precisely as you tell me," said Abbott. Morton then fiddled with the glass retort, making sure the ether had wetted the sponge, and put the spigot carefully in Gilbert's mouth. He had never practiced with this device, not knowing how much or how long an administration would be required. Nonetheless, he told his patient to breathe deep and slow and in four or five minutes Abbott was asleep.[16]

Morton removed the wooden mouthpiece, stood back and declared, "Your patient is ready, sir." Warren immediately made a three-inch incision and proceeded with surgery, "without any expression of pain by the patient." Having completed the surgery in about ten minutes, Warren turned to the enraptured audience, many of whom had been at the Horace Wells 1845 fiasco, and declared, "Gentleman, *this* is no Humbug." A short silence and then loud clapping and cheering resounded in the operating theater – soon to be named the Ether Dome. Abbot, on waking up from surgery, would repeatedly attest that he felt nothing, only a slight scraping at the end, "much like a hoe," as he was awakening.

The first published report of the public demonstration of a surgical anesthetic, dated November 16, 1846, would take the medical world by storm, Dr. Henry Bigelow concluding, "...what now promises to be one of the important discoveries of the age."[9] General anesthesia provided the transformational spark that surgery needed. Within less than a decade surgeons could do more complex, precise and far more invasive procedures, such as hysterectomies, proving that the abdomen could be safely invaded.[2]

In the week of October 16, 1846 there were only two scheduled patients for surgery in the single operating room of the Massachusetts General Hospital. Surgery was rarely performed. Today there are more than fifty-four operating rooms with over 200 surgeries daily at this hospital.

Edward Abbott fully recovered from the surgery, but discharge was delayed until December 7, 1846, with little evident change in the size of the tumor. He became assistant editor of the *Boston Herald*, but died at the age of thirty, from consumption, like his parents before him.

William Morton initially became a rich man, but controversy surrounded the ether question. He unsuccessfully petitioned Congress four times for tens of thousands of dollars in his claim for primacy in the discovery of anesthesia; competing with Horace Wells and Charles Jackson. He died a broken man on his way north to St. Luke's hospital in a carriage. He had pinned three decorations from foreign governments to his chest, seeking to escape the terrible heat wave that had afflicted New York City that summer. He was buried in Boston where his tombstone bears an epitaph composed by Henry Bigelow: *Inventor and Revealer of Inhalational Anesthesia: Before Whom, in All Time, Surgery was Agony: By Whom, Pain in Surgery was Averted and Annulled: Since whom, Science has control of Pain.*

Horace Wells, Morton's tutor and colleague, also came to an untimely end. Having stopped practicing as a dentist in a fit of depression after the failed nitrous oxide demonstration, he took up painting and invented a new bath shower. Becoming increasingly preoccupied with the claims and counter claims surrounding Morton, Jackson and himself, it eventually drove him crazy. Taking his claims as far abroad as the Académie de Medécine in Paris,* to no avail. Wells became agitated and frustrated, petitioning endlessly on the matter. To calm himself, Horace became a user of ether and then a chloroform addict. Moving to New York City to further his claims, and under the influence of chloroform, he bespattered a group of Broadway prostitutes with sulphuric acid in an attempt to get "all the bad girls out of Broadway." He was jailed, and in a state of great shame, left a suicide note to his wife, took some chloroform, cut open his femoral artery with a knife, and bled to death, aged only thirty-three.[13]

On a happier note, Gardner Colton, who introduced Horace Wells to nitrous oxide, fared much better. Despite Wells's failed demonstration with nitrous oxide, this gas is still used extensively in dental and anesthetic practice today. Colton largely responsible for this.[14] Joining the California Gold Rush in 1849, but failing to find enough gold, Colton returned to the East. After a stint as a correspondent for the *Boston Transcript* and the invention of several devices, Colton resumed his lecture-demonstrations with nitrous oxide in 1861. He had observed that the dangers of ether and chloroform were making them less popular as anesthetics and so resolved to reintroduce the use of nitrous oxide for dental practice. Together with two prominent dentists he established Colton Dental Associates in New York, providing nitrous oxide anesthetics for tens of thousands of dental patients.† In 1867, Dr. Colton travelled to Paris to attend the First International Congress of

---

* The French Academy being the center of European Medical development and an arbitrator on such matters.
† Reputedly 193,000 in the seven dental offices he established around the country.

Medicine. Here he demonstrated his apparatus and nitrous oxide anesthesia to the scientific world – much more successfully than Wells did two decades earlier.

One of the problems with William Morton's claim for primacy in the discovery of anesthesia, was that he wasn't the first. That was Crawford Long, who only belatedly published his case histories in 1849.[17]

Crawford Long (1815-1878) was "exceedingly modest in his pretensions."[17] After medical school at the University of Pennsylvania, he returned to Georgia, the state of his birth, to establish his country practice in the small town of Jefferson. A hard worker, he was absolutely dedicated to the welfare of his patients. Late for his own wedding, he returned after the ceremony to continue the care of a sick patient, not seeing his new bride for a full day afterwards. Soon after the wedding, in early 1842, friends asked him to make some nitrous oxide for a laughing gas party. Not knowing how, he made ether instead and introduced ether frolics to his companions. While under the influence of ether, he noticed the same thing Horace Wells had noticed with nitrous oxide: that he never felt any pain from bruises or cuts. One of the regulars at the ether frolics, James M. Venable, a pupil at the local academy, had two jaw tumors that he was fearful of having excised. On March 30, 1842, he visited Long, who suggested administering ether to minimize the pain of surgical removal. That evening after school was dismissed, Long's case history reads, "The Ether was given to Mr. Venable on a towel; and when fully under its influence I extirpated the tumor. The patient continued to inhale ether during the time of the operation; and when informed it was over, seemed incredulous, until the tumor was shown him." In turn Venable relates, "I commenced inhaling the ether before the operation. I did not feel the slightest pain and could not believe the tumor was removed until it was shown me."[17] Two witnesses testified to being present at this historic event. Dr. Long administered a further two ether anesthetics that year but did not consider publishing his findings until reading about the primacy controversy between Wells, Jackson and Morton in 1847. Delaying doing so, as usual, because of pressing needs to attend to his patients.

Nevertheless, March 30, the date of ether's first administration as a surgical anesthetic is now annually celebrated as Doctors' Day in the United States.

*

We return to England for the next step in the anesthesia story. Ether becoming known across the Atlantic through a letter written by Dr. Jacob Bigelow, Henry Bigelow's father, to Dr. Boott, an American doctor. As early as December 21, 1846, just two months after Morton's demonstration, Dr. John Liston performed the first operation under ether anesthesia in London. Liston was known for his speed, amputating the leg of a butler named Fredrick Churchill in an amazing twenty-five seconds. As the amputated leg fell to the floor, he turned to the assembled audience in the theatre and declared "This Yankee dodge beats mesmerism hollow." Liston was reputedly so lightning fast, that at one amputation before general anesthesia was available, he cut through his assistant's fingers as well as the patient's leg, before anyone could stop him. Both subsequently dying of sepsis. In the audience someone witnessing this tragedy died of shock. The first and only operation on record with a 300% mortality.[2]

With the new discovery of ether anesthesia, surgeons could take more time and care with their operations, avoiding such complications in the future. But not everyone was impressed with sulphuric ether as an anesthetic.

James Young Simpson (1811-1870) assumed the chair of midwifery in Edinburgh, under a cloud of hostility, having spent five hundred pounds sterling canvassing for the esteemed position.[18] But his prowess as a lecturer made up for this – as he soon attracted large classes of students. First to administer sulphuric ether for the pain of childbirth, he did not like it as an anesthetic. Ether smelled, made people sick, was flammable, and worst of all, was made in America! (The British were indignant that the discovery of ether had not occurred in the Old World.) He set about trying to find alternatives, taking suggestions from his students. A robust man, who liked to eat, Simpson favored dinner parties. Often concluded, much like a dessert menu, with suggested chemical compounds inhaled around the table. As these dinner parties were held on Thursdays – late into the night – a friend visited Fridays, at breakfast time, to see if anyone was dead. Simpson selecting the suggested chemicals based on their volatility,* correctly believing that upon inhalation they would more readily transmit to the bloodstream.

On Nov 3, 1847, chloroform was on the after-dinner menu. The guests inhaling it deeply from a vial.

---

* Tendency to evaporate.

Early Friday, Simpson woke up under the table to the sound of snoring friends; the next anesthetic had been found. It was quick in action, non-flammable – in an era when naked candle flames supplied artificial light – and was cheap and potent. Chloroform also did not have the same sickly smell or cause as much vomiting as ether did* However there was one problem for Simpson, as the chair of midwifery, the Church forbade pain relief for child birth. Only after Queen Victoria requested and received "that blessed chloroform," as she put it, for the delivery of her eighth child, Prince Leopold, was 'chlory' readily accepted. Chloroform use spread like wildfire through Europe and Germany and across the United States; becoming in many places the primary anesthetic over ether.

However, there was one big problem. Chloroform killed. Unpredictably.

Hannah Greener, only fifteen, dreaded the prospect of having the nail of her big toe removed. The fact that she had received ether anesthesia for a similar operation on the other foot, just a few months before, did not calm her.[19] On the day of the operation in late January 1848, she fretted a great deal, sobbing as she took her seat in the operating chair. Dr. Meggison pouring a teaspoonful of chloroform onto a handkerchief and gently placing this over her mouth, sought to calm her fears. "Hannah, put your hands on your knees and breath quietly," he said. Half a minute later, he pinched her cheek and finding her insensible, the incision of the toe was begun. She kicked briefly, "her lips became blanched, and she spluttered at the mouth as if in epilepsy." Attempting resuscitation, Meggison threw down the handkerchief, dashed water on her face and tried some brandy without the least effect. She was dead. "The whole process of inhalation, operation, venesection and death, did not occupy more than two minutes."† Hannah Greener's case was the first report of a death from chloroform anesthesia. There were to be many more.

Fifteen years later in 1863 the number of *known* deaths in England from

---

* Chloroform has the chemical formula: CHCL3 and is a naturally occurring substance produced by seaweed and fungi. In the 1850s it was produced by combining chlorine bleach with alcohol. Today it is produced in industrial quantities by heating a mixture of chlorine and methane. Chlorine is toxic to the liver and can convert into phosgene gas. It is no longer used in modern anesthetic practice. It has abuse potential and is implicated in 'sudden sniffer's death'.

† In 1911, studying cats, Dr. Alfred Goodman Levy demonstrated that the cause of death with chloroform, given in light doses, was that this anesthetic sensitized the heart's nervous conduction system, resulting in deadly ventricular arrhythmias. This was precipitated by the high levels of adrenaline circulating in the blood caused by the surgical incision. The toe is an especially sensitive area of the body and so there would be a large release of adrenaline if the patient was not fully anesthetized as probably occurred in Hannah Greener's case.

chloroform administration numbered 123, prompting the Royal Medical and Chirurgical Society to appoint a committee to investigate this tragedy. They suggested combining the administration of ether and chloroform.[*] Nonetheless the deaths continued. Fully forty years later, in 1909, more people died from chloroform than were murdered in England.[20]

Another, safer general anesthetic needed to be found.

Cyclopropane[†] might well have been that anesthetic. In 1929 this chemical compound was under investigation to evaluate its toxic potential. There was concern that cyclopropane might be a toxic by-product of propylene, a gas in commercial use. Surprisingly, when 14% cyclopropane was administered to cats in a box, they fell asleep and did not die, waking up none the worse for wear. Sufficiently reassured, a pharmacologist named Professor Henderson asked an assistant to administer some to himself – with good results. By 1938, cyclopropane was a readily accepted anesthetic, unfortunately with often tragic outcomes. Cyclopropane proved to be explosive – extremely so. That year, at the Baptist Hospital in Boston, Mary Lahiff, an Irish immigrant's daughter, received cyclopropane via a face mask for surgery to remove a tumor from her breast. As the surgery was drawing to a close, a loud bang, like an explosion, resounded in the operating theater, emanating from Mary's throat. Cyclopropane had exploded from a spark caused by the build-up of static electricity on the anesthetist. Mary died, not immediately, but from a rip in her trachea, air leaked under her skin and she blew up like a balloon, with subcutaneous air. Mary was the first of many.

In 1939 there were ninety-three recorded deaths from cyclopropane-induced explosions in the U.S. alone and in the following forty years of use, literally hundreds of explosions occurred, killing patients, surgeons, nurses and anesthetists alike.[20, 21]

Another, safer, non-flammable, general anesthetic needed to be found.

---

[*] This foreshadowed the concept of "balanced anesthesia," the attempt to administer differing combinations of anesthetic agents to minimize individual anesthetic agent toxicity to be embroidered on in Chapter 6.

[†] Cyclopropane has the chemical formula: C_3H_6. It is no longer used in modern anesthetic practice, although I used this in the early 1980s in England when it was readily used outside of the operating theatres in induction rooms to induce anesthetics in children. It rapidly provides anesthesia in two to three breaths when administered in 50% concentration. In circumstances where static electricity builds up on clothing and equipment or where cautery is used in surgery, it is explosive when administered with air, oxygen or nitrous oxide. Cyclopropane also caused arrhythmias like chloroform with multiple recorded deaths. Because it stimulated rapid breathing and did not result in a decrease in blood pressure it was readily adopted in anesthetic practice for close on 40 years.

Nineteen fifty-six heralded the modern era of anesthetic design, delivery and care with the introduction of halothane* into clinical practice.

Not found serendipitously like nitrous oxide, ether, chloroform and cyclopropane before it, halothane had been specifically designed – synthetized by C. W. Suckling for Imperial Chemical Industries to provide safer anesthesia. Marketed as fluothane, it was the first fluorinated and so non-flammable hydrocarbon compound. Reporting on five hundred successful anesthetics, Dr. Michael Johnstone from the Royal Infirmary in Manchester noted the salutary effects of halothane: no deaths despite many patients being already sick with renal failure and jaundice before the operation.[22]

Halothane foreshadowing the continuous improvement in anesthetic drug design, delivery and monitoring, which would propel the nascent practice of anesthesia to become the recognized medical specialty and the essentially safe practice it is today. Halothane and refinements in anesthetic delivery, making possible surgical procedures unimaginable before, in patients who would have been considered too sick to "take the ether," thus, hopefully, ensuring that in future years patients would be "waking up safer" no matter how infirm they were, nor how extensive the operation.

---

* Halothane has the chemical formula: CF_3CH, Cl, Br. It was specifically designed to be non-explosive through the fluorination of this ethane molecule, setting the stage for further development in anesthetic agents in the future. While not used in the developed world today, because of rare instances of liver toxicity, it is still extensively used internationally and is on the World Health Organization's List of Essential Medicines. It is relatively cheap, potent, fast in onset of action and recovery, but still causes arrhythmias and depresses the heart, blood pressure and respiration. This is in contrast to nitrous oxide, ether, and cyclopropane which stimulates the sympathetic nervous system, while halothane suppresses this system.

3

Senior House Officer – Anesthetics

English anesthetic practice and training, 1984 to 1987

Sculpture of John Hunter in the portico of the Royal College of Surgeons,
Lincoln's Inn Fields, London.

When you breathe, you inspire, when you do not, you expire.

– Anonymous

John Hunter (1728-1793) sits languidly on a raised marbled chair, chin propped on hand, staring out across the sea of faces congregating to hear the outcome of their final examinations for the Fellowship of the Faculty of Anaesthetists of the Royal College of Surgeons in London.

In 1745, surgeons separated from the barbers to form the Company of Surgeons, which received a Royal Charter, establishing the Royal College of Surgeons of England by 1842. The College building, quartered at Lincoln's Inn Fields in London, is resplendent with a fine porticoed entrance lined by imposing pillars sufficiently large for hopeful examination candidates to lean against or hide behind.

Hunter sees nothing of course because he is a marble statue of the great anatomist and surgeon who collected thousands of the human specimens housed in the building's museum. These specimens often forming the basis of the viva voce (oral examination) conducted by the College in the hallowed halls of the storied building, as part adjudication of a candidate's suitability, to be awarded a Fellowship of the College.

I remember one such viva voce session. Having already been subjected to an unremitting cross-examination, a glass box containing a pathology specimen drowned in formalin was thrust across the table by one of my two examiners. The glass box contained what looked like the larynx and trachea of a very small child, probably just born. Precariously, a small tumor was attached to the larynx. In life, the tumor was likely to have popped into the airway opening of the larynx as anaesthesia was administered, killing the child – the probable reason that this was now a formalin specimen.

"Dr. Mets, how would you anaesthetize this child?" the examiner asked, adding in a gruff voice, "if you knew what is evident from this specimen." He was referring to the fact that there was no way of knowing that this lethal tumor was there – hovering over the larynx – as it would be impossible to see this in the child by looking at him and no radiological way of identifying the problem preoperatively. I looked at him and took a deep breath, because what I was about to say might not sit well with the demanding examiner. "Sir, I would not anaesthetize this child, until I was sure that I had secured the airway. I would wrap the child in a blanket to restrain it and place the breathing tube without anaesthesia." A pregnant silence ensued, I waited anxiously for a response. "Yes," he said, "that's what they should have done!"

The Faculty of Anaesthetists in the Royal College of Surgeons was formed in 1948. The development of a separate specialty of anaesthetics had its roots in the Association of Anaesthetists of Great Britain established by Dr. Henry Featherstone in 1932. At that time anaesthetics were mostly given by general practitioners, poorly paid, receiving little to no respect from other specialities. By 1987, when I was taking the examination, the Faculty of Anaesthetists was now garnering increasing respect and would break ranks with the Surgeons becoming the College of Anaesthetists the next year; gaining a Royal Charter as the Royal College of Anaesthetists in 1992. The college's motto *"Divinum sedare dolerem"* "it is divine to alleviate pain."

Well, the Royal College was not alleviating our pain as we waited in the portico, surveyed by John Hunter, to hear whether we had passed our examination. The pass rate was reputed to be only 19% that year. Success would confer on us two benefits: a Fellowship signifying our undoubted suitability to practice anaesthetics and also the right to put FFARCS (Eng) – Fellow of the Faculty of Anaesthetists of the Royal College of Surgeons of England – after our names.

We had been summoned at 6p.m. to this traditional gathering place in front of Hunter's statue, concluding an intense day. Not only had we completed two viva voce examinations, we had also visited a nearby hospital at Queen's Square to examine patients specifically drafted for the purpose. Many of these patients were regulars in the examination process, not acutely ill, but with interesting, and often very rare, chronic conditions with clinical signs that would need to be found and reported on to our examiners. Patients brought in on the day of examination, were paid a small stipend, offered a cup of tea and sandwiches to sustain them, and then assigned to a cordoned off area – separated by traditional hospital bed dividers – where they undressed and took their place under a sheet on a hard bed; awaiting the arrival of an eager trainee.

FFARCS candidates allocated a patient, seemingly at random, were given just thirty minutes to question and physically examine them before being asked to report to two examiners. This was a high stakes nerve racking affair, given the reputed pass rate. For me it was especially taxing as I had taken vacation from my registrar position in anaesthetics, travelling from South Africa to London, to sit this test.

My patient was a young lady. She really looked quite well, but there was obviously something to be found, otherwise she would not have been drafted.

I set about asking the usual questions, then fully examined her, concentrating especially on her heart, listening with my stethoscope to the heart sounds (a combination of snaps and murmurs) that pointed to mitral stenosis.[*]

I wanted to be able to say confidently to the examiners what my diagnosis was, rather than a bumbling presentation about the different clinical findings and pulses, and heart sounds that I thought I heard with my stethoscope. This would clinch the examination. I had practiced for this exam, repetitively, on many patients back in South Africa and had diagnosed mitral stenosis before. But it was very unlikely in England. I turned to the patient and said, "I have come a very long way. Is there something you are allowed to tell me, that I have not yet asked?" "Yes," she said. "I had Still's disease as a child." This was revelatory because Still's disease is a chronic arthritic condition occasionally associated with heart disease. My presentation to the examiners was suitably confident; hopefully my success was assured.

To get to this stage of the final examinations for the FFARCS (Eng) was the culmination of an arduous training path in anaesthetics.

First, the coveted senior house officer (SHO) in anaesthetics post had to be secured.

"Call Roger," said Steve McVittie, a Scottish doctor practicing at Edendale Hospital in South Africa. "Who?" I asked, peering across the drapes while administering an anaesthetic, late one afternoon. "Dr. Roger Eltringham in Gloucester. He is always keen to have foreigners apply for SHO jobs in his anaesthetic department and serves as the faculty tutor. He is great fun to work with. Tell him I recommend you."

That certainly seemed like an opportunity. During the first three months as a medical officer in anaesthetics, I had decided that I enjoyed the practice so much that I would seek to start training in England. Seeking an SHO position, I had scoured the Job Listings section, in forlorn back editions of the *British Medical Journal* populating Edendale's sparse library, but had come up with nothing. Word of mouth seemed to be the way these things

---

[*] Mitral stenosis is a thickening of the leaflets of the heart valve separating the left atrium from the left ventricle. Like a purse string being slowly pulled tight, mitral stenosis causes obstruction of blood flow in the heart, with the result that patients become increasingly short of breath and tire easily. Commonly found in the tropics from rheumatic fever, mitral stenosis is only very rarely found in temperate climates.

were arranged. I wrote to Roger and was accepted, sight unseen, to start in February 1984.

There was a problem. This all-important SHO post, the foothold into anaesthesia training in England, would not begin for at least a year after I had finished the medical officer year at Edendale in 1982. And, a year after, Dr. Ulane Neveling, a fellow medical school graduate from Stellenbosch University, had completed her internship year at the nearby Grey's hospital in Pietermaritzburg. This offered a great opportunity. We decided to pool our limited financial resources and travel for the intervening year. We backpacked Southeast Asia, eurailed Europe, and bussed through North America, stopping off in Canada for three months to do locum general practitioner jobs in St Alban's and at the outport of Burgeo. Here, one fine Newfoundland morning, a cold breeze blowing off the sea, we were married. The St. John's Episcopal Church, prominently ensconced on a rocky outcrop, a blue sunny sky as a backdrop, provided the ideal setting. That day, after a suitable celebration, we left Burgeo by helicopter and have engaged in this life's adventure, together, ever since.

Roger Eltringham (1939-), inventor of the Glostavent anaesthesia machine, captained his high school cricket team on a trip to Holland. Upon hearing that the opposing side's captain, a surgeon, was delayed because one of his patients needed resuscitation for hemorrhage, Roger changed his career plans. Instead of becoming a physical training instructor he became an anaesthetist, thinking this would be much more exciting. Ideally suited to be a faculty tutor – training young doctors for the FFARCS (Eng) examination – because, as he said, "Berend, I am an expert at the examination. I failed it three times."

Roger was redoubtable; short in stature and balding, he always had a ready smile, a twinkle in the eye, and a funny story to tell. Every problem could be resolved over a glass of beer at the local pub. A renowned anaesthetist, he welcomed trainees from all over the world to his department. "Welcome to the Gloucestershire Royal Hospital, your first job will be to man the intensive therapy unit. This is a good way to get to know how the hospital works before you start training in theatre." This was indeed a good idea. I busied myself learning a new medical system and practice, having of course never worked in England before. As a surgical house officer in anaesthetics, I soon learned what the "house" part meant. Weekend in-house call – you were not to leave the hospital – started midday Friday and ended midday

Monday; a full three days. Here I learned not only how to manage very sick patients requiring cardiac and respiratory support – often using ventilators – but also how to support their families through this most difficult time. Another valuable lesson was learning to work with nurses, called "sisters" in England. Any young house officer did well to gain the ITU sister's confidence and trust. Once that was established, the sister would be an enormous source of information and would protect you, only waking you at night during the three-day marathon if an extreme emergency occurred that they could not handle by themselves. As an example of such an emergency, consider another ITU experience in South Africa.

I staggered out of the ITU sleep cubicle at around 2a.m. having been urgently called by the sister. A ventilated patient's ventilator alarms were shrieking that the device was malfunctioning. No oxygen was being pushed through the endotracheal (ET) tube into the patient.

The patient was an elderly South African dying of Klebsiella pneumonia. This bacterium eats away at the lungs, creating gaping holes which can burst. Dying patients often need respiratory support so that the prescribed antibiotics can take effect. Nonetheless, mortality is extremely high. I stood at the patient's bed. Lighting was poor. Still there was just enough light to see that he was struggling to breathe. "Air hunger": his chest and abdominal muscles heaved with the effort of inspiration. To no avail. He was starting to look terminal. The ventilator alarms continued shrieking; no oxygen was going through the red rubber tube down into his trachea and lungs. What to do?

Roger had told me: first let down the balloon cuff around the ET tube* (it may have herniated around the opening of the tube), then suction out the tube to see if it is obstructed, and if…"still in doubt, take it out!" I followed suit. I let down the cuff and disengaged the ventilator from the tube, equipped to suck it out with a suction catheter readied in my right hand. The patient took one very deep breath, now possible because the deflated cuff surrounding the tube left space in the trachea to inhale ambient air through, then – an explosive cough ensued. A six-inch Ascaris worm shot out

* Endotracheal tubes, have a circumferential balloon or "cuff" which can be inflated via a pilot tube using a syringe with air. These inflated cuffs, which are positioned close to the end of the tube, in the trachea, properly seat the ET tube allowing no air to escape alongside the tube. This allows positive pressure ventilation of the lungs through the tube without letting any gases escape alongside.

of the tube, landing deftly in my hand, ready to suction if that step had not worked. The patient recovered immediately. The Ascaris worm had blocked the tube, preventing any oxygen from being delivered to the patient, almost causing him to die from asphyxiation. I learned later that Ascaris worms, a common parasitic infestation of the stomach, attempt to leave dying patients, much as rats leave a sinking ship. But this one took a wrong turning into the patient's trachea instead of out of the mouth, thus causing a life-threatening obstruction of the tube when the worm realized its mistake and was turning back on its way out.

Those are the kind of emergencies the ITU sister would call the house officer for.

After a month in the intensive therapy unit in England, I started learning practical anaesthesia in the operating theatres. For the first week or so I was assigned with the anaesthetic registrar rotating from Bristol University to learn the ropes. Registrars have two or three years of anaesthetic training under their belt and have passed the primary examination for the FFARCS (Eng). This primary examination, the first in a sequence of examinations, comprised a written test on the basic science of anaesthesia and the physiology and pharmacology of anaesthetic practice. On passing this written section of the primary examination, a further intense viva voce examination in London would follow. Success in the primary examination provided an SHO like myself with the necessary leverage to apply for a top registrar position. A further two to three years as a registrar supplied the required clinical experience to qualify to sit the final examination, the outcome of which we were awaiting beneath Hunter's statue in the portico at Lincoln's Inn Fields.

Learning practical anaesthetics is like learning to cook. It is part art and part science. A cook mixes ingredients in a big pot and then adds to taste. Depending on what produce or ingredients are available that day – or to enhance the taste – she may alter the composition, often changing the amounts of different ingredients. She may add or subtract. She may bring the pot to boil or just let it simmer at a lower temperature. There is great scope for experimentation and refinement!

So too, in learning how to administer anaesthetics. There are many ways to combine different anaesthetic drugs to achieve the unconscious state. Different levels of unconsciousness are necessary for different types of surgery and patients.

Compare a robust rugby player with a frail octogenarian in a wheel chair. They have very different sensitivities to anaesthetic drugs.

Contrast cardiac surgery, where the chest must be opened, with eye surgery, where only a small incision is made to perform the operation. Unlike cookbooks however, anaesthetic textbooks give a range of doses for individual drugs and agents, but do not describe doses for administration when drugs are combined or for different types of surgery. That is left up to the individual anaesthetist, and therein lies the art.

The anaesthetist must determine the depth of anaesthesia required in the particular setting, adjusting the concentrations of gases and doses of administered drugs, much as a cook adjusts temperature and ingredients. Just enough and not too much. Anaesthetists, just like cooks, must learn to deal with the anticipated consequences if the pot boils over.

Ether or chloroform alone can provide anaesthesia. However, modern anaesthetic techniques require more than just the production of unconsciousness. Anaesthetists must paralyze the patient's muscles and stop patients breathing so that a breathing tube can be placed in the trachea and the abdomen can be cut open to allow surgery. The required muscle relaxation ensuring that muscles are not ripped when they are pulled apart with a large retractor to allow the surgeon access for the procedure.

Surgery is not innocuous. The anaesthetist must learn to manage the insults to the body. Sawing open a patient's chest or cutting open the abdomen for surgical access causes overwhelming increases in blood pressure that must be blunted by the anaesthetic techniques. As they go about their work, surgeons pull on organs such as eyes, intestines and the heart – interconnected through the nervous system – sometimes stopping the heart completely, other times, depressing heart function and rate, often needing treatment to counter.

If this were not enough, there is more. Anaesthetics not only depress the brain, they disable many vital functions and systems. The anaesthetist must learn how to compensate for these consequences, artificially, to minimize undesirable effects on the body.

While just one anaesthetic like ether or halothane could be given at sufficient depth to assure unconsciousness, blunt negative effects, and paralyze the patient, this would be at great expense in safety.

Consider the unrestrained administration of halothane in overdose. After unconsciousness, the patient's breathing and the heart would slow, blood pressure would drop and continue dropping, and then the patient would stop breathing. Lacking sufficient oxygen, the heart would stop, heralding imminent death.

Since John Snow's meticulous description of how to administer ether anaesthesia in 1847[*] – the science of anaesthetic practice and training has developed.[1] Safety has been hard won through meticulous research, teaching and the refinement of anaesthetic drugs, techniques and monitoring in favor of using multiple different medications to minimize the toxicity from individual agents. We call this "Balanced Anesthesia."

Despite these improvements, complications still abound from the very nature of surgery and anaesthesia, requiring the trainee anaesthetist to learn her craft, often still, unfortunately, by trial and error.

"Complications" was the name Roger Eltringham assigned to the weekly round-robin anaesthetic training tutorial that he hosted.[†] Over steaming cups of English tea, the SHOs gathered around him early on Tuesday mornings before theater started. Any complication was grist for the mill of discussion. Australian, South African, American, Indian, Chinese and a few English and Scottish doctors would be questioned, if not grilled, on the interesting cases that had occurred the previous week.

So we learned that deepening anaesthesia can in some instances be safer for patients.

Witness the recent patient I presented. A stout rugby player, grown fat with the years, presenting for an orthopedic procedure on the foot under general anaesthesia. I was using halothane, and this being early in my career, I was scared of deepening the anaesthetic, fearful of further depressing the heart and blood pressure. The surgeon struck at the foot much as with Hannah Greener who died from a similar procedure under chloroform.[‡] I had kept him too "light" and the foot incision must have released a torrent of adrenaline into the rugby player's circulation, because suddenly, volleys of irregular heartbeats occurred. Halothane was notorious for this complication – just like chloroform. It sensitizes the heart, provoking arrhythmias in the face of high circulating levels of adrenaline, which could end up in ventricular

---

[*] Considered one of the first textbooks of anaesthesia.

[†] I still use this teaching technique with residents and medical students.

[‡] This historic case study is recounted in Chapter 2.

fibrillation, the putative cause of Hannah Greener's historical death.

"Jonathan, what would you do in this situation?" Roger asked one of my English colleagues, Dr. Cooper. "I would deepen anaesthesia with a further bolus of thiopentone," was the correct answer.

We also learned that the common practice of directly injecting thiopentone using only a needle, placed in the brachial vein at the elbow, was indeed quite dangerous. Penetrating the artery below would result in inadvertent direct intra-arterial injection of thiopentone with gangrene of the hand and a possible need for amputation the result.[2] A possible safer alternative – placing an intravenous indwelling catheter first – had its problems too. Venflon was just such a newly developed intravenous catheter, which allowed repeat bolusing* of different drugs through an injection port hub.

I presented the next complication, the result of a remnant dose of succinylcholine retained unwittingly in this hub.

The patient was pregnant. Unfortunately she had suffered an intra-uterine death at around eighteen weeks' gestation and now needed removal of the uterine contents urgently to avoid infection. I had induced anaesthesia through the Venflon catheter, starting with thiopentone, then administering a paralytic agent, succinylcholine, so that I could quickly place an endotracheal tube to protect her lungs from the possibility of aspirating stomach contents – a complication that was very likely at this later stage of pregnancy. Once the patient was anaesthetized, the anaesthesia assistant and I readied ourselves to push her stretcher from the induction room, where I had started the anaesthetic, into the adjacent theatre, and then transfer her to the theatre table. We moved her onto the table, but just as I connected the EKG to monitor her heart rhythm trace, she started moving. She was too light! I needed to increase the depth of anaesthetic quickly. I injected a second dose of thiopentone through the Venflon catheter as Jonathan had suggested. To my horror, the EKG trace flatlined after the injection. What had I done? Thirty seconds passed, an eternity, then I saw a stirring. A tentative heartbeat was displayed on the EKG, and then another and another as her heart returned slowly to its normal rhythm.

Roger asked, "Chris what happened?" Chris Orlikowski, another South African-trained doctor, knew the answer immediately. "When Berend injected

---

* Administering a defined amount of a drug.

the thiopentone, a small remaining dose of succinylcholine,* was injected into the patient, causing cardiac arrest. He should have flushed the catheter immediately."

By 1984, the Gloucestershire Royal Hospital, where I was receiving SHO training in anaesthetics, was considered a state of the art National Health Service District General Hospital. With fourteen operating theatres and an obstetrics unit it served as a training center for anaesthetic, orthopedic, general surgery and gynecology and obstetrics senior house officers and registrars.

While there was no standardized anaesthetic equipment throughout the hospital, the basic equipment was of the class to be expected at such a training site.

This consisted of a Boyles machine; a two-level aluminum trolley on four anti-static wheels backed by an open metal frame forming a crossbar.† This anaesthetic machine accommodated an intricate set of metal pipes allowing delivery of anaesthetic agents and gases to the patient. The bottom level housed a Manley ventilator,‡ which could be connected to the patient via a set of corrugated rubber hoses, allowing the anaesthetist to mechanically assist breathing when necessary.[3]

The middle level contained a complex pipe system covered by aluminum sheeting which doubled as a work surface for masks, breathing tubes, syringes filled with anaesthetic drugs and other anaesthetic paraphernalia.

The cross bar housed anaesthetic gas piping that fed into a cylindrical halothane vaporizer, hanging above the work surface (quite a few machines also still had ether vaporizer bottles; we ignored those).

Oxygen, air, carbon dioxide and nitrous oxide cylinders hung on either side of the Boyle's machine in cages. Attached by yokes, these gas cylinders connected through a flow rotameter allowing precision delivery of quantitated

---

* Succinylcholine, was introduced in 1954, and is still used today, as no better alternative has been found. Its structure is that of two acetylcholine molecules linked together. This structure explains this complication. Acetylcholine is the physiological mediator which stimulates the muscarinic receptor in the sinus node of the heart. It is reported that five minutes after first administration, the breakdown product to succinyl-monocholine may sensitize the heart to cause severe heart slowing (bradycardia) with possible cardiac arrest when a second bolus dose is administered.

† See Chapter Six for picture.

‡ In the future, stand-alone ventilators such as the Manley ventilator would become superfluous as ventilators were incorporated into anaesthesia machines.

flows of these gases through the vaporizer. Capping the top of the stainless steel vaporizer, filled with liquid halothane, was a red circular gradated dial which could be adjusted to provide varying concentrations of halothane vapor.* Administered gases, after passing through the vaporizers, would flow into a system of corrugated rubber hoses – the anaesthesia delivery system – that was connected to a mask or endotracheal tube for inhalation by the patient. By throwing a switch, these hoses could also connect through a circle system of hoses that incorporated an absorption canister – containing calcium oxide granules – used to absorb exhaled carbon dioxide gas from the patient.

A very important part of anaesthetic training was to develop a keen understanding of the working of this complex equipment: the interplay of gas flows, vaporizer concentrations and ventilator settings, interacting with each individual patient's respiratory mechanics. There was scope for plenty of mistakes with this complicated equipment. And I, for one, made quite a few.

Worth mentioning though, was that there were already notable safety features on the anaesthesia machine and delivery system in 1984.

Features like a polarographic oxygen sensor, which alarmed if oxygen levels going to the patient crept too low, was present on some machines.† And, a pin index system had been newly incorporated on the Boyle's machine yokes so that a lethally wrong gas cylinder, say, nitrous oxide, could not be connected to an oxygen cylinder yoke.

To assure that life-saving oxygen was always available, this gas was piped from a central gas supply and fed to the Boyles machine.‡ If for some reason this oxygen supply became disconnected from the anaesthetic machine a "Bosun's whistle" – an oxygen failure alarm – would sound – loudly.§

Nonetheless, there was much room for error and many pressing safety

---

* Halothane, a volatile anaesthetic agent, is provided in bottles as a liquid and has a saturated vapor pressure of about one third of the atmospheric pressure at sea level. As soon as it comes in contact with air it vaporizes and mixes with air. This vapor is delivered to the patient to provide anaesthesia. The problem is that the ensuing concentration of around 30% would be immediately lethal. Hence vaporizers are constructed to allow only a small amount of planned gas delivery to pass through the vaporizing chamber. This fully saturated gas then joins the bypassed gas to deliver a concentration of halothane dialed into the vaporizer (0-8%).

† The polarographic oxygen sensor described by Clark was an important safety step in monitoring of anaesthetic gas delivery. (It was not very reliable at the time; the batteries would run out.)

‡ No matter what type of general anaesthetic is provided, additional oxygen is always needed. Ambient air contains only 21% oxygen concentration and the depressive effects of anaesthetic agents guarantee that patients will become hypoxic if additional oxygen is not available. Hence the emphasis on monitoring the adequacy of oxygen delivery.

§ We were instructed to check the Bosun whistle before every day of anaesthetic delivery.

enhancements yet to be made over the next thirty years or so.

For example, there was room for improvement in the way drugs were identified and administered to patients to avoid giving the wrong drugs to the patient – a very common error in anaesthesia.

At that time, different drug classes used for anaesthesia were often drawn up into syringes of different sizes: 20ml or 10ml or 5ml to identify them later when they needed to be administered. (e.g. 5 ml syringes were used for muscle paralytic drugs). Anaesthetists relying on the color of the liquid in the syringe (yellow for thiopentone), or the size of the syringe, to remind them what drug was present. The more fastidious anaesthetist would affix a piece of plaster around the syringe and write the drug name on it.* Others would just place all the syringes with their needles attached – for quick injection† – on a plastic tray; the position of the syringe on the tray hopefully reminding them of the drug within.

Basic equipment for standard monitoring, at the time, consisted of an EKG – to assess heart speed and rhythm – and intermittent blood pressure assessment. A blood pressure cuff was wound round the patient's arm and attached to rubber tubing, which fed into a circular blood pressure gauge – twelve inches across – prominently displayed and attached to one post of the Boyles machine.

A paper anaesthetic record was used to document these vital signs, as well as the drug doses administered, using a clipboard chained to the machine.

As patients often vomited from the anesthetics delivered, standard essential equipment was a suction device, usually with a large container attached. Larger Boyles machines might have the benefit of sets of drawers in which were placed emergency drugs, airways, bite blocks and other tools of the anaesthetic trade, readily available, at a moment's notice, when an emergency occurred.

My training progressed by leaps and bounds, trial and error, complications occurring regularly.

"Am I going to be all right then?" asked the patient I was visiting on the

---

* Today we have colored labels with printed medication names available to affix to the syringe. Or better still, syringes, color code labeled, prefilled with the anaesthetic medication, adding immeasurably to the safety and sterility of drug administration. See Chapter Five for picture.

† Many iv sets have rubber (now latex free) "bungs" through which a syringe needle can be pushed to administer the drug directly into the infusion line through which intravenous fluids are administered to patients.

ward to do a preoperative assessment. I wasn't so sure myself; taking a person's life in one's hands with limited experience is truly terrifying. She had fractured her hip, slipping on an icy pavement, and now needed to be anaesthetized for surgical repair.* I examined her and thought she might have early heart failure. Listening with my stethoscope I found that she had some crackles resounding in her lungs when breathing in deeply. This suggested that her heart might not be pumping as well as it should and so her lungs were starting to flood with extra fluid. I was not absolutely sure, but putting on a brave face, I reassured her as best I could, and went down to theatre to prepare for the anaesthetic.

There were two anaesthetic techniques that could be applied.

I could administer a spinal anaesthetic – under sterile conditions a thin spinal needle is introduced through the skin in between the lumbar vertebrae and into the fluid-filled sac surrounding the spinal cord. When spinal fluid backs out of the needle, confirming correct placement, local anaesthetic is injected, numbing all the nerves below. This includes the hip where surgery is to occur. The anaesthesia lasting for three to four hours, after which the patient recovers sensation.

The alternative anaesthetic technique was general anaesthesia, which I regrettably chose. I misjudged the fact that her incipient cardiac failure could be worsened by the cardiac depressant effects that general anaesthesia entailed. Administering thiopentone and halothane, I precipitated pulmonary edema (water in the lungs) which was now clinically apparent. The patient's already enfeebled heart muscle – weakened further by the administered anaesthetic agents – could no longer pump with sufficient strength to avoid the complication of fluid backing up in her lungs. Diuretic therapy, and prolonged respiratory support by ventilation was now needed to allow the heart muscle to recover and the lungs to clear before I could remove the endotracheal tube after surgery was completed. Fortunately, she recovered fully, and I learned a valuable lesson in patient frailty, medical optimization, and the need to administer anaesthetic agents that depress the heart less in such patients.

As demonstrated by this patient, whom I looked after late one night, SHOs' training in anaesthetics in the 1980s was largely unsupervised. Occasionally

* Anaesthesia for surgical repair of a fractured hip in an elderly frail patient continues to be controversial still today. The patients are often sick with heart failure which needs to be treated, but surgery needs to take place as soon as possible. The anesthesiologist and surgeon need to balance the uncertain risks in determining the time when the patient can best have the operation.

though we might have a consultant anaesthetist helping us with a list. Consultants would either anaesthetize alternative patients in the same theatre or have us helping them with more complex cases. As we progressed, we would run our own theatre list and often, especially on call at night, we were left to our own devices. We could call the consultant at home, but would often be told, "Get on with it."

Notwithstanding my list of complications, or because of them, I seemed to be progressing favorably; after six months as an SHO I was allowed to advance to do more complicated and risky anaesthetics.

I could now do obstetric anaesthesia on my own and visit outside institutions to provide anaesthetic care.

Dr. Roger Eltringham's confidence in my abilities did not do justice to how terrifying the first six months had been. I had lost five kilograms in weight, mostly, I believe, from the anxiety and worrying – especially the night before – in planning the next day's anaesthetics to be delivered.*

Sir Fredrick Hewitt, in 1896, while lobbying for the development of the specialty of anaesthesia in England described it exactly: "The anaesthetist of experience recognizes certain types of subjects, and knows that certain methods will be appropriate in certain of these types and inappropriate in others. He knows that certain subjects will represent certain difficulties. He disregards symptoms which possibly alarm the tiro, and *he feels anxious when the casual and untrained observer sees no need for alarm.*" Hewitt went on to say, "There are several operations in which 'the risk', so far as the procedures of the surgeon are concerned are practically nil, whilst that *of the anaesthetic is a tangible one, especially in the hands of an inexperienced practitioner.*"(emphasis mine)[4]

Roger, some ninety years later, also said it well. To provide safe anaesthesia, preparation and anticipation is paramount, while "being ready for anything" is essential.

Nonetheless, I was now a senior SHO in anaesthetics allowed to visit and cover the obstetric theatre no matter how anxiety-provoking that was.

Here we were still using trilene, a particularly toxic anaesthetic agent.†

---

* In some instances, with certain patients, this worrying never leaves you.

† Trilene or trichloroethylene has the chemical structure: $CCl_2=C.Cl.H$ Trichloroethylene, introduced in the 1920s, was used to extract vegetable oils and decaffeinate coffee. Subsequently it was found to have anaesthetic properties.

Trilene was another chemical, serendipitously found, to have very good anaesthesia and especially analgesic properties. Reason enough, at the time, for its use in obstetric anaesthesia. The only way to use this safely was to remember to exclude the circle anaesthetic absorption system when using this agent.

Was my nightly worry about the next day's cases warranted? Consider the sporadic and unpredictable development of malignant hyperthermia, a fatal disease caused by anesthetic administration.

In 1960 a young man fractured his leg bones in a motor vehicle accident in Australia.

He was not particularly worried about the surgery but was petrified of the anaesthetic. Ten close family members had died from anaesthesia after only minor surgical procedures.[5] The newly synthetized halothane was tried, as ether had been the killer anaesthetic in the past. Soon after halothane administration had started, he became intensely ill. His blood pressure fell, his heart rate climbed; becoming blue from cyanosis, he felt hot to the touch, while the circle absorber system used for anaesthetic delivery, became over heated. If the anaesthetist had looked closely, he would have found that the patient's muscles were rigid. The anaesthetic was stopped and iced cloths were applied to the patient's fiery body. Recovering fully – routine diagnostic and biochemical tests revealed nothing of note.

Nine years later, a fifty-one-year-old patient presenting at the same hospital was not so lucky. Administered halothane and succinylcholine, he became rigid and overheated, dying in less than twenty-four hours. This time however, routine tests showed severe muscle damage, identifying the problem as originating in the muscles. This syndrome, of overheating and muscle contracture after the administration of volatile anaesthetic agents and succinylcholine, would be called malignant hyperthermia, and had a mortality of seven in ten patients afflicted with a genetic predisposition to the disease.[6]

When used with a carbon dioxide absorption system, the heat generated in the chemical reaction causes the break-down of trichloroethylene to trichloroacetylene. This toxic product injures nerves, particularly the cranial nerves and more specifically the trigeminal nerve, which supplies the eye and side of the face. Anaesthetic techniques using trichloroethylene could lead to this untoward complication. Phosgene gas (used in chemical warfare) was a further toxic byproduct from trilene. This anaesthetic agent is no longer used today for these reasons.

Fortunately, speaking to the research that has made anaesthesia so much safer, an animal model, the Landrace Cross Large White Pig was found at the University of Cape Town in South Africa. This "Hot Pig" model, which reacted similarly to humans, when halothane or succinylcholine was administered, would be used to test drug therapy to attempt to treat this problem.[7] In 1975, the drug dantrolene was found to be the therapeutic breakthrough – paving the way for treatment of this condition with a concomitant decrease in mortality to around 5% in the present day.[8*]

With this cautionary introduction to the ever-present unpredictable threats facing an anaesthetist and his patient, back to my second six months as an SHO – allowed to do more complicated cases in obstetrics and outside hospitals.

General anaesthetic administration for a pregnant patient facing an emergent caesarean section to deliver a baby is always worrying. Especially for a newly minted "senior" SHO on his own in the delivery suite. There are not one, but two patients to worry about: the mother and the unborn child. And, anaesthetic agents affect them both, while the mother's body physiology and response to medications has changed to accommodate the growth and birth of the child.[†] This, in particular, can make endotracheal intubation – to ensure adequate lung ventilation and protection from vomiting – much more difficult than in the non-obstetric patient.

My pager had gone off; I was called urgently to the obstetric unit. Drugs had been drawn up previously and readied for just such an occurrence. As a first step, we give extra oxygen by face mask before inducing anaesthesia, asking patients to breathe in deeply – 100% oxygen for three to five minutes.

---

* Malignant hyperthermia is still a major problem but the mortality is around 5%. There is a familial pre-disposition which can be identified by genetic testing, but not absolutely excluded. Hence anesthesiologists today always ask for a family history of problems with anaesthesia. An absolute diagnosis of the condition can be made by taking a muscle biopsy and performing a caffeine-halothane contracture test. There are however only currently twenty-one centers around the world where this specific test is performed. If the test is positive, the patient will be labeled as having MH (malignant hyperthermia) and specific anaesthetics, such as volatile anaesthetics and succinylcholine will not be administered. At the first signs of MH, anesthesiologists will start the administration of dantrolene and follow a checklist protocol of therapy which includes ice-packing and other measures to decrease the patient's temperature. The first original research on dantrolene was carried out at the University of Cape Town laboratories by Professor Gaisford Harrison and his associates. I subsequently completed my PhD in these laboratories, studying the same strain of pigs used in the aforementioned seminal research.

† More specifics about the physiology of pregnancy will be provided under the section describing subspecialty anaesthesia (Chapter 7).

This is called pre-oxygenation and completely fills the mother's lungs with oxygen. All important, because we are about to stop all breathing and both the mother and baby need extra oxygen at this critical time. But there was little time to do this properly as the case was now emergent; fetal distress! The baby was in trouble and needed to be cut out immediately by Cesarean section to preserve its life.

I quickly gave some thiopentone and succinylcholine, my assistant then pressed on the mother's throat to make sure that no fluid from her stomach ran back into her lungs, while the muscle relaxant took effect. Paralyzing the muscles would allow me to open her mouth, put in a laryngoscope, visualize the airway opening to the trachea, and place the breathing tube. I removed the mask and tried opening her mouth. Impossible: she was rigid! I could not open her mouth; her face muscles clamped down tightly. Was this malignant hyperthermia starting?* Did this explain why I couldn't open her mouth to place the laryngoscope? Now we were all in real trouble. She was paralyzed and rigid, not breathing; oxygen supply was running out. I needed to see if I could push some air into her lungs by pressing the face mask down on her face and inflating her lungs using the Mapleson A breathing system that I had used to pre-oxygenate her. No matter how hard I tried, I could not. Her whole body was rigid. This is the most feared situation an anaesthetist can find themselves in. We call it: cannot ventilate, cannot intubate and it is a crisis! I called for help. A registrar anaesthetist was somewhere in the hospital and could be called for backup. I do not recall if the mother was going blue from lack of oxygen, but I decided to turn her on her side. I hoped in this way to allow her to wake up from the administered thiopentone and recover from the succinylcholine induced paralysis and rigidity. And it worked. Slowly, painstakingly, I forced oxygen into her body, pressing the mask tightly to her face while my assistant pressed the back of her head. She started to wake up on her side, sobbing and confused, but breathing. Haltingly at first, but with increasing vigor, soon after.

Why was the baby not yet born when she was waking up from anaesthesia, she spluttered? As she was breathing and recovering – this was one problem solved – but the baby was still in distress, still needing emergent delivery by Cesarean section. The anaesthetic registrar came in to the theatre

---

* Various degrees of muscle rigidity associated with muscular syndromes that can provoke malignant hyperthermia are well described. Particularly with the use of succinylcholine.

and immediately identified the crisis. Noting that she was already on her side, he busied himself with placing a spinal anaesthetic, as the mother was awakening, to allow rapid delivery.* The baby came out crying: a 10 out of 10 APGAR score, the score used to assess how well recently born babies are doing. The mother now fully conscious, sobbing with pleasure at seeing her first child born expeditiously by Cesarean section under spinal anesthesia. And I am forever grateful for the two of them and my registrar colleague who saved the day.

All's well that ends well. We sent off for tests for malignant hyperthermia and they turned out to be negative, leaving unexplained the extreme rigidity the mother experienced – occasioned by the induction of anaesthesia – that had posed a threat to her and her baby's life.

Professor Bill Mapleson (1926-), trim and nicely dressed in his signature Harris tweed jacket and tie, described the five different anaesthesia breathing systems he lettered: A, B, C, D, and E on the chalk board behind him. Lecturing to us as a faculty member for the Primary Course in Anaesthetics, held at the University of Wales in Cardiff, he was the undisputed expert on the subject. The problem to address was the amounts of nitrous oxide, air or oxygen in liters per minute, we would have to administer to patients through the different systems he had described – to ensure enough oxygen and avoid the build-up of exhaled carbon dioxide – so poisoning the patient. This was a complicated affair, different if the anaesthetized patient was breathing by themselves or assisted by inflating their lungs; delivered using the attached anaesthesia bag that was a component of the Mapleson anaesthesia systems. Lectures such as this formed the basis of the primary knowledge that was expected of anaesthetists. The described Mapleson systems were the state of the art at the time and depicted in every text book of anaesthesia since. Professor Mapleson was not an anaesthetist, but a physicist, who had been hired by the University of Wales' professor of anaesthetics, William Mushin, to study mechanisms of drug paralysis in human volunteers. Not surprisingly, few volunteers showed up to be paralyzed, so instead Mapleson investigated the physiology of breathing

* This was a relatively uncommon anaesthetic technique for Cesarean section in 1984. Today, and for the last twenty years or so, spinal anaesthesia is the preferred technique to avoid some of the problems I experienced. General anaesthesia is only performed if there is a specific indication to do so, and is still faced with trepidation by many, because they are not as practiced in the technique.

systems, the subject of his lecture to us that day. Thrilled to receive a lecture from this world-famous erudite man, I timidly walked up to the lectern during question time. "Professor Mapleson," I asked, "what is it like to be so eminent in your field?" He humbly replied, a faint smile expanding on his face, "I am the only man to become famous for writing down the first five letters of the alphabet!" A, B, C, D and E!

Bill's lecture was one of many by noted experts on the two-day course organized by the University of Wales to prepare candidates for the grueling primary examination for the FFARCS (Eng). Senior house officers in anaesthetics from the west of England and Wales were granted leave from their normal duties to attend the course, which featured multiple lectures on the basic science of anaesthesia, including physics and anaesthesia equipment, as well as the physiology and pharmacology of anaesthetic practice. Further preparation for the exam – which had both a written and oral component – was left to the faculty tutor at the home institution to arrange. At the Gloucestershire Royal Hospital, Roger Eltringham had the "Complications" sessions mentioned earlier and was ahead of his time in preparing candidates for the oral vive voce examinations by videotaping us while asking possible exam questions. Gloucester SHOs were thus well prepared for this all-important examination process, having gained experience in providing anaesthetics for all manners of cases, including psychiatric patients at the nearby Coney Hill Mental Asylum. Should we be asked the anaesthetic management of depressed patients presenting for electroconvulsive therapy, we would be able to provide a good example of how the refinement of anaesthetic techniques could enhance patient safety.

Electroconvulsive Therapy (ECT), or electroshock therapy, was introduced in 1934. Dr. Ugo Cerletti, an Italian psychiatrist, had observed the use of electrocution in slaughter-house pigs. Workers could better slit the porcine throat when the unconsciousness pig was lying still.* He extended the idea to human practice. Noting that depressed patients who convulsed often improved, he championed electroshock therapy to treat depression. However before the advent of anesthetic techniques this therapy was somewhat barbaric as prospective ECT patients needed to be shackled down and had electric

* This slaughterhouse technique would be important to my later pig research (Chapter 7).

calipers – with wetted electrode sponges – placed on each side of the head just in front of the ears at the temple. An attached electric wire connected the patient to a DC current generator box, readied to deliver a precise shock to the skull and brain. To protect teeth, a rubber gag was placed in the mouth and then a shock was administered; at a voltage sufficient to elicit a convulsion in the patient. The convulsion – an epileptiform seizure activity in the brain – was necessary to achieve a therapeutic effect. Unfortunately, although effective, patients suffered from extremely high blood pressure peaks, lack of oxygen, and many fractures of long bones and vertebrae occurred from the ensuing convulsions. To address these problems anaesthetic techniques had been developed by 1954.[9]

I drove to the Coney Hill Mental Asylum early so I could get everything ready in good time for the start of the list. Eight patients, lying on their stretchers in alcoves, faced the central wood-floored hall, like spokes in a half wheel. Light streaming down from the glass skylight windows lent eeriness to the ghastly proceeding. In the center of the cavernous hall stood a large oxygen cylinder, but little else. Attached, a Mapleson C, breathing circuit; I recognized it immediately, ready for my use. Little further anaesthetic equipment was in evidence but a small tray on wheels was beside the bed. I identified a waiting blood pressure machine, and cuff for the patient, and drew up multiple syringes filling them with methohexitone (MTX), an intravenous induction agent and succinylcholine (SUX), the paralytic agent. I labeled the syringes carefully and placed them on the tray ready for the first patient, whom I could spy in bed 1. ECT therapy then, as today, is provided in a series of six to twelve daily treatments; patients suffering short term memory loss and confusion coincident with the therapy. There is thus no point in taking an anaesthetic history (they can't remember anything), so in anticipation of the anesthetic I reviewed the patient's chart, to see what doses of MTX and SUX had been used previously, and whether or not the dose was considered right; just enough MTX to render the patient unconscious, but still allowing a perceptible convulsion to occur. This was critical. On the one hand the right amount of anaesthetic for the patient had to be provided so that the patient was just unconscious – but the seizure was not completely suppressed. On the other hand, sufficient SUX was required to arrest the physical effects of the convulsion, so protecting the patient from a long bone or vertebrae fracture.

My first patient, I will call him John, was in a catatonic state, with depression, and had received three therapies already, with minimal effect. Today the psychiatrist would up the electroshock dosage and I would lower the MTX dose slightly to allow convulsions to spread; it was all planned. But not an exact science. John was wheeled in and moved next to my rudimentary anaesthetic equipment and the waiting oxygen cylinder in the center of the hall. A cheery welcome on my part was greeted by a catatonic grunt. I let this ride, and started the now accustomed Venflon IV. The psychiatrist, placing the electrode calipers consulted his notes as to the desired voltage to administer and dialed this to the appropriate level. All he would have to do at the right time was push a button; the trigger had been set.

ECT was not a rare procedure in the 1980s. Fifty thousand patients a year receiving this therapy in England with around twelve hundred a year at Coney Hill Hospital. The large numbers of cases requiring anaesthesia was probably why "senior" SHOs were assigned to provide this service. The consultant anaesthetists having long tired of the need to provide multiple general anaesthetics in isolated scary places with no help available. Further adding to my trepidation was that a psychiatrist was no help in an emergency, and we were four miles from the nearest hospital. The Horton Hospital in Gloucester.

My job was to give just enough MTX to please the psychiatrist – a convulsion would form, but would be then immediately suppressed. And to time the SUX just right, so that the patient was partially paralyzed – allowing us to see the convulsion starting, but not allow progression, too viciously, to avoid bone breakage. SUX will stop the patient breathing, requiring oxygen assistance, hence the large tank festooned with the Mapleson C breathing circuit looming present in the center of the room.

John was drooling a bit. I injected 80mg of MTX, checked his eye lash reflex to ascertain when he was unconscious, and then administered 60mg of SUX.* Quickly placing the Mapleson C breathing circuit mask over his face and turning up the oxygen flow so I could inflate his lungs with the balloon bag filled with oxygen. Satisfied that I had provided sufficient pre-oxygenation to prepare John for the oxygen-depleting convulsion that

---

* Anesthesiologists always give the induction agent first (MTX), making sure the patient is asleep, before giving the paralytic drug, to avoid the patient being paralyzed and awake. Succinylcholine is a depolarizing muscle relaxant introduced in 1954 which causes painful contraction of the muscles that would hurt the patient if awake. After SUX administration, upon recovery from anaesthesia, patients, especially women, complain of myalgia – muscle pain. Some say it feels like they were in a road traffic accident.

would follow, I placed the rubber mouth gag, and with one finger held up his jaw, so keeping open his airway, indicating to the psychiatrist I was ready, but trembling. Zap! The electro shock was delivered to John's head with a buzzing sound emanating from the machine. A faint smell of electric burning wafted above the patient. John scrunched up his face from the shock. (Had I not given enough SUX or waited too long? The face muscle should have been paralyzed and not scrunched up.) Then slowly, his right hand started twitching and then the left, and then he started perceptibly, but not viciously, convulsing. The psychiatrist yelped with approval – I had done all right. John continued to convulse slightly as we turned him on his side to let his spittle escape from his mouth, and then he started coming to. Slobbering and confused but breathing – I made sure about that – I wheeled him back to the alcove whence he came from. A willing nurse recovering him further while I busied myself with the next patient, marveling at the anaesthetic technique, specifically designed to make this oft-performed procedure safer for the patient.[*]

Feeling sufficiently prepared to sit the written part of the Primary Exam, I made my way for the first of many visits to the Royal College of Surgeons building at Lincoln's Inn Fields in London. Lincoln's Inn Fields has the largest public square in London, deriving its name from the adjacent Lincoln's Inn, one of the four Inns of Court.

With the necessary clinical experience under my belt and hoping that I had devoted sufficient time to studying the anaesthetic text books edited by Miller, West, Parbrook, as well as Calvey and Williams, during the preceding seven months, I felt ready to try my hand at this demanding written examination. I had also benefited immensely from the described Primary Course held at Cardiff University.

Four weeks later, I received word in the mail that I had passed the written examination and was invited back for the second part of the test: the dreaded primary viva voce examination.

I was scheduled for the viva voce after lunch which turned out to be

---

[*] ECT is still regularly performed today. Having taken a dive in popularity after the film One Flew over the Cuckoo's Nest, there is a resurgence in interest for patients suffering from severe depression, catatonia, and paranoia. The same technique for anaesthesia is still used although the monitoring is more sophisticated and often a beta-blocker drug is administered to control hypertension not controlled by the MTX.

propitious. In fact, I credit this with the reason I passed. Lincoln's Inn Fields Square includes a lovely garden. In the summer months, tennis is played on its fields, a great spectator sport for the viva voce examiners seeking a break over lunch, especially when pretty girls are playing. I was summoned into the examination room exactly at 2p.m., and asked to sit down at a formidable table. Across from me sat Professor A.B., an anesthesiologist who knew a lot about the liver. The other examiner's seat was vacant. He had been delayed, I was told. Not surprisingly, I was asked extensively about the liver. This subject I knew well, to Professor A.B.'s evident satisfaction and pleasure. Things were going well until the second examiner arrived. Brusque, hot and flustered, Professor C. D. was known to be a fearsome examiner. He mumbled some apology about the girls and tennis on a hot day, and then proceeded to eviscerate me on an esoteric subject at best: the difference between osmolality and osmolarity, (the consistency of blood plasma constituents) and how this should be measured. I too became flustered and he appeared ever more agitated at my stumbling answers; I was sure I had failed. I left London for Gloucester despondently. Four weeks later I received an envelope marked with the Royal College of Surgeons letterhead. My wife called me at work to tell me. Too fearful to wait till I got home, I asked her to open it. I had passed! Saved by the bell or rather, the pretty girls playing tennis on a hot afternoon. There was no way Prof C. D. could fail me, despite my abject performance; he had not been present for the whole examination!

I was now ready for the next step in my anaesthetic training; an anaesthetic registrar position. Ulane and I had decided that we would return to South Africa to complete our specialist training.* We had family ties there and I had been accepted for a registrar position at the University of Cape Town Medical School. Groote Schuur Hospital, famous for the first human transplant performed there by Professor Christiaan Barnard in 1967, would be the next hospital that I would be trained in. Specialist training in anaesthetics in England and its former colonies like South Africa, while having a well-structured examination system, comprising a primary and final examination, was less structured in the requirement for clinical experience. In England in 1985 one needed at least seven years of experience before seeking a consultant post, while in South Africa around five years of documented anaesthetic experience was acceptable.

---

* She became a pathologist.

Fortunately, the primary examination that I had passed in England qualified me to sit both the South African specialist examination* as well as the English FFARCS. There was a problem, however. I had to return to England to sit this final examination. First to sit the required written final examination held again at the Royal College of Surgeons, and then if I passed that, I would be invited to the final viva voce scheduled around four weeks later. This necessitated five weeks of leave from my duties in Cape Town and so I had travelled back to England, with now three years of anaesthetics training experience, to try my hand at the final FFARCS (Eng) examination – in 1987.

We stood waiting beneath John Hunter's statue for word on how we had faired in this final examination held that day. Summoned to gather at the Royal College of Surgeons, we were not quite sure what to expect. Rumors abounded of course. Rumors that sometime after 6 p.m. the chief examiner would emerge from the Edward Lumley Hall, off to the side, where the other examiners were in waiting to congratulate successful candidates on their passing. Rumors that the only way you would know whether you passed or failed was on hearing your examination number called out loud by the chief examiner. Mine was 131. If your number was not called out you had failed, and could slink away in ignominy. The pillars surrounding the porticoed hallway providing convenient cover to hide behind. Out came the chief examiner, resplendent in a Royal College of Surgeons signature black gown, with the red silken border.

He started calling out the numbers in a loud stern voice, not a hint of emotion on display: 201, 189, 175, 174, 173, 168…and 140, 139…131! 127…123… I had passed.

I could now make my way proudly into the adjacent hall. There we had to sign our readied diplomas, already witnessed in signature by the College examiners. Upon entry into the hall, I was handed a glass of sherry, and joined the waiting examiners who mingled with successful candidates shaking their hands, and saying a few encouraging words. Dr. Ralph Vaughan, on pouring my second glass, remarked, "You did well, my boy, a bright future is assured."

March 17, 1987 was a proud day for me; I had become a Fellow of the Faculty of Anaesthetists of the Royal College of Surgeons.

I endeavored to have a few more drinks to celebrate.

---

* Fellowship of the Faculty of Anaesthetists of South Africa.

4

Lines of the Parachute to Safety

A synopsis of the key elements driving anesthesia safety

Medication Cabinet at the Old Operating Theatre (1822)
and Herb Garret, St. Thomas' Church, London.

The history of anesthesiology is the history of the struggle for safety.
– Dr. Gerald Zeitlin, 2011

We pause in the narrative to describe key elements in the development of the specialty practice of anesthesiology that have contributed to the anesthetic safety now much more common for surgical, diagnostic or therapeutic procedures.

I have briefly traced my, as well as the specialty's, fledgling beginnings, drawing on my own or others' records of practice to illustrate crucial points of knowledge, technique or science.

That anesthetic practice is safer is incontrovertible; in 1912 when Sir Frederick Hewitt assessed the situation, he recounted death associated with chloroform anesthesia as one in 3,000 patients.[1]* It took until 1954 for Professor Henry Beecher, the inaugural academic chair at the Harvard Medical School, to publish the first thorough assessment of anesthetic mortality. He prospectively reviewed more than 500,000 patients receiving anesthetics across ten hospitals in Boston, reporting that the death associated with anesthesia was one per 1,560 administrations.[2] Sixty years later, in 2014, death caused by anesthesia was only one per 140,000 anesthetics, a ninety-fold improvement.[3]†

Worth mentioning – as aviation is often compared to the practice of anesthesiology – still not as safe as flying in a commercial jet liner where the reported accident death rate was one in 2.3 million flights in 2013.[4]

The history of anesthesia has therefore been a history of the struggle for safety.[5] In this short chapter I will endeavor to summarize the lines of the parachute that together have provided the safer practice we enjoy today – the proverbial parachute to safety.

The first line of the parachute

The development of anesthesia from a craft to a discipline and then maturation to the specialty practice of medicine that it is today.[1]

Separation from the surgeons was necessary to progress!

As early as the 1890s in both London and New York a resounding cry for specialist "Public Anesthetizers" arose. Sir Frederick Hewitt in London

---

* Probably inaccurately.

† Computed as seven per 1 million anaesthetic administrations. However, the surgical trespass is far from safe, as one in 2,860 perioperative deaths are totally attributable to surgical misadventure.

remarking "the occasional administration of an anesthetic, even if spread over several years, cannot make a man a reliable anesthetist." He argued for "specialism" with every hospital having an experienced anesthetist. Recognizing early that anesthetics was not just a practical matter of skilled administration, he exhorted that the discipline be studied scientifically and taught by those practicing in the field – not by surgeons who were otherwise occupied performing their operations. To be safer, he announced, the delivery of the anesthetic had to be tempered by the conditions of the patient and the type of surgery.[6]

Anesthetic practice had to be separated from well-meaning but inexpert surgeons who had relegated the responsibility of this hazardous pastime to inadequately trained tyros. Witness Dr. George F. Shrady's description of the situation in New York: "Strange as it would appear to an intelligent layman, hospital surgeons, continue to delegate this important duty to junior assistants, dressers,* and medical students." The result: the almost dead patient at the end of the proceedings would require "hypodermatic stimulation with strychnine or digitaline" to avert total collapse. Thought unnecessary, Shrady continued, "if the proper vigilance and expertise had been applied, including the administration of a hot saline enema containing whiskey."[7] At that time, "Anyone can give an anesthetic" was the surgeon's rallying cry, and just about anyone did! Once drafted, these novices in the anesthetic craft received yelled instructions on anesthetic administration from inexpert surgeons. No wonder things went wrong! In turn, surgeons were distracted from anesthetic care by the need to perform the operations which required all their attention. Predictable failures and emergencies resulted which the drafted tyros were untrained to manage, resulting in a high mortality rate. Patients were categorized in three classes: those who "took" anesthetics well, those who "took" them badly (and died) and those who would not, or did not, "take" them at all – sometimes running screaming out of the operating theater.[6]

"Anesthetization as a Specialty: Its Present and Future" was the title of Dr. Ormand Goldan's talk in New York City, the evening of March 11, 1901.

Emboldened by his extensive experience in the administration of anesthetics, Dr. Goldan decried the fact that fifty years since the introduction of anesthetics, the discipline was still in its infancy. Pointing the finger at the

---

* Dressers, amongst other responsibilities, helped surgeons put on and take off their surgical coats in preparation for surgery.

surgeons, he lamented that they selected the anesthetic (ether or chloroform) without the concerns for safety that trained anesthetists "would give full consideration," resulting in "fatalities from ridiculously minor operations *obviously avoidable* if the proper anesthetic had been selected."[8]

Quite one thing to call for "specialism," quite another to develop a medical specialty!

For anesthetic practice to progress to a specialty, a unique body of empirical knowledge, learned through trial and error, would need to be bolstered by scientific investigations to advance the field. This in turn required meticulous documentation of outcomes as well as publication and teaching by anesthetists skilled in their craft to engender the necessary credibility that a new specialty branch of medicine deserved.

To further buttress specialty development, organizational structures needed to be established, allowing anesthetists to meet to discuss common problems and subsequently to develop educational, examination and certification procedures – as well as the evidence-based standards of care – that would underpin safe anesthetic practice.

One of the organizations that facilitated specialty development in London was the Association of Anaesthetists of Great Britain and Ireland established in 1932. Their stated aim, "the development and study of anesthesia and the recognition of anesthesia as a specialized branch of medicine." In England, the examination and certification process was first conducted, in 1953, under the auspices of the Royal College of Surgeons – successful candidates awarded a Fellowship in the Faculty of Anaesthetists of the Royal College of Surgeons in England (FFARCS[Eng.]).[*] After 1989 the Anaesthetists separated from the surgeons to form the Royal College of Anaesthetists.

Across the Atlantic, in New York, the Long Island Society of Anesthetists became the New York Society of Anesthetists by 1912; becoming the American Society of Anesthesiologists in 1945.

In America, too, the examination and certification process necessary to the development of the specialty of anesthesiology was first developed under the auspices of surgery. The American Board of Anesthesiology was created in 1937 through initial affiliation with the American Board of Surgery, but received full independence much earlier than in England, by 1941.[1][†]

---

[*] The author received the FFARCS (Eng.) in 1987.

[†] The author received American Board of Anesthesiology Certification as a Specialist in 1996.

In 1955 the World Federation Societies of Anaesthesiologists was established bringing together forty-two interested national anesthesiology societies at the first World Congress of Anaesthesiologists held at Scheveningen in the Netherlands. This organization spurred the worldwide development of the specialty practice of anesthesiology, now including 140 member nations as a testament to this progress.[*]

Both in London and New York the need to separate from surgeons to create the separate specialty of anesthesiology had been recognized. Counter-intuitively perhaps, the separate practice of anesthesiology so created, developed and then made known anesthetic approaches and techniques enabling advances in surgical practice hitherto unimaginable. A mutually interdependent virtuous cycle of surgery and anesthetic progress stretching over more than eighty years.

The second line of the parachute

This line can assuredly be assigned to the enhanced education, training and supervision that has been implemented in preparing candidates for anesthesiology specialty certification in many countries around the world.

The first university-based residency training program was established by Dr. Ralph Waters in Madison, Wisconsin in 1933.[†] Integrating clinical practice, scientific research and education, it would serve as a blueprint for residency training programs for others to emulate.

Having trained and received specialist certification in both England and South Africa, I subsequently served as the residency training director at Columbia University in New York, and as Professor and Chairman of Anesthesiology at Penn State University. In these capacities, I have been responsible for the training of close to four hundred anesthesia residents over the last two and a half decades. It is safe to say that over this period residency training and supervision has advanced. Not only because of enhanced teaching techniques incorporating, for example, simulation training – using computerized plastic human models – but also because of the prescribed knowledge and experience requirements demanded by the American Board of Anesthesiology and the Royal College of Anaesthetists. Both the American

---

[*] At the time of writing, the author serves on the Board of the World Federation of Societies of Anaesthesiologists.

[†] Anesthesiology trainees are called residents in the U.S.A. and registrars in the United Kingdom and former colonies such as South Africa and Australia.

and English systems also require certification of the training programs where residents or registrars are taught. And, ongoing verification of individual competency in anesthetic skills, knowledge and professionalism, for trainees to advance to the next level.*

The third line of the parachute
Advances in anesthesia apparatus design and development.

Consider Dr. John Snow (1813-1858), a pre-eminent English anaesthetist. Short of stature and balding, he had narrow set eyes, sharp features and a pinched appearance. As a member of the Royal College of Surgeons he was highly regarded by his peers. A teetotaler† and vegan, yet unfortunately in poor health, he was one of the first to adopt ether administration in London, less than a year after this was first introduced by William Morton in America in 1846.[9] Not satisfied with the handkerchief method of ether administration – citing the fact that this approach had killed a horse recently – he developed his own airway and anesthetic apparatus. This beautiful model of design allowed the administration of known quantities of anesthetic through a face piece, rather than the unknown, variable amounts that caused the reported equine death from diaphragmatic rupture. Assuring known concentrations of ether administration through an adaptable lead facemask, with an expiratory valve attached, enhanced immeasurably the accuracy of anesthetic administration – illustrating well how early and subsequent apparatus design has contributed to anesthetic safety.[10, 11]

The fourth line of the parachute
Design and research in anesthetic drugs.

As the reader by now knows, halothane was the first specifically synthesized anesthetic drug designed to provide safe non-flammable general anesthesia. Introduced in 1956, it was far from perfect. The ideal anesthetic would be

---

* I have described the situation in the U.S.A. and England as I am knowledgeable about these systems but recognize that throughout the world, training has been formalized in many other countries.

† John Snow proved that contaminated water from a pump in central London had caused an outbreak of cholera in 1854; removing the pump handle from the water pump in Broadwick Street to solve the problem. There is a public house called the John Snow in his memory at this address. It is a very nice pub, worthy of a visit.

quick to work, provide unconsciousness, pain relief and rapid recovery, while not causing heart depression nor loss of breathing. It must be neither explosive nor affect liver and kidney function nor cause heart arrhythmias. The ideal anesthetic should not cause nausea and vomiting and a few other things besides; such is the complex nature of providing a drug that allows reversible unconsciousness with minimal bodily harm. This was a tall order for halothane, the first designer drug. Liver failure became the concern with its use. Having previously determined that "perhaps" one in 10,000 patients might suffer severe liver damage from its administration, the National Halothane Study was performed in the United States to assess the problem.[12] Investigating the effects from over eight hundred thousand anesthetics, the study was found to be inconclusive.*[13] Nonetheless, halothane has been withdrawn from clinical practice in the United States, the newer drugs, isoflurane, sevoflurane and desflurane taking its place.

The fifth line of the parachute

The development of monitoring and recording devices to catalogue the effects of anesthetic drug administration.

A written record of the effects of anesthesia on blood pressure and heart rate was first performed by two Harvard medical students, Ernest Amory Codman and Harvey Cushing, back in 1894. This documentation was one of the first essential steps to allow improvements in anesthetic care. For only a permanent anesthetic record would allow an assessment of anesthetic techniques for improvement in post-operative outcomes. Remarking on the consequences from forcible dilation of the anus under anesthesia for a planned hemorrhoidectomy, Cushing stated, "When one sees recorded the great rise of pressure which may occur under these circumstances, the occasional hemiplegia† which has been known to follow supposedly simple operations of this sort need be no cause for wonderment." Cushing going on to champion the adjustment of anesthetic techniques to avoid extremes in blood pressure.[14] Presaging today's outcome research, which demonstrates that lower blood pressure during surgery is bad for patients, causing more kidney injury, brain dysfunction and heart attacks.[15]

---

* This study did show however that halothane was safer than the explosive cyclopropane which had greater mortality associated with its use.

† Stroke on one side of the body, a feared complication of very high blood pressure or prolonged low blood pressure.

Such research would not have been possible without the development of accurate monitoring devices and permanent anesthesia medical records of care.

Monitoring devices add a further extra level of safety as modern anesthesia machines also allow alarm systems to be incorporated – warning the anesthesiologist when vital functions might be compromised. If blood pressure drops, oxygen levels decrease or anesthetic levels are too high, an alarm will sound, alerting the anesthesiologist to address the situation – much like a pilot receives a low-altitude warning.

The sixth line of the parachute

The development of anesthetic techniques, which have made, especially more complex surgery, both possible and safer.

Consider the development of one-lung anesthesia for thoracic surgery.

Dr. Ralph Waters (1883-1979) credited with being the father of American academic anesthesia,* was a good-looking man with a bluff of blond hair and an expressive face. Born of a pioneer family, by the tender age of seven he was already riding a black pony, his dog Rover at his heels, tasked with herding cows and sheep on the family farm in Ohio. Graduating from Case Western University medical school in 1912, he established himself as a general practitioner, soon becoming the favored anesthetist of the local surgeons. He became so busy that he decided to limit his practice to anesthesia and developed the first "Downtown Anesthesia Clinic" in Sioux City, Iowa. By 1927 Ralph was appointed as an assistant professor of surgery in charge of anesthesia at the University of Wisconsin in Madison.†[16] Pioneering anesthetic techniques, one day he was providing an anesthetic for a lung operation. In 1932 lung surgery was fraught with hazard, because to approach the lung through the thorax, a deep surgical incision had to be made, collapsing the lung underneath as air sucked into the chest. Waters describes the problem: "This initiates a sudden circulatory disturbance which when combined with the radical alteration in respiration may bring about sudden and sometimes fatal circulatory collapse." Upon anesthetizing the patient, Waters inadvertently placed the endotracheal

---

* In turn Dr. Waters, credited John Snow with being "the greatest anaesthetist as well as the first."

† Six years later he was appointed the first professor of anesthesiology, the first position of its kind in America. Waters went on to develop the first fully academic residency training program enlisting basic science colleagues and initiating a research department of anesthesiology.

tube too far down through the triangular glottis opening in the larynx, not just into the trachea, where the tube belongs, but down on beyond the tracheal fork into one of the two main stem bronchi that go to the right and left lung respectively. Because the tube was beyond the fork of the trachea, in the right main stem bronchus, Waters – pressing his stethoscope to the patient's chest – could hear air going to the right lung, but none going to the left lung, when he squeezed the anesthetic bag. Realizing his mistake, he noted that this left-lung isolation might allow surgery to occur better, because the lung would not move; in fact, it would very slowly collapse on opening the chest, and the sudden decompensation he was fearful of was unlikely to occur.* So, through an error, he had developed a new approach to providing 'one-lung' anesthesia for thoracic surgery, going on to develop a special cuffed endotracheal tube for the purpose.[17]

This new anesthetic technique would allow future generations of thoracic surgeons to operate more safely on patients with lung disease.

The remaining lines of the parachute
Predicted to advance anesthesia safety even further
is the developing science of medical care delivery.

Whereas in the past, mistakes, complications, errors, or failures were blamed on the ineptitude of the anesthetist, faulty equipment, an act of god, or as a one-off rare occurrence, never to be seen again – increasingly now a systems-thinking approach is brought to the problem. The mistake, rather than being swept under the carpet, is seen as a learning opportunity to identify gaps in the process of delivering anesthetic care, safely. Incorporated extensively in the aviation industry, this approach is being determinedly copied by anesthesiology, bringing to bear attempts at standardization, practice guidelines, checklists, outcomes assessments and the study of behavioral, neuroscience and human factors design in developing approaches to the often high-stress emergency management situations that anesthesiologists, like pilots, encounter routinely in their practice. While the aviation industry has been able to enhance safety enormously through such, and additional measures like cockpit redesign, crew resource management, communication and simulation

---

* Slow collapse of the non-ventilated isolated lung occurs because of absorption atelectasis; oxygen is taken up into the lungs by passing blood and the alveoli collapse as a result.

training – anesthesia as a specialty still has a long way to catch up.

One of the crucial factors that has enhanced aviation safety is the quality of accident investigations and the reporting requirements that the airline industry has adopted. Critical incident investigations using a "black box" record of flight details, yielding valuable information that is distilled to its practical essence by aviation authorities.* To avoid similar mistakes in the future, these findings are then widely promulgated – while action steps for the affected planes and new procedures are mandated – throughout the industry by the Federation Aviation Administration in America and the Civil Aviation Authority in the United Kingdom.[4]

Following aviation's lead in enhancing safety, and informed by an academic anesthesia paper championing aviation critical incident monitoring as a way to improve anesthesia safety, the Anesthesia Patient Safety Foundation was established in 1985 in America.[18] This multidisciplinary organization, comprising anesthesiologists, equipment and drug manufacturers, engineers, regulators, insurers and attorneys, was established to counter the harsh spotlight that the American media had focused on anesthesia accidents that had injured many patients in the early 1980s. The foundation sponsoring research into anesthesia safety and producing a quarterly newsletter† providing safety-related news, ideas and opinions to the anesthesia community around the world.[19]

However, any anesthesiologist will tell you that while aviation might be used as a good model to help inform the further development of anesthetic safety, there are big differences in practice that must be considered.

Firstly, anesthesia and surgical care delivery is far more complex and much less standardized than aviation. There are over 300 different types of infusion pumps, multiple different anesthesia machine manufacturers, and minimal agreed to standardization, while there are only two major aircraft manufacturers,‡ allowing far greater predictability than is currently possible in healthcare.[4]

Secondly, pilots fly human-engineered equipment and are trained and licensed to fly in specific planes using flight simulators that can almost exactly reproduce the conditions of these man-made systems. A Boeing 737 pilot

---

* At the time of writing the International Civil Aviation Organization, the world's leading advocate for air safety and technical standards, is proposing that cockpit video recorders are installed. In our institution, video-cameras have been installed in the trauma bay so that we can review patient cases together with our surgical colleagues to review the quality of care performed and to develop strategies for improving the care going forward.

† The largest circulation anesthesia publication in the world.

‡ Boeing and Airbus.

is trained and licensed to fly a 737 and no other.

In contrast, an anesthesiologist looks after humans. We humans are far more complicated in design than a plane, and may be sick to boot, adding enormous variability and unpredictability to the situation.

Consider an anesthesiologist's variety of care: in the morning, she may be administering lethal drugs for anesthesia to a new-born baby with a defective heart, for lung surgery. In the afternoon, the patient may be a ninety-year-old, on multiple medications – all affecting bodily functions – with deranged liver, kidney and lung function, for surgery on the heart.

While full human patient simulation is indeed used in anesthesia training, the real-life fidelity of such training is always a question; the varied conditions that patient disease and surgical complexity bring cannot be faithfully reproduced with current simulation technology.

By comparison, during simulation recertification, pilots often cannot tell the difference between flying a plane or a flight simulator. That is far from the situation in anesthesia simulation! Training, using simulation, is helpful, but cannot replace the hard-won experience of the complexity of the operating-room environment.

Turbulence and bad weather!…you say, does not this need to be managed by the pilot? Any anesthesiologist you are questioning on the matter would respectfully agree. He might add that bad weather too can be simulated, and then tell you that during the liver transplant that he last provided an anesthetic for – five liters of blood were lost in as many minutes – after the surgeon tore a hole in a very large blood vessel. Or he might wince and tell you he had to manage an unrestrained patient from a car crash recently, whose head had gone through the windshield! Now confused and combative, blood spurting from her fractured face, the patient needs an airway tube placed safely before her ruptured aorta and fractures can be repaired under anesthesia. Current fidelity of computerized patient simulation equipment cannot allow one to practice for such events!

How then is anesthesiology to answer the siren call for patient safety levels approximating commercial aviation?

Predictably, further specialization is a part answer. Over the past twenty years subspecialty cardiac, obstetric, pediatric, intensive care, regional anesthesia and chronic pain management anesthesiologists have been Fellowship-trained. Undergoing an extra year of training after completing their residency, they receive

Fellowship certification upon successful examination in these subspecialties in the United States.

Further refinements of anesthetic technique, drugs, equipment and monitoring devices are also still to be made.

Far in the future, computer-assisted artificially intelligent systems will be incorporated to guide anesthesiologists as to the appropriate evidence-based care – further enhancing safety.

Industry standardization of the diverse electronic equipment, monitoring and alarm systems will also go a long way in avoiding accidents from lack of familiarity – or distraction – which regularly occur in the modern operating room.

Another answer to the question of patient safety is the renewed emphasis on preoperative medical optimization in preparing ever older and sicker patients for the onslaught of an operation – patient outcomes after surgery critically dependent on their preoperative state of health, fitness and nutrition.

Further enhancements in anesthesia safety will likely rest in replicating the aviation industries' approach. An example would be the development of a national mandatory critical incident reporting system incorporating a black box routine – videotaping and recording all perioperative events for later analysis. Bolstered by a requirement for the accurate reporting of all near misses and mistakes that occur in anesthetic practice (inadmissible in court proceedings), this would allow anesthetic care to be suitably scrutinized. To ensure that the findings are embedded in future anesthetic practice the reports so generated would need to be statutorily empowered to mandate systemic changes in industry design and standardization as well as in the processes of anesthetic care delivery throughout the country.

The Anesthesia Patient Safety Foundation was launched on principles that have enhanced airline safety. Anesthesiology, in its struggle for safety, would do well to emulate the sophistication of aviation investigations which has become one of the most powerful spurs to safety in recent years.

The failure to learn from mistakes being one of the single greatest obstacles to human progress.[4]

5

Magic! The Unfolding Mystery of Anesthesia

Anesthetics – How they work, how depth is determined,
and are there lasting effects?

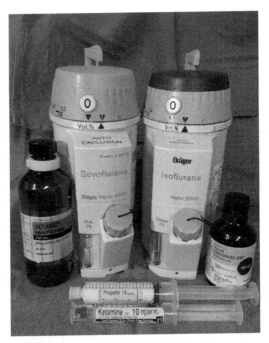

Two bottles of anesthetic liquid next to the vaporizers used to administer sevoflurane
and isoflurane, with two intravenous anesthetics, propofol and ketamine.

To sleep: perchance to dream: ay, there's the rub.
– *William Shakespeare*

We had all hoped that there would be a "unitary theory" of anesthetics – a simple explanation for how anesthetics worked to produce reversible unconsciousness in the brain. To no avail. It seems so simple: inject a syringe full of anesthetic or inhale a gas or vapor deeply, a few times, and the patient is asleep, like magic!

Consider a patient I anesthetized many years ago. Young and garrulous, she had experienced irregular vaginal bleeding and needed a dilatation (of the cervix) and curettage (of the uterus) under general anesthesia to diagnose the problem. In England, at the time, this was a very short procedure lasting no more than five minutes or so. But one that needs deep anesthesia to modulate the untoward effects of the cervical dilatation. And the patient must not move during the procedure to ensure that the curette does not perforate the uterus. To calm her, I started a conversation as I placed the intravenous catheter. She responded gaily to my series of questions, stopping in mid-sentence as the injected anesthetic, thiopentone, became sufficient to produce unconsciousness. Like magic – I am still often astounded by this – she stopped talking in mid-sentence! I gave some more anesthetic to ensure the necessary depth to allow the procedure to be performed, watching her carefully for any signs of awakening or movement. The procedure over, I allowed her to wake up. I switched off the halothane I was giving, allowing her to recover from the administered anesthetic spontaneously, the effects "wearing off."* Her eyelids fluttered a bit as she awakened and to my amazement she continued the interrupted conversation, picking up exactly, to the word, in mid-sentence, where she had left off, completely oblivious of the fact that she had just received a ten-minute anesthetic. She happily prattled on, clear-headed and awake, with no memory of the intervening surgical events, whatsoever.

That is the mystery of anesthesia, considered one of the great puzzles of medicine.[1, 2]

How do anesthetic agents produce these reversible effects in the brain?

How can we be sure that patients are 'deep' enough and will not have a lasting memory of events?

Are they truly unconscious during surgery or is there some subliminal

---

* Obviously far more complicated than that. Recovery from anesthesia is an interplay of anesthetic drug re-distribution away from the brain, metabolism and elimination in the body.

awareness that will haunt them postoperatively?

Indeed, what is consciousness? And what is sleep?

As anesthesiologists, we can only observe clinical signs in the patient that we have learned to associate with the insensate state we now call anesthesia. Is there a way of measuring the depth of anesthesia, so that we can minimize any potential for awareness during surgery?

Finally, are there immediate or lasting untoward effects in the brain and central nervous system from these powerful drugs?

I will attempt to answer these pressing questions in what follows.

General anesthesia can best be described as an unnatural, drug-controlled condition, administered so that surgical and medical therapies can be provided safely and humanely. Confusion arises because anesthesiologists incorrectly use the word "sleep" to allay anxiety in their patients. General anesthesia appropriate for surgery is not sleep; rather, it is a drug-induced coma or unconsciousness. Anesthesia, like sleep, is reversible and allows dreaming, but when at appropriate depth will not allow arousal, no matter how strong the stimulus. In contrast, when asleep, no matter how deep, patients can be aroused. Experiencing pain and recalling the events that occurred.[3]

At the heart of the puzzle of how anesthetics work to render people reversibly unconscious is the incredibly complex brain circuitry that exists to maintain the conscious or awake state, counterbalanced with complex neural processes needed for humans to be able to sleep – a restorative brain state necessary for human survival.[2]

We can be forgiven for thinking there would be a simple explanation for how anesthetics work. After all, ether, the first anesthetic, was such a simple compound* one might have thought there would be a simple "unitary theory" solution to the conundrum. Indeed, Claude Bernard, regarded as one of the pre-eminent medical scientists of the time, posited in 1870 that anesthesia might be a unified phenomenon; a unitary mechanism common to all forms of life. This idea was strongly supported by the work of Hans Meyerton (1896) – experimenting with tadpoles – and Charles Overton (1901). They independently demonstrated that the potency of anesthetics correlated directly with their solubility in olive oil. This Meyerton-Overton hypothesis of lipoid anesthesia was avidly taken up by researchers in the 1960s to 1980s

---

* Diethyl ether with the structure H_5C_2-O-C_2H_5 was synthetized by distilling sulphuric acid with ethyl alcohol.

to indicate that anesthetics were likely to work in tissue and organs that were rich in fat. The unified mechanism so proposed further bolstered by research that Dr. Edmond Eger performed at the time. Wanting to determine a way of comparing the strength or potency of different volatile anesthetics – such as halothane and isoflurane – he developed the concept of MAC.[4] MAC or the Minimum Alveolar Concentration of an anesthetic, was determined to be that concentration of the agent that would reliably ensure (in 50% of participants, mind you) that patients would not move under anesthesia when a skin incision was performed to start a surgical operation. MAC was found to be very useful to compare the potencies of different anesthetic agents; which in turn was shown to correlate closely with their solubility in oil, further sustaining the unitary theory of action. Hence researchers strove to identify a unitary lipid soluble site within the central nervous system and brain that would explain how anesthetics might work. Thinking this to be the lipid-rich cell membranes of central nervous system tissue and circuits, research was focused in this direction until it was recognized that experimental inconsistencies with these sites of action abounded and there might be other sites and mechanisms of action. Franks and Liebs[5, 6] subsequently demonstrating that a range of anesthetics worked at protein-like receptors (termed the Protein Perturbation theory of Anesthesia). Protein-based receptors located in neural tissue, when bound by anesthetic agents, unlocking an increase or decrease in neural circuit activity. Today, while there is widespread recognition that these critical signaling proteins are the most likely molecular targets for anesthetic drugs, many of the exact proteins still remain to be identified. Ongoing research now recognizing – far from Claude Bernard's hope of a unified phenomenon – that the induction of the anesthetic state is a very complex one; investigators seeking to identify not only where, but also how these anesthetics work at these sites.

Electroencephalography has been a great help in the quest to understand anesthesia. First used in 1937 to assess the effects of ether and thiopentone anesthesia, the electroencephalogram (EEG) has become a very useful tool in helping to appreciate the effects of anesthetics on brain neural circuits and in characterizing the brain electronic signals that allow us to assess anesthetic depth.[1]

Simply described, multiple electrodes are attached to the scalp and complex electric currents discharged by brain and central nervous activity are captured, computed, recorded and displayed for interpretation. Used extensively to evaluate both sleep and coma, Dr. Emery Brown has compared these electronic brain patterns with those produced by the anesthetic state, showing them to be very different.[7]

In order to understand this more deeply I have to introduce the reader to this complex field, which you can skip, but at your own peril, for fear of not fully understanding the inherent differences in sleep, coma and the anesthetic state.

As the state of sleep, coma, or anesthesia progresses, the displayed brain electric wave forms change their characteristic speed (frequency) and size (amplitude) as well as orientation over the brain. Different sections of the brain such as the cortex (outer shell), thalamus (in the middle of the brain) and brainstem (attaching the brain to the spinal cord) are involved. The EEG brainwave patterns allowing comparison of the similarities as well as extent or depth of the three different states – sleep, coma, anesthesia. For ease of identification the wave forms are defined by frequency (cycles per second or Hz) as: Slow (< 1Hz); delta, δ (1-4Hz); theta, θ (5-7 Hz); alpha, α (8-12Hz) and beta, β (13-25Hz) waves.

In the awake state, a person with wide-open eyes, will have a normal active EEG pattern, a composite of the afore-named waves, looking much like the fine, frequent, serrations on a hack saw.

As their eyes close, when a small dose of propofol is given, the wave pattern changes to predominantly δ wave types, looking much like the smooth sign sound waves an audiophile might appreciate.

Then, when anesthesia is deepened further, the patient experiences a paradoxical stage of brain activation, so-called because the EEG is activated rather than suppressed by the anesthetic: a very fine but taller agitated saw tooth pattern is displayed.

As anesthesia deepens to what is called Phase 1, there is more α and δ, but less β activity, resembling a mid-size serrated saw.

Deepening further, Phase 2 heralds further slowing of this brain pattern, looking more like a large-size irregular serrated saw with a few teeth missing here and there.[*]

Finally, in Phase 3 of anesthetic depth, known as the burst suppression

---

[*] Importantly this same state is seen in vegetative coma patients as well as during very deep (stage 3 non-REM) sleep.

stage, α and β waves predominate with long gaps in electrical activity, looking like a tree saw with whole sections of serrations missing – an EEG pattern found commonly in coma patients, but never in sleep.

Anesthesia sufficient for surgery is usually achieved at either the Phase 2 or 3 level of depth. If more anesthetic is administered to Phase 4, the EEG isoelectric phase is reached, where the electrical wave form is almost flat line, very common in coma and brain death. This isoelectric state is regarded as too deep a state for anesthesia as possible brain damage may occur. Yet EEG monitoring of anesthetic depth is not commonly used in anesthetic practice today.

In summary, deepening anesthesia can be monitored through a progression of brainwave EEG patterns: changing from a hacksaw to sign wave and on to an agitated saw-tooth pattern, culminating in a mid-size serrated saw wave appearance.

At levels deep enough for surgery the pattern progresses to a large-size serrated saw with "burst suppression" gaps in the saw pattern (just like those found in coma). Too-deep levels of anesthesia are demonstrated by a flat line also found in coma and brain death as mentioned above.

While it is said that patients may dream under anesthesia the EEG pattern during sleep is usually very different from that induced by anesthetics.

Sleep is characterized as either Rapid Eye Movement (REM) sleep or Non-REM sleep occurring in ninety-minute cycles. REM sleep is accompanied by irregularities of breathing and heart rate as well as skeletal muscle hypotonia (relaxing of muscles), all of which can occur in light anesthesia, although the EEG patterns are very different during these phases. Non-REM sleep occurs in three stages and is associated with a waxing and waning of muscle tone and decreased heart rate and body temperature. In the deepest stage (3) the EEG wave pattern looks similar to that found under anesthesia (Phase 2) and in vegetative coma, showing a large-size irregular serrated saw-type pattern with a few teeth missing here and there. During this deepest stage of sleep, the greatest decrease in pain perception occurs and the sleeper is least rousable.* But, crucially, with sufficient stimulation, will be roused to awakening and awareness, which cannot occur during this phase of an anesthetic (or coma) despite similar EEG-patterned waves. That is the magic of the anesthetic state,

---

* Similar to anesthetic effects this stage of sleep switches the thalamus (an important central brain relay station) to the 'off' mode, inhibiting transmission of pain sensations to the cortex (outer layer) of the brain.

allowing surgery to occur, usually without recall.

Coma is another matter. Often caused by structural brain damage from injury, stroke or terminal systemic diseases such as liver or kidney failure, the patient is completely unresponsive. Lying with eyes closed, even prodding or shouting may result in little to no response. Only rarely, and then only in response to a very painful stimulus, grimacing or reflexive body movements may occur. EEG patterns in coma vary dependent on the extent of injury, but are similar to those described during phase 2-4 of deep anesthesia, culminating in the isoelectric flatline stage which may herald brain death.

Before describing how the study of EEG wave patterns has helped researchers begin to tease out how anesthetics work, it is useful to describe the physical signs an anesthesiologist will see as his patient progresses through the different described EEG stages, upon induction of anesthesia. Closely watching these effects, the anesthesiologist uses these clinical signs to assess anesthetic depth.[7]

Outwardly calm at first, as propofol is administered for induction of anesthesia, the patient enters the paradoxical stage of excitement. There may be purposeless movements of the arms and legs, incoherent speech, euphoria or dysphoria, with irregular breathing attempts. Oral commands are no longer responded to and there is loss of skeletal muscle tone as she enters Phase 1. Obstruction of the airway or sudden vomiting may occur at this early stage. Usually the anesthesiologist will check the patient's eyelid reflex, lightly brushing his finger over the patient's eyelashes to see if they flicker. If they don't, we know that the patient is unconscious, and will start assisting her breathing to counter the inevitable respiratory depression that occurs. Heart rate increases and blood pressure may rise or fall. Further deepening the anesthetic, we enter the maintenance of anesthesia phase, (2 and 3), adjusting the anesthetic depth to counter effects of the surgical stimulation on the body. Signs that tell us that we are not deep enough – often called light anesthesia – are the physical signs in the body created by a sympathetic discharge, our body's fight or flight response to injury. The heart rate and blood pressure may increase rapidly and dangerously, the pupils will widen and the patient may perspire and tears roll from their closed eyes. Or worse still, they may move, eliciting loud complaints from the surgeon. At levels of anesthesia suitable for surgery, functionally, the patient approximates a state of brainstem death. They are unconscious, need cardiac, respiratory and thermoregulatory support, do not respond to extreme stimulation and have none of the usual brainstem reflexes to protect them from harm. Mercifully, this state of brainstem dysfunction is not permanent; reversing with recovery from the anesthetic in minutes.

Dr. Arthur Guedel (1883-1956), a self-made man, lived by the philosophy that one learns through one's mistakes. Too poor to go to high school, he apprenticed to a machinist, losing three fingers for his troubles, and yet made it to Indiana University, eventually becoming Chair of Anesthesiology at the University of Southern California. In 1917, during the First World War, he was sent to the town of Chaumont in France. As the only trained anesthesiologist he was told to manage anesthesia care for a number of base hospitals supported by the U.S. military on the Western Front. Recognizing that he could not single-handedly manage the flood of injured soldiers in these different hospitals, he trained corpsmen and nurses to give anesthesia. Ether was the anesthetic agent used, and key was the need to monitor anesthetic depth, so that these little-trained personnel would know when to lighten the anesthetic, so as not to have the patient stop breathing.

This, at a time when oxygen administration during anesthesia was unheard of, and there was no means of supporting breathing should this stop from an ether overdose. To address this problem, Dr. Guedel devised a chart diagramming stages of anesthetic depth from ether. Basing this on his own clinical observations; he outlined the eye signs and respiratory signs of deepening anesthesia that were consistent in every patient. Monitoring these changes would allow the drafted anesthesia personnel to determine when anesthesia was too deep and the patient would likely stop breathing. This "Depth of Anesthesia Chart" proved most useful in providing safe anesthesia, which Dr. Guedel in turn monitored by checking on each hospital where ether was administered – riding on a motor cycle from place to place.[8]

So how do anesthetics work? Isn't it about time that I started to answer the question?

Simply put, perhaps a little too simplistically, but useful to understanding; intense research indicates that anesthetics produce unconsciousness by disrupting the electrical connections between the thinking/remembering brain (cortex) and the feeling/sensing parts of the brain (limbic system). Exhaustive

EEG evaluation and interpretation suggests that the thalamus in the midbrain may serve as a relay, switching on and off the oscillatory brain circuits required for arousal.[7, 9, 10] Notwithstanding these theories, disruptions in cortical-cortical connections may also provide an explanation.[11] From this and many other investigations it has become apparent that because it is so critical that humans can be both fully conscious and yet able to experience restorative sleep (and be easily rousable if endangered) – there are an overwhelming number of brain circuits ensuring that these seemingly contradictory functions can occur. Part explaining why it is that diverse drugs – with varying mechanisms of action – have been shown to disrupt different circuits to achieve the same apparent anesthetic state.

Hence there is not one mechanism of anesthetic action but many different mechanisms by which differing brain circuits can be temporarily disrupted – causing the insensate state we call anesthesia. Take, for example, propofol and ketamine (pictured above), two well-known anesthetics that have very differing mechanisms of action. Ketamine, sold on the streets of New York as "angel dust" because of its often pleasant hallucinatory effects, is a very effective anesthetic and analgesic, used extensively to provide general anesthesia. Yet it works on different (opposing) receptor systems in the brain and spinal cord producing widely different EEG patterns in comparison with propofol and other general anesthetics. This is partially explained by the fact that different circuits are affected to achieve the same outward state of unconsciousness demonstrated with propofol anesthesia.[3, 12] One of the problems with ketamine is that patients may suffer dysphoria (an unhappy state) postoperatively. To minimize this, a benzodiazepine medication (midazolam) is often administered to oppose these effects by blocking the offending neural circuits causing the dysphoria. Yet midazolam by itself can be used as a general anesthetic, as can many other drugs in this class.

Further complicating our understanding of anesthesia and consciousness is the somewhat philosophical point that as anesthesiologists we can only assess the behavioral response produced by the administered anesthetic. We can only observe and verify signs in our patients that suggest that they are unconscious. We cannot truly know what they are in fact experiencing in their apparently unconscious state nor whether this will be remembered in any form.[13]

Another important phenomenon is amnesia, the inability to remember events that we experience consciously. Part and parcel of the mystery of anesthetic practice – many anesthetic agents cause this amnestic state in a dose-dependent fashion, varying significantly from patient to patient.

Consider the case of a resident in anesthesia training, who I took care of many years ago while I was at Columbia University. A strapping young man, he had asked me to look after him during surgery on his right foot. We had placed a regional anesthetic, injecting a local anesthetic medication close to the nerves supplying his foot, deadening sensation, so that when surgery was performed, he would experience no pain. Awaiting the surgeon's arrival in the operating room, I administered small doses of the anesthetic drugs midazolam (2mg) and fentanyl (100ug), which lightly sedated him. Nevertheless, as soon as the surgeon walked into the operating room, my patient, the resident, sat up on the surgical table and proceeded to tell the surgeon exactly what he should do for the operation on his right foot. Then he lay down and went back to sleep. From assessing the resident's behavior, I would have told you that he was fully conscious at the time of the discussion with the surgeon, however when I asked the resident about this event postoperatively, he had absolutely no memory of sitting up and telling the surgeon what to do. In fact, he was embarrassed to hear the story told.

Recovery from anesthesia has also been well studied using the EEG. It tracks nicely upwards, starting with recovery of brainstem functional paralysis and ascending through a vegetative state to a recovery of cortical functioning, when the patient can again respond to oral commands and open their eyes. Because recovery from anesthesia is usually slower than induction, the anesthesiologist can witness this upward migration in clinical physical signs in his patient as they appear in the reverse order from induction.

Blood pressure and heart rate rising as attempts at breathing start to occur. Painful stimuli of any kind at this time – such as the surgeon closing the wound with sutures – will result in a fight or flight response with further increases in these parameters. Salivation, tearing, gagging, coughing, and grimacing herald return of brainstem functioning, while defensive posturing and involuntary movements indicate passage through the vegetative state. Eye-opening and a clear response to verbal commands, "Lift up your head," demonstrating that sufficient cortical activity has returned to declare the patient awake and recovered from the short-term effects of the anesthetic.

*

Thankfully rare, but an extremely concerning problem, is that of "awareness under anesthesia" during surgery.

Sandra, twelve years old at the time, describes the problem:[14]

> Suddenly, I was aware something had gone very wrong. I could hear what was going on around me, and I realized with horror that I had woken up in the middle of the operation, but couldn't move a muscle. I heard the banal chatter of the surgeons, and I was aware of many people in the room bustling about, doing their everyday clinical jobs and minding their own business, with absolutely no idea of the cataclysmic event that was unfolding from my point of view. While they fiddled, I lay there, frantically trying to decide whether I was about to die, and what options were open to me.

Reportedly occurring in only one of 19,000 anesthetics, the fact of this happening is attributed to our imperfect understanding of how anesthetics work. Ensuing sometimes, despite sufficient anesthetic having been administered, according to usual criteria. At other times, when a mistake in drug administration has been visited on the patient. Awareness is also occasionally experienced at the start or close of an anesthetic as patients are going to "sleep" or recovering from anesthesia.

That is not the real problem. It is in the middle of surgery that it is most distressing to the patient. Sandra experiencing nightmares for a full fifteen years after the event: "A 'Dr. Who'-style monster leapt on me and paralyzed me," until she realized that she was reliving the feeling of muscle paralysis that she encountered when waking up during surgery. This fact, of the anesthesiologist's use of muscle relaxants, to paralyze the patient, is central to the issue.

Normally, if the patient was "light" – insufficient anesthesia had been administered – for the depth of anesthesia required for the particular surgical stimulus, the patient would reflexly move, indicating to the anesthesiologist that he should deepen the anesthetic. However, when paralyzed, the patient's muscles will not work and so the anesthesiologist has lost this sign that anesthesia is too light and that his patient might be experiencing awareness.

There are three surgeries where this is most likely to occur: cardiac, trauma and obstetric surgery, all for the same reason. The anesthesiologist has paralyzed the patient and is keeping the anesthetic "light" to minimize the detrimental effects of deep anesthesia – on the heart in cardiac and trauma surgery and on the unborn baby during Cesarean section. Under such circumstances, many anesthesiologists will use modified EEG monitoring techniques in an attempt to assure appropriate anesthetic depth to guard against awareness occurring. Nevertheless, modified EEG monitoring has not been shown to be a sure-fire guarantee that awareness will not occur.[15]

We turn now to the question, whether anesthetics might have long lasting detrimental effects in the brain. Dr. Emery Brown poses the issue well:

> The fact that general anesthesia can be functionally equivalent to brain-stem death indicates how deeply general anesthesia can depress brain function and perhaps explains why some patients do not fully recover consciousness for several hours after general anesthesia and why postoperative cognitive dysfunction could persist in elderly patients for several months.[7]

As early as 1955 this was a recurring question.

Having scrutinized the records of over four thousand patients receiving general anesthesia at Oxford, Dr. Bedford noted that in patients who had received anesthetics later in life, fully one third "had never been the same since operation" at least as noted by close relatives,[16] sparking the question whether general anesthetic administration might be detrimental to brain function or accelerate the brain's decline.

This would seem a simple problem to solve. It is not. One needs to separate out the effect of the anesthetic drug on the brain from the effects of surgery which causes a general neuro-inflammatory reaction. Then there are the effects of pain, low blood pressure and possible low brain oxygen levels that need to be considered. And the effects of the many other drugs that might be administered during the perioperative period. What is clear is that there is a spectrum of brain dysfunction occurring after surgery – starting with acute delirium and continuing as postoperative cognitive dysfunction, POCD for short.

Delirium, occurring as often as one in ten patients, is an acute cognitive disorder, characterized by inattention and disorganized thinking commonly having a fluctuating course that may be apparent immediately after surgery or develop over hours to days afterwards. Drugs like midazolam, commonly used as part of an anesthetic technique, increase the chance of delirium in elderly patients while greater depths of volatile anesthetic administration – assessed using EEG monitoring* – are also associated with more delirium postoperatively. These observations offer the very real possibility that administering anesthetics to defined depths, guided by EEG monitoring, could result in less delirium postoperatively.[17]

POCD is a syndrome defined as a decline in cognitive performance on a set of neuropsychological tests completed before and after surgery for comparison. There is much disagreement on how this decline in brain function should be defined – as well as the duration of assessment – but usually stretches to three months after the operation.[18] The causes are likely to be multifactorial, although POCD is clearly associated with increasing age, as well as inversely related to the patient's level of education. While there is no demonstrated advantage for propofol over volatile anesthetics, ketamine administration has been shown to be protective in patients undergoing cardiac surgery. What is of particular interest (and concern) is that EEG brain monitoring shows that greater depths of anesthesia administration are associated with more postoperative decline in cognitive function.[19, 20]

There is also an unanswered emerging question as to whether undue sensitivity to anesthetic agent administration, measured by EEG, is due to the direct effects of these agents on brain cells or rather a marker of the underlying frailty of the individual patient.[21] This is especially so at the extremes of life; the very old and the very young.

In the young, there has been a developing concern that anesthetics might cause actual damage to growing brain cells. Here ketamine, at least in young animal studies, appears to be a major culprit. While programmed cell death, termed apoptosis, occurs during normal development of the central nervous system, ketamine has been shown to worsen this process causing widespread neurodegeneration in the rat pups studied.[22] Further research indicating that many common anesthetic agents enhanced the demonstrated neurodegeneration with associated persistent behavioral and learning deficits in the preclinical animal models used.[23] No specific anesthetic agent could be considered safer than another, but because these studies were performed in animals, human

---

* Burst suppression ratio (Phase 3 anesthesia) as well as lower bispectral index levels, a processed EEG variable that can be quantitated using a special device called a BIS monitor.

studies were called for to establish if the demonstrated brain cell injury might also affect a child's brain development.[24]

The Smart Tots research program was established in 2010 to investigate this problem in children. Nagging questions needed to be answered. Are there short- or long-term detrimental neurocognitive, emotional, or behavioral outcomes resulting from anesthetic agents? Should non-emergent surgery be postponed till an older age when brain cell development is less rapid and less vulnerable? What age is safe? Four years and older? What drugs are safe? Because the outcomes of such difficult to perform human studies are years in the making, the Smart Tots program, through its website, has sought to reassure, while informing parents of progress. Some comfort is to be found in a study using sevoflurane, the most commonly used anesthetic in children. Children around one year of age, needing hernia repair surgery, were enrolled in an international study performed over a six-year period.[*] The interim two-year analysis, comparing neurodevelopmental effects between children randomized to receive either general sevoflurane anesthesia or spinal/caudal anesthesia,[†] suggested that there were no profound differences to be found.[25] Nevertheless, caution in interpretation of such preliminary findings is always warranted; the study authors warning that assessment of two year olds for neurological changes is inexact and that the duration of approximately one hour of anesthesia for hernia repair, fell far short of the time period of anesthetic required to injure young animals. Hence this might not be a sufficient period of exposure to demonstrate an injurious effect in the children studied. Reporting further that in the future the authors are planning to publish an assessment at the five year time point after the anesthetic, which will provide a much better evaluation of the long-term detrimental effects of sevoflurane administration at one year of age. In the meantime, the Smart Tots Program informs potentially worried parents on their website thus:[‡]

> Although research in animals is often very helpful, it may sometimes cause undue concern and prompt changes in medical practice that have unintended consequences that are not in the best interest of children.

---

[*] Feb 9, 2007 to Jan 31, 2013: 722 infants, 28 hospitals.

[†] Spinal or caudal anesthesia, introduces a local anesthetic, using a sterile needle, into the spinal fluid encased by a spinal sheath, below the spinal cord. This deadens all sensation below the umbilicus, allowing hernia surgery to be performed without the need for a general anesthetic.

[‡] Smart Tots: (accessed, Dec, 2017) http://smarttots.org/faq-for-parents/

Much more research is needed to provide parents with additional information about the safe use of anesthetic and/or sedative drugs in children. Until more information is available it is important that children continue to receive any necessary surgery and anesthesia.

In summary, there are clearly many lasting questions that ongoing research in anesthesia is trying to address. Not only on how anesthetics work, but whether, in producing reversible coma, anesthetics have detrimental effects on the brain. The fringes of life are currently the areas of focus for human research: the very young, where the developing brain is most vulnerable, and the elderly or frail, where brain function is deteriorating. Here we are learning that greater depths of anesthesia, as assessed using the electroencephalogram, may be associated with greater damage.

Anesthesiologists are only recently becoming aware of this research, paving the way for the much greater use of EEG monitoring and the selective use of anesthetic agents in attempts to minimize the detrimental effects of anesthesia on brain function and patient outcomes.

6

Drugs, Equipment and Monitors – An Alarming Situation

The role of drugs, equipment and monitoring in enhancing patient safety

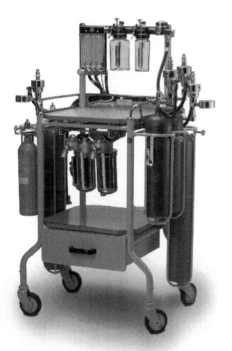

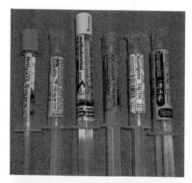

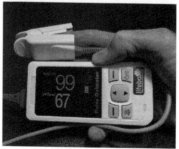

Left – Boyles Machine. Top right – IV medications used to administer anesthesia.
Bottom right – Pulse oximeter used to monitor oxygen saturation of blood.

Many Intravenous agents have collapsed and few have been resuscitated.
– David A Davis[1]

Drugs (i)

"Balanced Anesthesia," using three drugs, rather than the blunderbuss approach of using just one anesthetic, like inhaled chloroform, was the goal. This to minimize the need to administer near toxic levels of a volatile* anesthetic like chloroform to achieve all components of the triad of anesthesia required for surgery. Narcosis,† muscle relaxation and analgesia are needed. If this can be provided using three specific drugs – one for each of these states – so much the better for the patient.

The search for an intravenous anesthetic was on.

John Lundy (1894-1973), who coined the concept of "Balanced Anesthesia," carefully taped a fluffy cotton strip to the patient's upper lip.[2] It would flutter much like a butterfly, as the patient inhaled and exhaled through the nose, indicating that the experimental drug thiopentone had not stopped the patient's breathing. Although not the first intravenous anesthetic, the administration of thiopentone on March 8, 1934‡ was as important a date in anesthetic practice as that of ether's first public demonstration by William Morton on October 16, 1846 – ushering in the ready acceptance of the intravenous route to provide anesthesia.[3] To ensure that he really was injecting thiopentone intravenously, Dr. Lundy pulled back on the glass syringe plunger, gently aspirating a little blood into the syringe containing the yellow-colored sulphurous barbiturate derivative. Then injecting two to three milliliters of the yellow solution, he asked the patient to start counting to ten and beyond. Closely observing the fluffy cotton strip, he injected another milliliter of thiopentone for every count of five; usually administering a total of five ml. to assure anesthesia. Recommending slow injection – over thirty seconds – to avoid overdosing the unduly frail or sensitive patient, he remarked that, as surgical anesthesia was produced, respiration was considerably depressed. Should the patient turn blue from lack of oxygen, he exhorted, "No time should be lost in administering

---

* Volatile anesthetic: a liquid like ether, chloroform or halothane that is readily vaporized to a gas at room temperature.

† Narcosis is a classic term for the insensate state we call anesthesia. In the Netherlands anesthesiologists are called Narcotiseurs. Before becoming an American, the author was Dutch by birth.

‡ Attributed to Ralph Waters in Madison, Wisconsin.

oxygen and carbon dioxide* in order to be sure of avoiding serious untoward results."

"Intravenous Anesthesia" was the simple title of Dr. Lundy's landmark paper describing his personal administration of thiopentone to more than 3,000 patients for all manner of surgeries. Noting that "patients answered questions during operations with apparent honesty and yet have no memory of having talked," he suggested that thiopentone, colloquially called "the truth drug," might be found useful "in the interrogation of certain individuals in medico-legal practice."

Many other drugs had been tried before as intravenous anesthetics, unfortunately with little sustained success.

Sir Christopher Wren, the renowned English natural scientist and architect, being one of the first to document intravenous anesthesia through a goose-quill needle embedded in the vein of a dog, in 1656. Fashioning a syringe made of another dog's bladder he injected a mixture of ale and wine, "making him drunk but soon after he pisseth this out." The dog happily surviving the experiment.

Ether too was administered intravenously to disastrous effect. Nikolai Pirogoff of St. Petersburg administering ether liquid to dogs in 1847, upon which many died. Another drug, chloral hydrate, was tested as an intravenous anesthetic for surgery in humans around 1874 by a Bordeaux surgeon, Pierre-Cyprien Oré. Unfortunately its prolonged effect led to respiratory compromise and death – Dr. Oré fired for his insistence that chloral hydrate was safer than chloroform. Next, a urethane compound, popularized as hedonal, was introduced in St. Petersburg for human use in 1909. It was however impractical, being slow of onset, not soluble (making it difficult to prepare for intravenous use) and had a very long duration of action.

Barbiturates, although synthetized as early as 1863, were only recognized to have hypnotic effects fifty years later. Nevertheless they were unsuitable: when administered intravenously, they either took too long to work, were too short in action, or lasted too long to be considered a practical intravenous anesthetic before the advent of thiopentone – which proved useful – but far from ideal.

---

* Carbon dioxide was administered to increase the patients respiratory rate, CO_2 acting as a respiratory stimulant.

An ideal[*] intravenous anesthetic would have the following characteristics: it would be rapid in onset of action, when administered into a large vein of the hand or arm, inducing unconsciousness, reliably, in close on thirty seconds. It would not "hurt" with injection. (This is an intractable problem because anesthetics work in the brain, which is like fat tissue in consistency. Hence all intravenous induction agents need to be lipid (fat) soluble to produce anesthesia. But for a drug to be introduced into the blood stream it must be "water soluble." Therein lies the problem. Induction agents have to be mixed with a water solubilizing agent – often painful on injection – in order to be administered intravenously.)[†]

It must render the patient unconscious with the minimum of excitatory effects, hiccoughing, coughing, tremor or movement of the arms, or worse still – actual convulsions.

It must be rapidly broken down and excreted from the body in an inactive form, so that the intravenous induction agent does not accumulate and result in prolonged activity.[‡]

It must not be toxic to the many organ systems in the body.[§]

The ideal agent would exhibit no impairment of breathing drive or mechanics.

It should be "hemodynamically stable" and not depress the heart nor blood vessel tone leading to hypotension, cardiac failure and shock especially in patients that have suffered blood loss.

Nor should the body's "fight or flight" response – partially mediated through the sympathetic nervous system – be unduly impaired for fear of causing cardiovascular collapse in such patients having lost blood from trauma or wounds sustained in battle. That was one of the key, initially under-appreciated problems with thiopentone.

Administered as a "safe" anesthetic to military personnel who were wounded,

---

[*] We use the word "ideal" a lot in anesthetic drug design. A few anesthetic drugs are now approximating this ideal, but many still leave much to be desired.

[†] This is technical, but important, because some patients recount feeling this pain when they go off to sleep. We often add in lidocaine (a local anesthetic) as part of the intravenous induction sequence to try to minimize this problem. Different induction agents are solubilized using diverse mediums. Propofol in intralipid, giving its white color. Etomidate in cremaphor EL. Thiopentone in an alkaline medium to avoid precipitation.

[‡] Thiopentone is very reasonable in this regard, except if more than a dose of around two grams is administered, when the metabolism of this drug changes and action can be much more prolonged.

[§] Brain, kidneys, liver, bone marrow, neuro humoral endocrine system, as examples.

and in shock, after the Japanese bombing of Pearl Harbor on December 7, 1941, few doctors at the time knew of the adverse circulatory effects of this new intravenous induction agent and so injected a relative overdose. Many unnecessary deaths ensued. Consequently thiopentone proved to be far from the ideal – paving the way for further research in the development of more hemodynamically stable intravenous anesthetic agents.

Methohexital, an oxybarbiturate, introduced in 1954, was considerably better with respect to hemodynamic stability and as it was metabolized more rapidly than thiopentone, has minimal lasting sedative effects. Both methohexital and thiopentone remain widely used intravenous anesthetics today.[*]

Ketamine, another intravenous induction agent which maintains blood pressure, increases heart rate and has very little respiratory depressant effects, was introduced in 1970, followed closely by etomidate (1973).[†] Intravenous induction of anesthesia with etomidate has the least detrimental effect on cardiovascular and sympathetic nervous system stability and so it is often used in cardiac anesthesia or in elderly patients who have compromised heart function. Etomidate has a drawback however, that has not been fully elucidated. This drug has been shown to impair the production of steroids in the adrenal glands, especially if prolonged infusions are used. Carbo-etomidate, a new version of this drug, which does not have these effects, is undergoing clinical trials.

Along the way there were many induction agents that were introduced and then withdrawn from the markets. A steroidal derivative, alphathesin (1972) found initial favor but was withdrawn because of associated deaths, while propanidid (1960), caused too much cardiac depression to be continued in practice.

Propofol, introduced in 1983, usurped thiopentone's throne as the most favored anesthetic agent. Its ease of use, and particularly the damping down effect on laryngeal airway reflexes that it accomplished, made induction of anesthesia, by and large, a smoothly reliable process. Propofol is still, however, far from the ideal, having the greatest effect of all current induction agents in

---

[*] Thiopentone is no longer available in the U.S.A. This intravenous anesthetic was used as the cocktail of drugs (with a muscle paralytic and high doses of potassium to stop the heart) administered for lethal injection. By report, fearing possible litigation, the companies that imported thiopentone into the U.S.A. stopped doing so. As a result this very good induction agent is no longer available for use.

[†] Designed and introduced by Janssen's Pharmaceuticals. Please see further text below.

depressing the sympathetic fight or flight response that patients rely upon to maintain blood pressure. In so doing, propofol causes severe cardiac and blood pressure depression which can significantly compromise frail patients if not used judiciously.

Accordingly the search for the ideal induction agent continues with unfortunately few new drugs on the horizon.

Drugs (ii)

Down as dead as if it had been struck by lightning.
—Abbé Fontana, 1781 (on the effect of curare injected into a rabbit)

Muscle relaxation is the second component of the balanced anesthesia goal. Weakness of a patient's skeletal muscles is important to allow the anesthesiologist to manipulate the airway and control breathing, while allowing the surgeon to comfortably open cavities such as the thorax or abdomen without tearing and injuring the muscles to do so.

Both intravenous and volatile anesthetics produce muscle weakness by causing hypotonia, a relaxation of muscle tone that skeletal muscles are maintained at. In addition, volatile anesthetics can produce relaxation of these muscles through a direct effect in decreasing the strength of contraction. The theory of "balanced anesthesia" posits that if a second, non-anesthetic drug can be found that provides muscular paralysis, then the untoward effects of the deep anesthetic state that would be required for adequate surgical muscle relaxation can be avoided.

The introduction of curare, a muscle relaxant, into anesthetic practice would prove revolutionary to this concept.

Ecuadorian jungle Indians knew that to immobilize birds during the hunt, tipping their arrowheads with a paste from certain liana vines that grew in the forest, was most effective. Curare lianas were taken back to Europe by early explorers to investigate what extract might be responsible for these "poison arrows" which proved so effective in hunting. Administering curare to a cat in 1812, the English surgeon Edmund Brodie kept it alive, despite its obvious muscle paralysis, using artificial respiration.[3] Three hours later, the cat suddenly woke up and walked away not impaired in the slightest. Nonetheless scientists needed to know how curare worked. Did curare just affect the skeletal muscle causing paralysis or did it affect other muscles like that of the heart?

Claude Bernard (1813-1878), a pharmacist by training, becoming a physician only later in life, was the pre-eminent physiologist in France in the mid-nineteenth century. A Chair of Physiology was created for him at the Sorbonne, where he studied French frogs, administering curare to tease out these questions.

Establishing that curare did not affect the nervous system as a whole, he found the amphibian's heart beating merrily despite total skeletal muscle paralysis immobilizing the frog. He made another crucial observation: "Curare paralyzes the motor nerves, particularly at the point where they make contact with the muscles." Later researchers would call this the neuromuscular junction, going on to explain how acetylcholine and curare interacted to cause reversible muscle paralysis.

Briefly, acetylcholine, one of the key mediators[*] in the central nervous and muscular system, acts in the neuromuscular junction which is to be found in all skeletal muscles. The neuromuscular junction, at its simplest, has one nerve ending enveloped by a muscle fiber, with a gap between the two known as the synaptic cleft. Upon conduction of a nerve stimulus from the motor cortex of the brain down through the connected spinal cord, and on to a peripheral nerve arriving at the junction, a packet of acetylcholine mediators is released into the synaptic cleft, and moves across to bind to a nicotinic acetylcholine receptor on the skeletal muscle fiber. This receptor binding transiently fires (depolarizes) the muscle, causing it to contract and then relax as it awaits the next packet of acetylcholine for further activation. The "used" acetylcholine is rapidly broken down by a local enzyme in the neuromuscular junction called acetylcholinesterase – breaking it off from the receptor – so that the receptor can be activated again. Curare gains access into the synaptic cleft by diffusing from circulating blood and blocks acetylcholine from binding to the nicotinic receptor. So, the muscle stays in a relaxed state and is not activated.[†] Over a period of time, as the concentration of curare diminishes in the synaptic cleft,[‡] acetylcholine can start to rebind to the receptor and muscle fibers start firing again.

---

[*] "Mediator" is a catchall phrase used in medicine and physiology for chemical compounds that are secreted by the body to bind to a receptor – a receptor being a protein structure, which when bound actuates a series of actions like muscle contraction in this case.

[†] Curare is called a non-depolarizing muscle relaxant in the anesthesia literature.

[‡] Curare diminishes as it diffuses back to a lower concentration in circulating blood; the result of liver metabolism of the drug.

There is another way of more rapidly allowing muscle fibers to recover from curare administration. Muscle-fiber recovery can be hastened by increasing the concentrations of acetylcholine in the synaptic cleft to compete for binding with curare. This is done by administering a "reversal" drug intravenously which is carried in the bloodstream, diffusing to the synaptic cleft and binding to the cholinesterase enzyme, so inactivating it. As a result, acetylcholine is not broken down, but increases in the synaptic cleft instead – with each new packet of acetylcholine release. Neostigmine is such a reversal drug, which Dr. Enid Johnson, a Canadian anesthesia resident at the time, had ready, just in case.

Harold R. Griffith (1894-1985) a resolute, merrily pudgy man, loved to smoke his pipe to relax. He mused that every anesthetist wished that he might be able to produce rapid and complete muscular relaxation in resistant surgical patients. Decorated in youth for bravery as a stretcher bearer in the First World War – having interrupted his medical training to undertake this service – Griffith subsequently established an anesthetic practice at McGill University in Montreal, Canada.* On viewing a film demonstrating the use of D-tubo-curare in paralyzing a psychiatric patient – to minimize skeletal injury from ECT[†] induced convulsions – he became convinced that this muscle relaxant drug might be used to aid anesthetic management. Harold thought of trying icosotrin, the newly available commercial form of kurare, in patients who were considered anesthetic "resistant" – straining their abdominal muscles unduly during surgical operations in the belly – making it difficult to perform the surgery efficiently.

Encountering just such a patient, on January 23, 1942. The patient, a 250-pound plumber, was undergoing an exceedingly tedious appendectomy; the surgeons struggling to open the abdomen enough to do the operation properly. Seizing the opportunity, Griffith instructed his resident, Dr. Enid Johnson, to administer five ml. of curare intravenously to see if it would work. Within a minute the abdomen was as "soft as dough." Dr. Griffith's subsequent report – describing the successful use of icosotrin to aid muscle relaxation – without the need for assisted ventilation, nor harmful effects – shook the anesthetic world to its core. Provoking both positive and negative reactions.[4] To boot, Griffith's curare administration allowed a decrease in the dose of the administered

---

* Griffith served as the founder and first president of both the Canadian Anaesthetists Society (1943) and the World Federations of Societies of Anaesthesiologists (1955).

† ECT, electric convulsive therapy.

cyclopropane; exactly the approach that the concept of "balanced anesthesia" wanted to achieve.

Muscle relaxation, using curare, soon became accepted anesthetic practice; fulfilling the second required component of the desired balanced anesthesia triad. However, curare as a muscle relaxant, was a rather crude drug, having both effects on the neuromuscular system as well as the autonomic nervous system causing serious drops in blood pressure. Administered curare binding not only to nicotinic receptors in the neuromuscular junction – achieving the desired muscle relaxant effect – but also to a similar nicotinic receptor in the autonomic nervous system, resulting in untoward effects like hypotension and the slowing of the heart beat. So much so that a patient's blood pressure could drop by 30% of its value as a result of curare administration. Adding this to the depressant effect of thiopentone injection used for induction of anesthesia, resulted in patients having very low blood pressures, which was unacceptable. Hence drug design was directed at a synthetic non-depolarizing muscle relaxant that would provide more selective blockade at just the neuromuscular junction to avoid autonomic nervous effects.

A further problem with curare administration was the fact that progressively larger doses of curare were being used in patients under anesthesia. While initial use by Griffiths and others was of low doses – which might have allowed the patients to continue breathing by themselves – safely; increasing doses of curare turned initial muscle *relaxation* into full muscular *paralysis* – where respiratory assistance was crucial to patient survival. These much higher doses also needed the reversal drug neostigmine to be administered. As stated previously, intravenous neostigmine administration blocked the acethylcholinesterase enzyme in the neuromuscular junction – causing a buildup of acethylcholine, which in turn displaced the remnant curare – allowing normal muscle activity to resume.

Another concern was that kurare was very long-acting because its breakdown by the liver was slow at best. Thus, the second impetus to new drug design was that the synthetic muscle paralytic be broken down rapidly in the body. These two drug-design requirements of selectivity and rapid metabolism spawned a plethora of new muscle relaxants in the intervening years. Today we use synthetic paralytic agents which have no negative cardiovascular effects and last for around thirty to forty minutes. Nevertheless, they still require reversal with neostigmine.

Drugs (iii)

The human mind is like a parachute, it works best when it is open.
– Paul A. J. B. Janssen

Dr. Paul Janssen (1926-2003), considered the most prolific drug inventor of all time, had an important idea.[5] If he could synthetize an opioid analgesic that had the chemical structure inherent to morphine,[*] but without all the baggage – a drug that was more selective and so more potent at the chief site that opioids worked at in the body[†] – this might provide the go-to analgesic needed in anesthesia. The third component of the anesthetic triad of narcosis, muscle relaxation and analgesia – that formed the basis of a balanced approach to anesthetic care – would thus be admirably satisfied. Janssen, whose Belgian physician father had established a medical products business in Turnhout, was a competitive chess player. Deciding early in life that he wanted to establish his own privately funded, research-based, drug-design company, he travelled to the United States to learn how to do so. Visiting established pharmaceutical manufacturers throughout the country, he financed the majority of his travels by winning pickup chess games.[5] Starting what would become the giant company, Janssen Pharmaceuticals, in a small space on the third floor of his father's medical product business, Dr. Paul, as he was affectionately known, pulled together a team of scientists producing fentanyl in 1960.

Fentanyl became the first in a line of fully synthetic opioids with Al-fentanyl, often called fentanyl's brother and Su-fentanyl, its sister, close on its heels – now incorporated into anesthetic practice around the world. These highly selective opioid analgesics – all specifically designed to have less side effects than the morphine, diamorphine (heroin) and pethidine available at the time. Over time, Dr. Janssen and other investigators, went on to establish that humans have so-called endogenous opioid and enkephalin receptors spread throughout our bodies, with intense concentrations in the pain-sensing centers of the brain and spinal cord. During the fight or flight response, the body releases endogenous opioids (endorphins) and enkephalins to minimize pain sensation automatically.[‡] Further research identified that there are at least five different

---

[*] The piperidine ring is considered essential to providing decent analgesia.

[†] Later to be determined as the mu opioid receptor, which was not yet established in 1960.

[‡] This endogenous release of endorphins and enkephalins is associated with the "high" that runners experience,

types of opioid receptors throughout the body, now named mu, kappa, delta, epsilon and dynorphin receptors. All mediating different analgesic and side-effect responses, such as respiratory depression, and nausea and vomiting. This finding spawned further synthetic opioid research designed to tailor different synthetic opioids to provide analgesia with as few side effects as possible. Thus, drugs such as pentazocine, buprenorphine, nalbuphine and others, were incorporated into anesthetic practice. Importantly, an antagonist drug, naloxone, a drug that could displace opioids like fentanyl from the mu receptor that caused respiratory depression, was found as early as 1961. This could be used at the end of an anesthetic if the administered opioids were causing too much respiratory depression – slow intravenous administration, titrated to effect, would allow the patient to start breathing again.[*]

Although Janssen died suddenly in 2003, fentanyl lives on as a testament to Dr. Paul's foresight in designing the go-to analgesic for anesthetic care. Five decades after its introduction, fentanyl remains the most widely used opioid in anesthetic practice in the world today,[†] usefully providing the third component of the balanced anesthesia goal.

Drugs (iv)

Balanced Anesthesia.
– *J. S. Lundy*

Balanced anesthesia, the concept that multiple anesthetic drugs might be used to provide general anesthesia, rather than relying on just one agent to

---

and speaks to the addictive nature of exercise. Some runners experience withdrawal if they do not exercise, further supporting the theory of endorphin action.

[*] Opioids depress respiratory drive by impairing the chemoreceptor response to carbon dioxide (CO_2) buildup in the medullary region of the brain. Dissolved CO_2 in the blood stream increases when a patient is not breathing adequately. This acts as a stimulus to the chemoreceptor reflex to increase respiration. Opioids blunt this response, requiring ever higher levels of CO_2 to stimulate respiration. Eventually the CO_2 receptor response levels are set so high by the opioid overdose that the CO_2 buildup causes coma in the patient and the patient dies from respiratory arrest. Naloxone is now widely available to treat respiratory depression in emergency situations where individuals may have taken overdoses of narcotic street drugs.

[†] It is safe to say that I have used fentanyl as a component of almost every one of the literally thousands of anesthetics I have delivered to date. But I am now changing my practice in the belief that minimizing intra-operative narcotic use may well turn out to be better for patients overall postoperative pain experience.

do this, has afforded anesthesiologists great flexibility in providing anesthetics calibrated to a specific patient's condition and the particular requirements of the surgical procedure that is performed. Previously, I have likened the provision of anesthesia to that of creatively cooking a fancy meal. There is no set recipe – the anesthesiologist decides what she thinks is best for her patient at the time. She balances the effects of the different agents, perhaps providing more intravenous than volatile anesthetic* on the one hand, and less of a muscle paralytic and more opioid – because the patient is reacting strongly to the surgical intervention – on the other. It is a dynamic situation requiring continuous monitoring of the effects of the anesthetic agents on measured parameters such as blood pressure, heart rate, oxygen saturation, muscle paralysis and anesthetic depth using modified EEG recordings. Anesthesiologists are the only true clinical pharmacologists in medical practice. Usually in medicine, a physician will prescribe a medication, and the prescription will be filled by a pharmacist and administered by a nurse. Not so in anesthesiology. We decide what we prescribe and give it at the same time, noting the immediate effect of our drug administration. In addition, we are ready to deal with the consequences of the detrimental effects of our anesthetic agents. Consider a very common situation: we induce anesthesia and the blood pressure continues to drop relentlessly because of the well-known interaction of anesthetics with the anti-hypertensive drugs the patient has been taking.[6] To counter this, we rapidly administer intravenous norepinephrine, replenishing blood levels of this life-saving hormone depressed by general anesthesia, so bringing the blood pressure and heart function back to a viable range.[7]

Clearly, there is no "standard anesthetic" approach, however there is a usual sequence that might be helpful for the reader:

- Anesthetic equipment is readied and checked in advance.

- Drugs are usually prepared in syringes before the start of the case.

- All standard monitors are attached to the patient before or during the anesthetic.

---

* Administered through a vaporizer at different concentrations.

- Using a previously placed intravenous catheter, one or two intravenous anesthetic agents are administered for induction of anesthesia while oxygen is administered by facemask.

- Should muscle paralysis be required, a suitable muscle relaxant is administered intravenously.

- The mask is replaced with an airway device, usually a laryngeal mask airway,[*] or the patient's trachea is intubated with an endotracheal tube.

- Anesthesia is then maintained with an intravenous or volatile anesthetic agent or both.

- At some time before the start of the surgical procedure, fentanyl or another opioid is administered.

- Anesthetic depth is maintained and monitored throughout the procedure and doses of agents adjusted as needed.

- The patient's temperature is monitored and maintained within normal limits.

- Blood loss occasioned by the surgical procedure is replaced.

- As the operation draws to a close, the anesthetic agent administration is stopped, allowing the patient to slowly awaken or "recover" as we more accurately call this process of anesthesia offset or eduction.

- The muscle relaxant effects are reversed with neostigmine.[†]

At the end of the procedure should the anesthesiologist believe that remnant anesthesia is due to fentanyl or other narcotic administration, naloxone can be given.

---

[*] A laryngeal mask airway will be described later in this chapter.

[†] Just before, or mixed with the neostigmine; atropine or glycopyrrolate is administered intravenously to counteract neostigmine's effect of increasing acetylcholine concentrations in the autonomic nervous system, which will cause

Should this remnant anesthesia be thought to be from another drug of the benzodiazepine class like midazolam, this can be reversed using a specific reversal agent flumazenil.[8]

Beyond these three reversal drugs in anesthetic practice, all other administered agents need to wear off spontaneously,[*] through redistribution, exhalation, elimination or metabolism.

The patient "awakens," gaining consciousness, and is allowed to recover from anesthesia usually in a recovery room specifically designed to look after patients postoperatively.

Equipment

With the very first anesthetics there was really no call for complex equipment for administration. Ether was simply dripped onto a readied towel or handy handkerchief, before application to the patient's mouth, followed by exhortations to deeply inhale.[†] William Morton, however, was in a quandary. Having been invited to give the first public demonstration of ether on October 16, 1846 at the Massachusetts General Hospital, with only a day's notice – he was going to use a liquid, ether, which had been around for over 500 years – really nothing new. So he needed an "invention," a piece of anesthetic apparatus for delivery of the anesthetic, that would bolster his claim for primacy of a general anesthetic administration for surgery.

As described earlier, Morton turned to A. A. Gould, a glass maker, who fashioned a globed, two headed retort, containing a sea sponge.[‡] Plugged into one side was a wooden spigot (at two o'clock) which Morton's patient, Gilbert Abbott, would be encouraged to suck on so drawing air through a second opening (at ten o'clock) over the sponge, steeped in ether, and on into his lungs to induce anesthesia. Gould can be credited with the first anesthetic equipment successfully used to administer anesthesia. His apparatus elegantly presaged two major directions for anesthetic equipment design. *The spigot* anticipated airway management equipment and apparatus, while

---

severe slowing of the heart, potentially leading to cardiac arrest, if not opposed by these so called anticholinergic drugs.

[*] There is now a specific reversal agent for the muscle relaxant drug rocuronium. This is known as sugammadex, a drug designed to envelop the rocuronium molecule, so inactivating its effect at the neuromuscular junction.

[†] Ether also stimulates respiration.

[‡] Pictured in Chapter 2.

the sponge-filled glass retort was the precursor of anesthetic delivery equipment. These two equipment design directions helped make anesthetic delivery the generally reliable and safe administration that it has become today.

The Spigot: Airway Management Equipment

The central problem to address is the fact that anesthesiologists need to ensure that during anesthesia the patient's "airway" – the pathway that administered gases and oxygen follow from the mouth or nose, down through the pharynx, larynx, and on through the glottic opening,* into the trachea and then lungs – remains open. This, despite the detrimental effects of anesthetics. Problematic because to varying degrees the induction and maintenance of anesthesia can compromise this "airway" at multiple levels – collapsing the airway – which needs to be then "opened" or maintained, using all manner of different airway devices. This problem has been the ongoing basis for equipment design advances.

A further focus of equipment development has been the design of tools (laryngoscopes) to introduce these airway devices as quickly as possible, either once anesthesia has been induced, or even before anesthetic induction, for fear of "losing" the airway once anesthesia has changed the airway configuration sufficiently that oxygen cannot be delivered in time.

It is all a matter of timing. Once the patient has been anesthetized and their breathing stopped, then no further oxygen delivery occurs until the airway is secured and ventilation (assisted respiration) starts. Five minutes or less! That is all we have. As un-replenished oxygen is depleted in the lungs and blood stream, the body goes into a fight or flight response to try and rescue the situation. There is a flood of circulating norepinephrine and epinephrine and the sympathetic nervous system goes into alarm mode, driving up the patient's heart rate, blood pressure and strengthening the heartbeat, all in a response to hypoxia – lack of oxygen – at the cellular level. The patient turning blue

---

* The glottic opening is the entrance from the larynx into the trachea. Overlying this is the epiglottis, a V-shaped structure attached to the base of the tongue at the valleculae. When the glottis is viewed by an anesthesiologist using a laryngoscope, placed at the valleculae, and so elevating the epiglottis, the glottic opening has a triangular shape, with on each side the white glistening vocal cords and at the base two cartilagenous, aryepiglottic folds of skin. Just below this glottic opening, two or three tracheal rings can often be seen. When seen as clearly as this, the glottic opening is the most beautiful sight in the world to an anesthesiologist, because she will be reasonably sure that she can safely pass an endotracheal tube, securing the patient's airway.

from cyanosis.* Brain cells are the most sensitive and die first. So the body shifts into overdrive, seeking to ensure that more blood – albeit depleted of oxygen – is sent to the brain to protect this vital organ as long as it can. If no life-saving respiration occurs however, the blood becomes completely depleted of oxygen and as the brain cells continue suffering, the heart starts to slow to conserve energy, and then, inevitably, cardiac arrest occurs. Usually by now, pandemonium reigns in the operating room, monitor alarms are shrieking their dire warnings, extra equipment is rushed in, and colleagues gather to assist the emergency situation.

In an attempt to avoid such scenarios, ever more sophisticated airway equipment has been developed over time. Starting with facemasks and oral "airways," then devices that could be placed into the trachea – endotracheal tubes – and finally appliances that could be positioned over, or above the larynx, like the laryngeal mask airway.

John Snow – as early as 1847 – declared that the administration of ether in England using a towel or handkerchief was inept. Contriving to remedy the situation, he designed an anesthetic delivery apparatus – as well as a face piece – to cover the mouth and nose made of thin sheet-lead, "the pliability of which easily adapted to the peculiar form of the features."[9] Connecting the face piece to the delivery apparatus using a three feet length of elastic tube, Snow noted that the tube needed to be wider than the trachea, to assure that resistance did not build up from the friction of breathed-in air. He noted too, that to manage the airway effectively, the patient should recline rather than sit in a chair as they would often slide off with induction of anesthesia – recommending that this should be avoided at all costs. If the patient turned purple he thought it proper to remove the face-piece for a short while, so the patient could breathe in "un-etherized air." If they snored, he took this as a good sign.

Sir Frederick Hewitt (1857-1916) decided to pursue anesthesia as a career because his eyesight had worsened. Holding a mask while feeling the patient's pulse for signs of life was not considered taxing. Hewitt being well known for his coolness and determination in difficult situations, like airway obstruction, designed the first oral airway in 1908 to deal with this problem. It had a circular metal ring, grooved to fit between the teeth, attached to a short

---

* Cyanosis, the blue tinge seen in the tongue, lips and finger tips first, is due to the depletion of oxygen bound to the hemoglobin in the arterial blood. The so-called deoxyhemoglobin is blue in color rather than the red of oxygen bound hemoglobin: oxyhemoglobin. That is why venous blood is blue and arterial blood is usually red.

rubber tube and was intended for use only when respiration was obstructed. Snoring or "seesaw" movement of the chest and abdomen indicating to the anesthetist that this was the case.[10]

These newly designed masks and oral airways helped relieve some of the airway problems encountered by the anaesthetists of the day when anesthetics were provided for peripheral operations like amputations. But what if the surgery was to be performed on the face or even worse the mouth, pharynx or larynx and involved breaking the jaw bone to gain access? Then, a "cut in the throat" – making a hole in the trachea – was required, allowing a metal tube to be inserted, so protecting the lungs from the inevitable bleeding that would ensue, while assuring that the patient kept breathing.*

Sir William Macewen (1847-1924) thought there must be a better way. A tall, handsome man, who tolerated fools badly, he had practiced on cadavers, passing a tube through the mouth, and on through the glottic opening into the trachea. Noting that with a little practice this was easy to do, if he put his finger into the "subject's" mouth, pressing the overlying epiglottis to the tongue, and so finger-guided the tube into the larynx through the vocal cords. Soon putting this to the test in a live patient, Macewen described the successful placement of an endotracheal tube under chloroform anesthesia in a fity-five-year-old plasterer with invasive oral cancer, back in 1880.[11] The patient recovering fully and suffering no detrimental effects to his voice or larynx from the intubation. Joyous about the success of his newfound technique, Macewen expounded prophetically in an article "that as long as the tube which went below the vocal chords remained patent, there could not possibly be any fear of asphyxia, and the most frequent cause of fatality under chloroform would be avoided."

Nevertheless this technique of securing the airway was not widely adopted – if at all – probably because of the largely unappetizing need for finger placement of the endotracheal tube in an era when surgical gloves were not widely used.

Sir Ivan Whiteside Magill (1888-1986) had a different approach. Drafted in 1919 to anesthetize patients with gross facial trauma requiring reconstructive surgery, he noticed that tubes passed "blindly" through the nose, sometimes perchance ended up in the trachea. With much practice, he established that the ideal position for blind passage through the nose was with the patient's head

---

* In abject airway emergencies during anesthesia, when all other methods have failed to secure the airway, this approach is still recommended to save the patient's life today. (See Chapter 10)

positioned as a man would adopt in "draining a pint of beer." This position allowed easy endotracheal tube placement in conscious patients and obviated the need for some of the crude laryngoscopes already developed at the time.

Laryngoscopes usually have two key components. The laryngeal blade with a light at its tip, to be placed on the back of the tongue to help visualize the glottic opening; and the handle which contains batteries to power the light. Patients need to be anesthetized before a laryngoscope can be introduced into the mouth and pharynx because often painful airway and other protective reflexes are provoked by the placement of a blade close to the glottis. The pharynx area has a rich supply of nerve endings and well developed involuntary reflexes to protect the lungs from food and fluid that pass through this common pharyngeal passage on their way to the esophagus and stomach, on the one hand, and the larynx and lungs on the other. Hence, the placement of a laryngoscope is almost impossible in an awake patient without anesthesia, because he will start gagging, coughing, fighting, and sometimes vomiting as a result of these reflexes. Under too-light anesthesia there is also a danger of laryngospasm; the complete closure of the larynx from these hyperactivated reflexes tuned to avoid any aspiration into the lungs.*

Magill, although championing "blind nasal intubation" had in fact also designed a laryngoscope that he called an "intubating spatula." U-shaped, it featured a straight blade and battery-filled handle with an intervening straight connector. The straight blade was designed to press down the epiglottis much like Macewen's finger, so that an endotracheal tube could be passed into the glottic opening. The problem, that no one realized at the time, was that pressing down the epiglottis in this fashion was a setup for laryngospasm under light anesthesia, especially thiopentone anesthesia.

Sir Robert Macintosh (1897-1989) designed the laryngoscope still most used today. Witnessing, that under deep anesthesia for tonsillectomy, a curved device, the Boyle Davis gag – placed at the base of the tongue – allowed an excellent view of the glottic opening by pushing the epiglottis away; he added a laryngoscope handle to the gag to complete the design. Thus the Macintosh laryngoscope, popularly known as the "MAC," was born – now available in five

---

* Anesthesiologists are well trained to deal with the life-threatening problem of laryngospasm. If nothing else works we use a paralytic agent like succinylcholine to paralyze the laryngeal nerves causing this reflex activity, so that the larynx will open up and we can assist respiration to avoid asphyxiation.

sizes (MAC 0-4) to accommodate children and adults alike. The so-designed MAC launching endotracheal intubation as a well-accepted airway technique – performed at the time using re-useable red rubber tubes, which came in different sizes to accommodate patients' differing tracheal dimensions.

While endotracheal intubation created a safe passageway for inhalation and exhalation, and avoided the feared respiratory obstruction and asphyxia, this airway technique could not completely protect the lungs from aspiration of fluid, blood or stomach contents in the pharynx that leaked past the tracheal tube, alongside the tracheal walls, and on into the lungs. Indeed, the possibility of aspiration was made worse because the patient's laryngeal and tracheal protective reflexes were impaired by the anesthetic state.

Although others had dabbled in solutions, Arthur Guedel, in America, took the problem seriously, designing endotracheal tube "cuffs" – cut from the fingertips of rubber gloves – that could be inflated, so surrounding the tube and closing off the trachea completely. Nevertheless, many of his anesthesiology colleagues remained skeptical of the value of these "cuffed" endotracheal tubes to assure airway protection; requiring a dramatic exhibition to popularize this technique for avoiding lung aspiration. Guedel took to the road and presented a series of "dunked dog" demonstrations, using his pet terrier "Airway," at medical conventions and meetings. Anesthetizing Airway, Guedel intubated the dog with the now cuffed endotracheal tube, turning him on his back and completely immersing the terrier in a large aquarium filled to capacity with water. Only the endotracheal tube remained sticking out above the water so that the dog could continue breathing anesthetic and air through it. (All could see the dog upside down in the aquarium through its glass windows). Without a cuff, of course, water would have leaked into Airway's mouth and pharynx, and passed down the trachea alongside the tube, drowning the dog. After an hour or so Guedel removed his pet. Waking up in front of the audience, still wet from the dunk tank, Airway got up groggily, shook himself vigorously to get rid of excess water clinging to his coat and then trotted out of the auditorium to loud applause. Retiring from the road show, Airway's work done in popularizing cuffed endotracheal intubation in America, the terrier happily lived out his life in the Guedel's family home.

People are not all the same, in fact we are all distinctly different. So too are our faces, jaw structure, tongue and pharynx, that constitute our airway leading down to the trachea.* Hence anesthesiologists evaluate every patient's facial characteristics and peer into their mouths asking them to stick out their tongue to help to predict whether their "airway" may be difficult to manage using a conventional laryngoscope like a Macintosh. We do this before taking the irreversible step of administering a general anesthetic, for fear of losing (not being able to manage) the airway after induction; with the dire consequences previously noted.

The problem of the "difficult" airway has spurred the design of multiple different aids for intubation – like bougies or stylets (put inside the tubes) or laryngoscopes (placed in the mouth) – to help visualize the glottic opening better; all in an attempt to help negotiate compromising facial characteristics safely.†

Most important in making airway management safer over the last thirty and fifteen years respectively have been the incorporation of fiber-optic bronchoscopy and video laryngoscopy into anesthetic practice.

The fiber-optic bronchoscope – now usually attached to a large video tower displaying a wide-screen view for all to see in the operating room – allows an anesthesiologist to intubate a patient before administering general anesthesia. Upon anesthetizing either the nasal passages, or the mouth, with local anesthetic, the anesthesiologists passes this thin camera tube down the airway to the laryngeal glottis, while the patient is still completely awake. Then, after visualizing the glottis through the bronchoscope, some local anesthetic is sprayed on to the vocal cords and down the trachea (so numbing the airway further), allowing an endotracheal tube to be placed with minimal discomfiture to the patient. Connecting the tube to the breathing system, the anesthesiologist then "tests" that appropriate ventilation of the lungs can occur before starting the anesthetic. The patient and anesthesiologist remaining secure in the knowledge that the airway is safe – and will not be lost – after induction of anesthesia.

Video laryngoscopes, like the Glidescope however, require general anesthesia to be administered first. Nonetheless the Glidescope – which has the laryngoscope blade angled at sixty degrees to the handle – allows us to visualize the glottis on a video screen, more easily, in difficult airway patients, making an enormous difference in enhancing the safe management of anesthesia. So

---

* This is one of the reasons why simulation training is inadequate to the task for training to manage the "difficult airway."

† Protruding teeth, small jaws, obesity, radiation damage, former surgery, acute trauma.

much so that when conventional laryngoscopy using a MAC fails, video laryngoscopes are now the most commonly used devices to rescue the situation.[12]

Another technique that is recommended to save the patient, is placement of a supra glottic airway, better known as a laryngeal mask airway.

Dr. Archie Brain (1942-), a dapper always well-dressed man with a mischievous glint in his eye, never planned to go into medicine. Born in Japan to a father who was a knighted diplomat, he had a penchant for the arts; studying linguistics at Oxford before becoming fascinated by science and invention. Upon completing medical training at St. Bartholomew's in London, he got into anesthesia quite by accident. The job he was interviewing for had been taken, so he was offered an anesthetic one instead. Saying, "I might as well have a go, why not?" After six weeks he was hooked. "I just loved it." Becoming a lecturer in anesthetics at the London Hospital in 1980, he started work on some of his planned inventions, contriving to establish what was really missing in anesthetic practice that would make it safer. Remarking, "All this holding of facemasks does seem to me to be a bit awkward," at a time that he was doing a lot of dental anesthesia using a Goldman nasal cone mask. With his artistic eye he recognized a match between the triangular shape of the glottic opening of the larynx and that of the skull bones surrounding the nose – formulating a plan to see whether the Goldman cone could cover the larynx (it covered the nose nicely, so why not the larynx?); in so doing inventing the laryngeal mask airway. Visiting London's Institute of Laryngology, he borrowed pathological specimens, putting them in his suitcase – smelling of formalin – to carry them home on the Underground; testing his prototypes on his kitchen table over weekends. Connecting a Goldman nose cone to a sawn-off endotracheal tube, he tried it on himself: "I coughed and spluttered a bit but I could breathe through it. It was a very exciting moment." Then, when he had summoned up enough courage to do so, he tried the prototype on one or two patients under anesthesia, fearing that he might hurt the patients. "It was really a very exciting moment, because they just breathed happily through this. And then I tried squeezing it* – a bit – and then I found I could actually also ventilate [the patient]." The so invented – Laryngeal Mask Airway (LMA) – became commercially available in 1987 and it is fair to say that this airway device was to prove to be an inflection point in anesthetic safety – revolutionizing anesthetic

---

* The anesthetic reservoir bag.

practice. There was now an alternative to holding or attaching a mask to the patient's face – the norm for short anesthetic cases – before its introduction.

The LMA is placed simply without the need for laryngoscopy. After anesthetic induction, the patient's mouth is opened and the soft pear-shaped device is gently pushed over the tongue and seated over the larynx – noted by the easy air exchange that occurs through its plastic connecting tube when it is in the right place. The connecting tube, similar in design to the proxymal side of a conventional endotracheal tube, is attached to the anesthetic breathing system for anesthetic delivery and gas exchange.

The LMA can also serve as an easier alternative to endotracheal intubation, neither requiring laryngoscopy nor muscle paralysis to place, while causing much less cardiovascular and respiratory tract reflex responses.

An "intubating" laryngeal mask airway has also been developed which can be used in an emergency situation when the airway cannot be easily secured using alternative means. Also designed by Archie Brain – Archie tells me that he is now most pleased when he hears stories of how the LMA has helped save yet another patient's life.

"That's really what it's all about." Isn't it?

Anesthetic Delivery Equipment
The Sponge-Filled Glass Retort

The sponge-filled glass retort used to deliver the first ether anesthetic was ingenious in design. It was portable and realized a key feature: how to deliver a concentrated amount of this volatile anesthetic to the patient. Anesthesia requires the delivery of precise quantities of a mixture of an anesthetic vapor and a carrier gas like oxygen to the airway of the patient. But as a volatile anesthetic like ether turns from a liquid to a vapor it cools, decreasing its own velocity of vaporization; so the large surface area provided by the wetted sponge compensated for this fact.

Ever since, the development of anesthetic apparatus has incorporated two main features: an anesthetic vaporizer that can deliver precise temperature-compensated concentrations of anesthetic agent, and, a system to deliver exact volumes and concentrations of carrier gases like oxygen, nitrous oxide and air reliably to the patient's airway.

Vaporizers, unique to anesthetic practice, are designed with a specific volatile anesthetic agent like sevoflurane in mind.* This is because the different currently used anesthetic agents, halothane,† enflurane, sevoflurane, desflurane and isoflurane, have distinctive biochemical properties, conferring different potencies, onset and offset times, and volatility. Volatility is reflected, importantly, in the described anesthetic agent's wide variability in saturated vapor pressures. Agent-specific saturated vapor pressures govern how many anesthetic molecules will be released from a liquid to form a vapor at a specific temperature, and also impact how quickly the anesthetic liquid cools – losing temperature as molecules need extra energy to escape from the liquid to become a vapor. As this is different for every agent, precise compensating mechanisms need to be adopted in each agent-specific vaporizer to achieve the exact concentrations of anesthetic demanded by the anesthesiologist as she sets the anesthetic concentration dial, prominent on the top of the vaporizer. In turn the color-coded vaporizer, is connected to the anesthetic gas delivery apparatus, which provides the carrier gas that will deliver the vaporized anesthetic to the patient.

How these carrier gases, such as nitrous oxide, oxygen or air, are delivered in exact quantities through the vaporizers, picking up the volatile agent on the way to the patient, has been a further focus of apparatus design.

A great leap forward occurred in the 1870s when nitrous oxide and oxygen was first compressed into cylinders. This was a boon and a bane. A boon because it allowed portability of anesthetic gases. A bane because the very high pressure that these gases were compressed at would be too dangerous to apply directly to a patient's airway. Hence a system of pressure regulators and high-pressure tubing needed to be designed to safely provide such carrier gases, allowing them to pass through the vaporizer, pick up the right amount of anesthetic and convey this to the patient. The delivery system also needed to ensure that both the exact concentrations and the precise volume of gases (measured in milliters per minute) could be provided. A flow rotameter was the final solution to this problem. An inspired device – again, color-coded according to the gas supplied – it comprised vertical glass tubes, one for each gas delivered,

---

* They are called agent-specific vaporizers. Named and color coded for the specific agents, sevoflurane is yellow, isoflurane, purple. Newer vaporizers have color-coded uniquely shaped filler connectors which are attached to the bottles of anesthetic and then used to fill the vaporizer's tank with anesthetic liquid. This makes it virtually impossible to place the wrong anesthetic in a modern vaporizer, which could have catastrophic results.

† Halothane is still used extensively worldwide as it is relatively inexpensive compared to the other agents. Ether is also still occasionally used.

below which was a small knob. Turn the knob clockwise and more of the delivered gas would flow through the glass tube causing an enclosed bobbin to rise up a gradated scale indicating the exact amount of gas that the patient would receive. Pretty soon all the required design modifications and additions turned the rather simple anesthetic delivery *apparatus* into ever more complicated anesthesia *machines*. These now incorporated gas cylinders, high and low pressure systems of tubing and hoses, vaporizers and rotameters and usually, because they were becoming heavy, wheels!

Edmund Gaskin Boyle (1875-1941) was one of the first to add this necessary feature. His 1933 version, Boyles machine – combining all these components with a two-level working surface – becoming the blueprint for anesthesia machine design in the future.[*] To this day anesthesiologists suffer from the fact that rotameters are placed on the left side of anesthesia machines because Boyle was left handed.

What had not been addressed however was a reliable method for managing respiratory depression. Before the 1930s, if the patient stopped breathing there really wasn't much that could be done. Anal stretching, electrocution, a splash of water or brandy on the lips, or vain attempts with a bellows in the mouth rarely resulted in a change of course. Yes, insufflation anesthesia, a catheter placed in the larynx feeding oxygen to the lungs had been invented, but positive-pressure ventilation was not yet established practice to remedy the often terminal respiratory depression from anesthetic administration.

The Pulmotor, termed the first ventilator, was a positive-pressure ventilatory device that might just solve the conundrum of respiratory arrest. Introduced in 1907 by Bernard Draeger to resuscitate drowning victims at swimming pools, it found utility in ambulances but unfortunately did not find favor in operating rooms. Iron lungs weren't the answer either. Developed in 1928 to combat the respiratory paralysis from polio, they surrounded the patient completely, exerting negative pressure to inflate the lungs, making surgery impossible. The Spiropulsator, the first specifically designed ventilator for the operating room, was deployed in some theatres in Sweden in 1933, but was far too complicated and so not widely adopted. So, until the 1930s, on the occasions that anesthesiologists encountered respiratory failure, attempts would be made to compress the chest by squeezing hard on each flank, but if that failed to rally the patient's

[*] A fuller description of a Boyles Anesthesia Machine is provided in Chapter 3 and a picture heads this chapter.

breathing, that was that! The patient did not take the ether well! And often died an untimely death.

"Personally, I can see no danger in controlling ventilation," declared Dr. Nosworthy. "This may be performed mechanically by the Spiropulsator, or more simply, and just as effectively – if the anaesthetist appreciates what he is doing – by hand." This proclamation, in a well-known medical journal, changed the approach to this problem forever.[13] Encouraged further by the fact that as muscle relaxation using curare was increasingly adopted, anesthesiologists were becoming ever more tired of having to ventilate the patient by hand – either via a mask or endotracheal tube. Consequently the introduction of a simple mechanical ventilator was keenly received.

John Blease (1906-1985) started his career as a butcher boy, before designing his own 1000cc motor bike, "the Blease Special," and becoming the uncontested champion sand racer for six years running at Southport in northwest England.[14] By now, owning a car repair business, an anesthetist friend, Dr. Roberts, asked him to improve his dental anesthetic machine. Blease did so with good effect, and upon Roberts's untimely death, took over his dental anesthetic practice becoming highly skilled in the art of clinical anesthesia. So much so, that during the bombing of Liverpool in the Second World War he was pressed into service as an emergency anaesthetist, a practice only performed by trained doctors in England! Which he was not. In answer to the drudgery of "bag-squeezing" that controlled ventilation required, he designed and produced his first positive-pressure mechanical ventilator, the Blease Pulmoflator, incorporating motorcycle technology to drive the "bag in bottle" piston that inflated the patient's chest. Teaming up with Roger Manley, they produced the elegantly simple Blease Manley ventilator, widely adopted for controlled ventilation around the world. Such a free-standing ventilator could be placed on the Boyles machine and was easily connected with breathing hoses to the patient. It was simplicity itself.* Consisting of a bellows on a box, all the anaesthetist had to do was adjust a weight on a hinge to a sufficient height along the hinge arm to assure enough downward pressure on the bellows to inflate the patient's chest. Then, he would set the tidal ventilation – the volume of each controlled breath – that he wanted the patient to receive (say 600ml) and adjust the number of breaths per minute

---

* The author used this ventilator at the Gloucestershire Royal Hospital in 1984.(If the patient was too big, and the weight insufficient to adequately inflate the patient's chest, anaesthetist's were taught to attach a liter bag of saline on top of the weight to help matters along.)

by setting the total volume of gas (oxygen and nitrous oxide) flow delivered a minute.* This was a simple matter of adjusting the rotameter flows to the required amount of gas, because the ventilator was connected into the breathing circuit – leading to the patient – by throwing a simple switch,† Hey presto! The patient was ventilated with good effect, relieving the anesthesiologist from the tedium of bag-squeezing, and freeing him up to attend to other pressing matters.

Pressing matters such as administering intravenous drugs and fluids, adjusting ventilator and anesthetic settings to adapt to the changing surgical situation, while monitoring progress of the patient, and documenting these on an anesthesiologist's record of practice. Initially such a record was just a sheet of paper on a clipboard, but eventually, a fully electronic computerized record would be generated which automatically downloaded most if not all of the physiological parameters used to monitor the patient's well-being and anesthetic state.

Today, anesthetic machines have grown into behemoths on wheels, weighing in at around 200 kilograms with incorporated ventilators, gas cylinders and electronic monitors. Fully integrated, the machines help anesthesiologists deliver anesthetics while presenting monitored parameters on wide-screen displays and automatically downloading data to an interactive electronic medical record usually attached as a laptop computer to the machine. Equipment and monitoring alarm systems are a major feature. Initially, alarm settings are preset by anesthetic machine algorithms. However, during the anesthetic they can be adjusted or silenced by the anesthesiologist, only to recur a minute later should the problem persist. Drawing on ergonomic display features used in airplane cockpit design, an anesthesia work station looks much like what a pilot might have to contend with in flying a modern aircraft. Not surprisingly these sophisticated anesthesia machine and monitoring devices can cost in the order of $100,000 each, close to what a second-hand private plane can

---

* We call this total delivered gas a minute, the minute volume. If we set it at six litres, then, with a tidal ventilation of 600 ml, the Manley ventilator would deliver ten breaths a minute. This is called a minute volume divider ventilator. Ventilators have become very sophisticated, allowing the addition of baseline pressures to keep the airways open at all times, and allowing adjustment of inspiratory flow rates, and the monitoring of the exact volumes of tidal and minute ventilations delivered, displaying the varying pressures developed in the lungs. While ventilators from the 1960s to late 1980s were often free-standing, now they have been incorporated into anesthesia machines, making some of the monitoring of respiratory parameters mentioned possible.

† And reconnecting one of the rubber hoses to the circuit.

be bought for. Fortunately these planes fly better, nevertheless, we often talk of "flying the anesthesia machine," drawing on parallels between aviation and anesthesia.

Monitors: An Alarming Situation

Monitare
– *Latin: to warn*

John Wright Clover, wearing an overcoat and gloves, sat himself down in a high-backed wooden chair ready for a picture to be taken. Balding, and quite old, his remaining hair stood out, windblown from coming in out of the cold. His son, the famous anaesthetist of London, Joseph Clover (1825-1882), stood closely by with a large silk bag – much like a pillow case – filled with chloroform, slung over his shoulder. Turning to his father he put a mask gently to his face. With the other hand he felt for his radial pulse at the wrist. "Pick up your arm so I can demonstrate the monitoring technique," he must have said. Then the senior Clover closed his eyes and Joseph looked gravely down at his forebear. Flash!... In the dissipating smoke, a daguerreotype photograph was taken. The posed picture so created in 1862, reputedly used, to advertise Dr. Clover's technique of continuously monitoring the patient's pulse under anesthesia.

Physical signs like breathing, pupil size, skin color and pulse (rate, volume, regularity) are useful, but often inadequate for assessing the patient's state under anesthesia. Far better to develop instruments specifically designed to measure or detect changes in physiological parameters with much greater accuracy and sensitivity. Such instruments are called monitors, used in anesthesia, often with alarms, to warn us when things are going wrong.*

Back in the 1950s better monitoring devices were needed. Especially for the heart, as doctors realized – from treating surgical casualties with thoracic injuries during the Second World War – that the heart could be manipulated

---

* A permanent record of parameters such as heart rate and blood pressure was crucial to determining both the effects of anesthetics as well as the associated outcomes from anesthetic practice. Drs. Harvey Cushing and Ernest Codman at the Massachusetts General Hospital are credited with the first anesthetic records of practice. First used, as early as 1894, when they recorded pulse and respiration frequency.

with relative impunity; propelling innovations in cardiac surgery. Today still, the monitoring that I could use as a cardiac anesthesiologist will serve to explain the state of the art.

"The heart is just a pump," Dr. Christiaan Barnard[*] famously asserted. Nonetheless, anesthesiologists are critically concerned with monitoring this vital organ's well-being during an anesthetic.

Routinely, we attach a five-lead electrocardiogram (EKG), applied to the chest, using sticky electrodes, so that we can electronically assess the heart's activity – monitoring for irregularities of beat or acute changes that might suggest impending cardiac damage. This tells us little, however, about how well the heart is pumping; so we attach a blood pressure cuff around one upper arm and place an intra-arterial catheter in the radial artery, at the wrist, in the other. This radial artery catheter provides a pressure tracing, displayed in red, on the video display monitor allowing second to second assessment of blood pressure – dependent on both heart function and blood vessel tone.[†]

This extent of monitoring would be more than good enough for most surgeries, but in heart surgery we monitor more, introducing a few more devices, as the anesthetic progresses.

Once the patient is asleep we insert (through a central vein in the neck under strict aseptic conditions) a central venous catheter and then place a Swan-Ganz catheter through this.[‡][15] Usually yellow in colour, around fifty centimeters in length, and affectionately known as "the Swan," this catheter allows measurement of pressures in the heart as well as a determination of pump function – cardiac output – using a technique of intermittent intravenous saline injection to compute. As we "float" the Swan, intra cardiac pressure waves are displayed on the monitor, identifying the correct position of the balloon-tipped catheter in the heart.[§]

Next, after the patient is intubated, we introduce a transesophageal echocardiographic ultrasonic probe, through the mouth, into the esophagus and sometimes down into the upper regions of the stomach. This allows us to view,

---

[*] Dr. Barnard performed the first human heart transplant at Groote Schuur Hospital in Cape Town in 1967.

[†] If blood vessels in the body dilate from anesthetics, or blood or fluid is lost, blood pressure will drop, no matter how well the heart is working.

[‡] Introduced by the cardiologists H.J.C. Swan and W. Ganz.

[§] The key insight that Dr. Swan brought to the design of this catheter was the placement of an inflatable balloon at its tip – an idea generated by watching sailing ships in Santa Monica Bay – allowing the catheter to "float" in the

assess, and record, the functions of the heart valves and four heart chambers, before and after, the cardiac surgical procedure. Serving not only as a guide as to how well the surgical procedure was performed, but also how effectively cardiac strengthening drugs, like norepinephrine, are working.

How well the lungs are functioning, in providing oxygen to the blood and clearing carbon dioxide from the body, is also of critical importance and is exactly monitored using both a pulse oximeter and an end-tidal carbon dioxide monitor.

The pulse oximeter, an early warning system, is a monitoring device that has arguably contributed the most to anesthetic safety since its introduction in the 1980s. Applied as a clasp or plaster around one of the fingers of the hand, it works by transmitting light waves through the digit, computing the difference between oxygenated and deoxygenated blood, then displaying a blood oxygen saturation value on a monitor for all to see and hear – far earlier and better than the clinical sign of cyanosis (blue blood) that was relied on in less monitored times. One of the required standard monitors for anesthesia administration, the pulse oximeter is an essential item, included in the Surgical Safety Checklist, developed in conjunction with the World Health Organization, helping set the standards for safe anesthesia practice world-wide.[*16] Walk into any operating theater in the developed world[†] and the singular sound you will hear is the beating heart pulse of the pulse oximeter. Instantaneously recognized, the pitch of the sound adjusts as the patient worsens. Fresh and bright in sound when blood saturation is 100%,[‡] if this deteriorates, in say an airway emergency, each 1% drop in measured saturation results in a pitch change; going down to a low growl – a sound we hate to hear – indicating that the patient is in real trouble and the saturation is in the fifties or less!

blood stream through the right heart chambers and on into the pulmonary artery.
*   More about this in Chapter 8.
†   This is however not the case in many countries around the world. The Lifebox Program, a charity, seeks to place a Lifebox pulse oximeter (pictured) in every operating room around the world – having determined that there are over 77,000 theaters that lack reliable pulse oximeters. The author has travelled to Guyana, Guatemala and Nicaragua, to train local clinicians in Lifebox pulse oximeter use as part of this program.
‡   We speak loosely of blood saturation. It is actually not the blood but the iron containing hemoglobin in blood that binds oxygen, which is fully saturated when the monitor reads 100%. As oxygen is used up in the body and not replenished, it unbinds from hemoglobin (Hb) and so the % saturation declines. Anemia, low hemoglobin content of the blood, does not affect saturation directly, so the monitor can read 100% saturation because the available Hb is fully saturated. The oxygen content, the total amount of oxygen carried in every 100ml of blood is dependent on two factors: how much Hb there is to bind oxygen and how much oxygen is dissolved in the other components of

The average human uses up 250ml of oxygen a minute during cellular respiration, producing 200ml of carbon dioxide in the tissues of her body. The pumping heart, circulating blood, transports this dissolved carbon dioxide back to the lungs to be eliminated. Breathing in and out allows exchange of one for the other, and is as much about bringing in oxygen (O_2) as it is important to eliminate carbon dioxide (CO_2) from the body. Hence we monitor the inspiratory and expiratory concentrations of both O_2 and CO_2. Inspired O_2 concentration[*] to make sure we are giving enough. Expired CO_2 to confirm that adequate ventilation is eliminating the carbon dioxide waste produced. We call this "end-tidal CO_2 monitoring."[†] Introduced in the 1980s, this exhalation is diagrammed graphically on the monitor, allowing interpretation of the wave form so generated, helping diagnose and treat such acute conditions as bronchospasm (tightening of the airways of the lungs) that may occur under anesthesia.[‡]

The humble stethoscope, often draped across the anesthesiologist's shoulders for convenience, is an especially useful monitoring device. Standard practice after intubation, or LMA placement; listening to the lungs helps confirm correct placement and serves to assess whether or not bronchospasm has occurred.

Once the airway device is connected via disposable tubing[§] to an incorporated

blood, like plasma. In anemic patients the oxygen content is therefore lower and the ability to deliver oxygen to the cells is limited. In such circumstances of a low Hb, should an airway emergency occur in patients where the blood oxygen content is thus lower, oxygen will be used up quicker and consequently the oxygen saturation will decline earlier. This is why anesthesiologists are always concerned by patients who are anemic.

[*] Inspired oxygen (O_2) should be at least 21% (and can be set higher) or an alarm will start sounding. In fact many modern machines will not allow administration of nitrous oxide (which contains no useable oxygen) unless oxygen is also administered to ensure that at least 21% inspired concentration of oxygen is administered to the patient. O_2 is piped to all modern operating rooms and provided from a central gas supply often maintained outside the hospital for safety reasons. (O_2 is explosive and is stored in a massive liquid oxygen tank kept at -160°C). Piped oxygen is connected into the anesthesia machine by color-coded tubing connected into a pod gas supply (often hanging from the ceiling) with specific connectors for each gas supplied through the pod to ensure that the wrong gas cannot be delivered to the patient. As a further safety measure, oxygen, air and nitrous oxide cylinders are also attached to the anesthesia machine to provide emergency supplies should the central supply system fail. Piped and cylinder pressure readings, for these three gases, are prominently displayed on the anesthesia machine console allowing the anesthesiologist to verify that he has enough gases available to look after the patient.

[†] "End-tidal," because it occurs at the end of a tidal breath, i.e. normal cyclical breathing or ventilation if the patient is attached to a ventilator.

[‡] Endotracheal intubation, especially in asthmatic patients and smokers may cause acute severe bronchospasm, which needs to be treated with deepening anesthesia, albuterol or, if life-threatening, epinephrine. The end-tidal CO_2 monitoring trace will show the effects of such therapy.

[§] Involving a circle system with a carbon dioxide absorption device.

modern ventilator, innumerable other respiratory parameters can be monitored and are displayed on the anesthesia machine console. Parameters such as respiratory rate, minute ventilation, tidal ventilation, inspiratory and expiratory pressure, derived pressure volume loops – for most of which alarm settings are automatically set. At last count around fifteen possible alarms can be set on a modern anesthetic machine. A truly alarming situation, as many of the alarms are known to distract hyper-vigilant anesthesiologists from the care of their patient.[*][17] So they switch them off.

Of critical importance, however, is the disconnect alarm, which starts sounding if an inadvertent disconnection of the breathing system occurs from the airway device.

This should never be switched off!

Using monitoring to determine the depth of the anesthetic state is still far from perfect. Although the inspired and, especially, the expired end-tidal concentrations of anesthetic agents like sevoflurane are monitored, they can only serve as a guide as to what the anesthetic state might be in a particular patient when compared to the MAC requirements for that specific agent[†] – giving only an idea of the likelihood that the patient is unconscious and amnestic. Far better would be real-time electroencephalographic (EEG) monitoring of anesthetic depth, but this is not routinely performed. Instead, the bispectral index monitor (BIS) is widely used, especially in cardiac surgical patients where there is higher risk for awareness. The BIS is an electroencephalogram-derived device and the most commonly used depth of anesthesia monitor in anesthetic practice today.[18] An electrode strip is applied to the forehead and the BIS monitor processes the frontal EEG signal, using a proprietary algorithm, to calculate a dimensionless number prominently displayed on a monitor. BIS values range from 100, the awake state, to 0, where all brain activity is suppressed. It is intended to indicate the patient's level of consciousness. A target range between 40-60 has been advocated to avoid awareness and excessive depths of anesthesia administration. Unfortunately, despite its widespread use, this BIS monitor has

---

[*] In hospitals the pervasive presence of "nuisance" alarms which have caused alarm fatigue and associated "sentinel events" have provoked The Joint Commission, an accrediting agency in the United States, to issue a Sentinel Event Alert addressing concerns around Medical Device Alarm Safety. In our own department we have developed an Alarm Setting Policy to ensure that all essential alarms are activated.

[†] MAC or minimum alveolar concentration, is defined as that end-tidal concentration for a specific agent at which 50% of patients will not move when a surgical incision occurs.

not been shown to be better at ascertaining lack of awareness during anesthesia than end-tidal anesthesia concentration determination.[18] Notably inexact at best.

The anesthetic state lowers your temperature. Partly this is due to anesthetics depressing the thermoregulatory center in the hypothalamus. And then there are the effects of conduction, convection, radiation and evaporation in a patient who is lying completely still in a cold operating room.

Hypothermia, especially under anesthesia, can have multiple detrimental effects, increasing wound infection rates, impairing blood coagulation and at the extreme, less than around 32°C, causing ventricular fibrillation leading to cardiac arrest and death.

Not surprisingly we monitor temperature as a standard of anesthetic care, using an electronic thermometer – called a thermistor – which can be placed in any orifice, but more usually in the mouth or nose. We don't just monitor of course, but pro-actively use different stratagems to maintain a patient's temperature. So for example, disposable, inflatable, upper and lower body warming devices are applied. Heated air pumped through the system, keeping the patient warm. While humidifiers are included in the airway equipment to guard against temperature loss from the latent heat of vaporization needed to humidify the dry gases we administer – in so doing also minimizing damage to sensitive tissues lining the airways.

A critical monitor in the operating theater is a neuromuscular transmission monitor.

After the administration of a muscle relaxant drug like rocuronium, we seek to determine whether a sufficient dose has been administered to paralyze the patient adequately for the surgery to be performed, as well as whether additional doses are required for long operations to proceed. In addition, at the end of the surgery we need to know what dose of the reversal agent, neostigmine, needs to be administered and assess whether, after the determined dose has been given, the patient has gained sufficient strength to allow extubation. If we get this wrong the patient could be weak post-operatively, which might in turn result in lung aspiration, increasing respiratory failure, and a greater risk for post-operative lung complications. A recent publication in the leading journal *Anesthesiology,* puts it well: "Muscle relaxants are often essential components of a balanced anesthetic technique; yet they may produce life threatening complications if not dosed and monitored appropriately."[19]

A neuromuscular transmission monitor (NTM) achieves that goal. At its simplest it consists of two electrodes applied over a nerve supplying a set of muscles. We often place two EKG stickers over the ulnar nerve at the wrist connected by electric wires to the NTM to achieve this. Activating the battery-operated NTM, by pressing a button, sends four quick electric impulses to the ulnar nerve. We call this a train of four (TOF). It hurts, so we only do this when the patient is anesthetized. We then look at the effect of this TOF stimulus on the muscle set supplied by the ulnar nerve. In the absence of prior muscle relaxant administration, four vigorous twitches – the patient's hand closing in on itself – is the result. With increasing muscle paralysis from rocuronium administration, the four twitches become ever weaker, then disappear one by one, until there is no response from the TOF stimulus. The patient is now totally paralyzed. As the muscle relaxant wears off, first one then two, then three and eventually four twitches return, telling us how much neostigmine we need to give to fully reverse the patient. Ensuring their ability to breathe adequately post-operatively and so avoiding many unnecessary complications.

Lastly, a monitor, or warning system, we don't yet have, but could use, is one that reliably identifies the risk of fire or of explosion in the operating room.* Although we no longer use highly flammable anesthetics like cyclopropane and ether, there is still a risk of operating room fires ignited by the use of high oxygen concentrations, lasers, combustible materials and the density of electronic equipment that fill a modern operating room – that just might short-circuit or produce the spark that causes an explosion.

One of my own cases, many years ago, illustrates the point well.

On call at night as a locum registrar in England, I was informed that emergency surgery for a ruptured abdominal aortic aneurysm had been scheduled. When a patient suffers such a ruptured aneurysm, with the excessive blood loss this entails, surgery can rarely save the day. A week earlier, surprisingly,

---

* During the current "time out" process in the U.S.A., that is mandated before each operation, where the patient and planned procedure as well as the consent for operation and management of required prophylactic medications (antibiotics and anticoagulant therapy) is formally discussed, any possible fire risks and the location of a fire extinguisher is also established.

I encountered a similar patient, not quite as sick, and on calling my consultant – safely at home – I was told, "Get on with it," so I did. With good results, I must add.

Today, suspecting the same response, "I got on with it," summoning the senior house officer to help with this all too difficult case – having everything ready, by the time the patient was emergently transferred to the operating theatre, at around 2a.m., in the morning. Placing an arterial line quickly we sent off an arterial blood gas analysis sample to the laboratory fearing extreme acidosis* of the blood indicating that this patient was indeed terminal. We planned to induce anesthesia, the surgeon standing poised over the patient, ready to make a quick incision to get into the abdomen as rapidly as possible. Placing a lifesaving aortic clamp, deftly, around the aorta would stop further bleeding. As is often the case in such patients, the abdomen is full of blood and tense and distended, and this tamponades (compresses) the aorta. Although burst, this stems somewhat the blood leaking from the ruptured aneurysm. We induced, he incised, releasing the tamponade and the bleeding from the ruptured aorta recurred unabated – the patient's blood pressure crashing as the surgeon struggled to see, and clamp, the aorta through the torrent of blood. Administering copious quantities of blood and fluids, we kept the patient alive, against all odds, while the surgeon completed the complex procedure.

Extreme acidosis was indeed present, as we had feared, and was getting worse as the surgeon closed the abdomen, ending the case. Planning to transfer the patient to the intensive care unit for further monitoring, we were told that a bed was not ready. The surgeon suggesting that we transfer the patient to the recovery room instead. This was not a good idea as our patient was becoming increasingly unstable as the acidosis continued to progress – so I said so – and not a minute too soon. Looking up at the EKG monitor, I saw the start of a few irregular heartbeats, then runs, and then ventricular fibrillation. The saw-tooth pattern readily apparent on the green electronic EKG trace; heralding completely chaotic heart action and cardiac arrest.

---

* Acidosis is due to shock and inadequate blood volume perfusing vital organs like the liver and kidney. As the so produced lactic acid builds up in the bloodstream the pH value measured in a patient's blood sample decreases. This acidosis causes enzyme systems in the body to fail, resulting in unresponsiveness to drugs like norepinephrine and epinephrine that we administer to resuscitate the patient, the heart becoming unstable and often degenerating into irregular rhythms, presaging certain death.

The treatment: defibrillation, using two highly charged electronic paddles, placed over the heart. One on the patient's sternum and the other over the rib cage on the left, making quite sure that the two do not touch for fear of the 1,000-volt charge sparking between the paddles. I applied electrode gel to the chest quickly, covering the areas where I would place the paddles* and asked the nurse to press the charge button on the defibrillator. Placing the paddles, I asked everybody to stand back – fearing electrocution of bystanders – as I discharged the paddle electrodes on the patient's chest; 200 joules of electric energy released to re-stabilize the cardiac rhythm. Stand back! Discharge! The patient heaving slightly from the discharged shock. Looking up at the monitor, the EKG showed a straight line and then a few disorganized beats. Giving some IV epinephrine we tried again. Placing the paddles again over the gel on the patient's chest: Stand back! Discharge! Another heave, to no avail; ventricular fibrillation persisted. External cardiac massage was the next step, for one or two minutes as we readied ourselves to provide another shock. Repeating this process over and over ineffectively. Worried, I started monitoring the patient's pupil size. Looking for fixed dilated pupils – unresponsive to light – a sign of imminent brain death. Which was the situation here. We tried once more. By now there was quite a lot of gel already on the patient's chest, so I did not need to put on more, before I applied the paddles. Stand back! Discharge! Bang! A blinding flash – and an almighty explosion illuminated the scene, smoke filling the room, as 1,000 volts leaped between the paddles, through the gel now smeared across the patient's chest. The smoke clearing, slightly blinded by the explosive flash, I saw nurses running towards the operating theater exit doors. Running to get a fire extinguisher. And someone was heard to mutter haltingly, through the smoky haze… "Now he is really dead." And, unfortunately, he was. Despite our very best efforts to the contrary.[†]

* Electrode gel, at that time, came in tubes, and is necessary to avoid burns to the patient, ensuring there is proper conductivity between the paddle surface and the patient's skin lowering the resistance to the discharging charge. Nowadays self-adhesive electrodes are often applied to the skin allowing discharge of the defibrillator remotely.

† Discharge of electric current from paddle to paddle as occurred here is known as "arcing" and unfortunately happened regularly in this clinical scenario. It does not injure the patient because there is no charge into the patient but instead is dangerous for bystanders. Fortunately no one was injured by my error in not clearing the gel on the skin between the paddles.

7

Specialization – Anesthetic Registrar, University of Cape Town

Specialist anesthetic practice and research training, 1985 to 1992

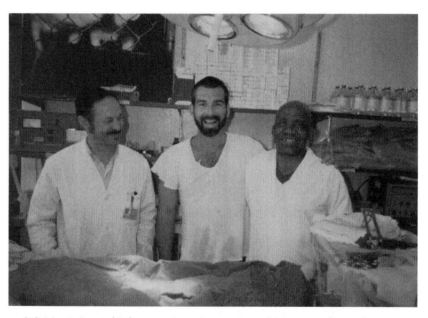

J. S. Marais Surgical Laboratory. Brian Sasman, Berend Mets, Hamilton Naki, 1990.

Finally what is the future of Anaesthesia? The first step should be an educational one. By sending out into practice men who have a proper appreciation of the responsibilities and requirement in anaesthetizing, a notable saving of human life will inevitably result.

– *Sir Frederick Hewitt, 1896*[1]

Professor Gaisford Harrison (1926-2003) stretched back in his comfortably imposing office chair. Internationally known for his research work on malignant hyperthermia and anesthesia outcomes, he had thrust the department of anaesthetics at the University of Cape Town on the world stage.[2] Balding, mercurial in temperament, but distinguished in a bowtie, he peered quizzically through his large framed spectacles at me. His impressive office intimidating me somewhat, I asked again, louder this time, would he consider me for a registrar position in the department in two years' time. I had explained that I had been offered a job as an anaesthetic SHO at the Gloucester Royal Hospital and wanted the opportunity to come back and complete my specialist training in South Africa. He harrumphed, "Don't you know that I only have three registrar positions a year and twenty-five applicants?" I didn't. However, I thought it might be a good idea to go and introduce myself, before leaving the country, and told him so. He harrumphed again, a little more friendly now, and asked me whether I understood what specialization meant. I wasn't too sure, so he told me. "Well, young man, it goes like this. I know that you have done three months of anesthetics at Edendale Hospital, but that was in a district general hospital. Groote Schuur Hospital is a specialist hospital. Here we have to manage specialist type cases such as cardiac patients, as well as complex pediatric and obstetric patients who have been referred for care in this tertiary hospital center. These patients, because of their condition, have altered physiology and pharmacology that has to be understood in order to be able to administer sophisticated anesthetics to manage both simple as well as complex surgeries such as heart and liver transplants. Anesthetic practice has to be adapted to take account of these conditions and complex operations, so this is what you will learn to manage as a registrar specializing in our department. You will need at least five years of training, rotating through the different specialty disciplines like obstetrics, cardiothoracics, pediatrics, neurosurgery and trauma anesthesia. And, oh yes, you will undergo training in intensive care and, if you want, I will teach you research as well. We have a Medical School pig facility across the way in the Jan S. Marais Surgical Laboratories, where I do all my work." Suitably impressed, I took this as heartening news, thanked Professor Harrison, and told him I would apply from abroad, should the time come.

Groote Schuur Hospital, famous for the first human heart transplant that was performed there in 1967, was opened in 1938 to great fanfare. Perched on the steep slopes of Devil's Peak, its two hospital wings spread out like arms, reaching out to the city below, and the vast Cape Flats beyond. Crowned by a sculpture of the goddess Hygea and flanked by two turrets with an ornate water tower rising dizzyingly in its center, the hospital looked as much like a place of worship as of healing. Named Groote Schuur (Big Barn) in defer- ence to the large estate of the same name, bequeathed by Cecil John Rhodes, the 850-bed hospital was to become the pre-eminent teaching and research hospital in the country.

It was thus with mounting excitement that I accepted the position as regis- trar in anaesthetics at the University of Cape Town, starting work in July, 1985. Fresh from six months backpacking through Southeast Asia, after completing my SHO job in England, I was raring to go. By now, Groote Schuur Hospital (GSH) had been extended; a separate maternity block and cardiac block with a chapel in their midst had been added. Twenty-one operating theatres and 1,400 beds were vital statistics. Pediatrics had moved to the nearby Red Cross Children's hospital and a busy trauma unit fronted the hospital with two ded- icated operating theatres readied to take care of the injured and wounded.[*3] Intensive care had expanded and the University of Cape Town Medical School, built adjacent to the hospital, was garnering increasing international respect for its research.

Obstetric anesthesia was the first specialty discipline I needed to master.

The Obstetric Patient

Pregnancy prepares the aspirant mother to grow, sustain and ultimately deliver the baby within. Both delivery by the normal vaginal route or via Cesarean section is a high-risk endeavor.[†4] Consider that two lives are at stake and a liter

---

[*] In the 1980s South Africa had a traffic injury rate ten times worse than the U.S.A. while deaths due to interpersonal violence were six times higher than in America.

[†] Hence peri-partum mortality is considered a major indicator of the state of a country's health services worldwide. Maternal mortality is ten times higher from a Cesarean section than associated with a vaginal delivery. United

of blood may be lost in the process. Much more blood if there are complications. Pregnancy visits physiological and anatomical changes on the mother that have profound effects on the approach to delivering anesthetic care. And that is in the "normal" patient. Never mind if she has other pregnancy-induced problems like gestational hypertension or cardiac disease.* Driving these changes is progesterone release initiated by implantation of the fertilized ovum in the endometrial wall of the uterus. Increasing progesterone levels result in maternal water retention which often manifests outwardly as edema of the skin. And inwardly, not so visible but nevertheless important, blood volume increases substantially, diluting hemoglobin levels. Creating the anemia of pregnancy, this cleverly prepares the mother for the inevitable blood loss with delivery. Cardiac output also increases by half as the heart beats both stronger and faster, so providing a sevenfold increase in blood flow to the uterus, allowing this organ to increase in size as the fetus grows. With a passenger on board, mom needs more oxygen delivered and more carbon dioxide exhaled and so starts breathing deeper and faster as pregnancy progresses. But as the uterus grows, her "oxygen tank," her residual lung volumes, become smaller, compressed by the increasing mass below. The stomach is also pushed up and progesterone and estrogen cause pyloric muscles to relax resulting in more acid in the stomach and reflux up the esophagus. We call this a "full-stomach." These two uterine mass effects result in a high probability for hypoxia and lung aspiration, necessitating special anesthetic techniques to avoid these complications. A further problem in pregnancy, and this is a big one, is that the patient's "airway" becomes much more challenging to manage. The associated edema, engorgement and friability of the upper airway blood vessel capillaries, especially after the patient has experienced a "difficult" labor and has been "pushing" to deliver the baby, takes its toll. These factors and the substantial weight gain and increased breast tissue associated with gestation, may make a simple airway a very difficult one to negotiate.

Quite apart from the alterations in anatomy and physiology, pregnancy and the fact that there are two recipients of the planned anesthetic, have

States data from 1997-2002 have demonstrated that this risk from a Cesarean section delivery is greater if a general anesthetic is provided rather than a spinal or epidural anesthetic (neuraxial anesthetic). Since the early 1990s, in the U.S.A. and many countries around the world, most Cesarean sections are now performed using neuraxial techniques, unless contra-indicated, or emergent in nature. At the time of the case report to follow, most, if not all, C-sections were performed using general anesthesia.

* Five to ten percent of patients have pregnancy-induced hypertension and/or pre-eclampsia, worldwide.

profound effects on the pharmacology of anesthetic drug administration. Firstly, the mother is more sensitive to administered anesthetics, probably due to the circulating progesterone. Secondly, while we seek to anesthetize the mother, we do not want to subject the baby to these drugs; allowing the babies to come screaming into the world with a great APGAR* score and no remnant anesthetic effects. This wish is complicated by the reality that many anesthetic drugs cross easily from the uterus through the placenta – the baby relatively more acidotic than the mother – administered drugs congregate at higher concentrations in the undelivered child. Anesthesiologists stingily administering drugs during a Cesarean section – keeping the patient as light as possible – so as not to depress the unborn child unnecessarily. Notwithstanding the fact that there is higher mortality associated with Cesarean section than a vaginal delivery, in many instances it can be lifesaving, for example when obstructed labor occurs. Especially when there are twins, and three lives are at stake.

Case One

I had drawn the short straw once more! On call on New Year's Eve, I was working again with Dr. Mark Slack, now the obstetric surgical registrar, reprising his role as a surgical intern colleague on New Year's Eve at Edendale Hospital, some seven years earlier. On this occasion we were in charge of the obstetric unit at a maternity hospital, one of the hospitals in Cape Town served by the University. My role was to provide anesthesia for laboring patients and all obstetric surgical cases for twenty-four hours. As Ulane and I had spent too many New Year's evenings apart, my wife, now a registrar in pathology, joined me for the evening. Planning to see in the new year together at midnight – the evening turned out to be altogether different from what we expected.

After a busy day, having first anesthetized four patients for tubal ligation surgery and then a further three for Cesarean section delivery, Mark and I had hoped to have a break in activities at midnight. Finishing our last case at around 10.45p.m. together, he told me he needed to check on one last parturient, with twins, laboring in the delivery suite. I woke up the

---

* The APGAR score (out of 10) is a way of assessing how well the baby is doing immediately after birth, as well as five and ten minutes afterwards, and has been standardized and is used universally around the world. (A score of 8-10 is good) More about Dr. Virginia Apgar and the APGAR score in Chapter 8.

patient as he investigated the situation, calling me urgently that we had to turn around the single operating theatre quickly as he had found obstructed labor and we needed to proceed with another Cesarean section immediately. He confirmed that while the situation was urgent, it was not emergent, as the twins were not in fetal distress, requiring immediate extraction. If we could stop the labor, we had time to proceed. Consequently, he had switched off the pitocin infusion, a drug which had been used to enhance uterine contractions, to assure this.

I worked quickly to turn around the room, readying thiopentone and succinylcholine and checking that the enflurane vaporizer was filled. Two working laryngoscopes and a set of smaller endotracheal tubes were ready in case the intubation proved difficult. The suction equipment had been tested, should the patient vomit on induction. I looked at the clock on the wall, a feature of all operating rooms, hanging high above the anesthesia machine. 11.35p.m., twenty-five minutes to midnight and the new year, as Slacky,* wheeled the patient into theatre. She was larger than usual, bearing twins – fortunately the labor pains appeared to have subsided from stopping the pitocin drip. Hoisting her on to the operating room table, we placed her in a left lateral tilt to avoid the now very large pregnant uterus from obstructing her blood flow to the heart.† Reassuring the expectant mother, I made sure to pre-oxygenate her with 100% inspired oxygen, using a well-fitting mask placed over her face, encouraging her to breathe in deeply for the full five minutes required. She was a little frightened, as was I; both of us acutely aware that there were now three lives at stake. I induced anesthesia with thiopentone and administered succinylcholine. SUX, we like to call it, works in less than a minute. As a fast-acting depolarizing muscle relaxant it causes all the patient's muscles to contract perceptibly. We see this as movements and twitchings, particularly in the face muscles and arms and legs. We know the patient is properly relaxed and ready for intubation when the twitching stops – safe in the knowledge that thiopentone will keep her asleep for around five to ten minutes, so she is completely unaware of this muscle

---

* Dr. Mark Slack's nickname, a friend and colleague of many years.

† Placing the obstetric patient in this left lateral tilt position is standard procedure. At this late stage of pregnancy, if the patient is kept supine on her back, the heavy uterus presses down on both the inferior vena cava blood vessel leading to the heart – decreasing cardiac output – and the descending aorta, resulting in less blood circulation to the uterus, which can precipitate fetal distress.

activity.* Fortunately, she was intubated easily and so I started administering nitrous oxide and just a little enflurane anesthetic so as not to depress the two unborn babies. Scrubbed and ready, Mark quickly cleaned her stomach, before placing drapes so surgery could begin.

The critical time period for the two babies, still nestled in mom's uterus, is incision to delivery time. Not anesthesia induction to delivery time, as we provide a very light anesthetic to the mother. Cutting the skin and then the uterus with a scalpel, causes the placental blood circulation to dwindle and the two babies can then become slowly asphyxiated.† Hence, the surgeon strives to perform this incision quickly. Never stopping to mop any blood, just cutting swiftly through the uterine muscle in order to scoop out the waiting baby without delay. Clamping the placental cord as fast as possible, which often provokes the first deep breath; bringing needed oxygen into the child's waiting lungs. This should all take about two to three minutes tops, but with a second baby to deliver, this would be much longer for the second. We looked up at the clock together to note the time, five minutes before the middle hour. Not enough time to complete both deliveries before midnight.

"Stop!" I said. "Mark, what would happen if we delivered the first child before midnight, in the old year, and the second in the new. Would they be condemned to be different ages for the rest of their lives?"

"Yes!" he responded, "and there is a cash prize in South Africa for the first registered birth after midnight."

We could time it perfectly – we were completely ready to start. We waited the three remaining minutes, and as the wall clock struck twelve, Mark incised the uterus, delivering one then two babies rapidly, both born with a welcoming cry in the same new year. Surely the parents would receive the prize for the firstborn baby?‡

---

* Thiopentone also crosses the placenta to the baby, having a peak effect around five minutes after administration to the mother, so this drug has usually worn off by the time the baby is delivered, with no untoward effects. Should a patient be given succinylcholine, by mistake when she is awake, these muscle contractions would be very painful indeed. Patients often feel some muscle pain after the operation, called myalgia, from the contractions caused by succinylcholine administration. We have no good alternatives to this drug so we still use this regularly today for general anesthesia for this surgery.

† That's why Cesarean section for multiple babies is always a problem, one has to come out first, and the other may suffer from this decreasing placental circulation, caused by incision of the uterine wall.

‡ As far as we could ascertain, they never did, which we found difficult to believe, as the first was born not two minutes after midnight.

The Cardiac Patient

The cardiac patient is always a problem. Whether presenting for a cardiac surgical procedure such as a valve replacement or for surgery not involving the heart directly. The engine that maintains life, the heart, is a problem when it is not working well. The heart's job is to pump blood around the body. Comprising four muscular chambers, two on the right and two on the left, blood drains from the lower body blood vessels into the inferior vena cave and from upper body vessels, into the superior vena cava, attached to the right atrium. The right atrium contracts, pushing blood through the tricuspid valve, into the waiting right ventricle. As the right ventricle contracts to pump blood, to the lungs, the tricuspid valve balloons up, like a parachute, to stop blood running back into the right atrium, blood pulsing on through the pulmonary valve and artery to the lungs to be oxygenated. From the lungs, through four pulmonary veins attached into the back of the left atrium, red oxygenated blood is pumped on to the left ventricle. The mitral valve between the two, opening up to let this happen, in turn floating up when the left ventricle contracts to expel blood into the massive aorta. The aortic valve opens, just at the right time, to let blood shoot up out of the left heart and into the body beyond. Then, the aortic valve closes to stop blood running back after ejection. The left side of the heart, often thought of as the pressure side, can adjust to accommodate high or lower systemic pressures, literally pushing blood around the body through the arteries, into smaller arterioles, and then through capillary beds – networks of tiny arterial vessels – to feed oxygenated blood to every organ and tissue in the body.

Then, after oxygen has been taken from the blood, now turning blue, it courses through capillaries which again widen to form venules, then veins, ultimately disgorging into the two vena cavae leading back to the right atrium. The right side of the heart is often thought of as the low pressure "reservoir" of the heart serving to accommodate blood from the body draining back to the pump.

While I have tracked the pathway that deoxygenated blood follows to be re-oxygenated in the lungs and then ejected into the body as a series of steps, in fact this is coordinated through the cardiac nervous system. The right and left heart working in parallel to pump blood into the lungs and body simultaneously.

This cardiac muscular action is coordinated by the heart's conduction system. An electric discharge starts at the sino-atrial node adjacent to the right atrial wall, travels across the atrium, stopping for a brief period at the atrio-ventricular node situated in the septum, separating the right and left ventricular chambers, before discharging across the ventricles, causing these to contract and so pump blood. This electric depolarization activity, travelling across the heart, is captured by the EKG machine, showing as a trace and spikes seen on an electrocardiographic monitor. This is all it is. An EKG shows only the electrical activity that is migrating across the heart and cannot show whether the heart muscle is actually contracting as a result.

There are thus three components to effective heart function.

First, the electronic discharge must occur in a coordinated fashion.

Second, the heart muscles must contract forcefully as a result of this. If the heart muscle is damaged due to chronic or acute ischemia the heart cannot pump successfully (heart failure).

Third, the valves must not leak (be incompetent) or be constricted from fibrosis (stenotic) obstructing blood flow, no matter how well the heart muscle beats.

The cardiac patient is a problem because he may have only one or all three of these essential heart components affected. Consider a patient with ischemic heart disease. Inadequate blood supply to the heart through narrowing of coronary blood vessels can affect all three heart functions. The conduction system can be impaired, the muscle wall damaged, and the mitral valve can become leaky.* Now add the fact that anesthesia with, for example, halothane, can also affect all three components. Halothane† depresses myocardial contractility, slows electrical conduction, and if sufficient hypotension results, can compromise coronary blood flow causing ischemia. It should not be surprising that we tread carefully when we manage cardiac patients and have developed anesthetic techniques over the years to minimize the detrimental effects of anesthetic administration on cardiac function.

---

* "Cor" is Latin for heart. Hence "coronary arteries" describe the arteries supplying the heart which can become chronically narrowed and acutely obstructed causing a heart attack or acute myocardial infarct. This can cause cardiac muscle to become permanently damaged or temporarily malfunction. The mitral valve, in the left ventricle, consists of two cusps, looking like a "mitre," a headdress worn by bishops. As the mitral valve floats up, during ventricular contraction, to stop blood flowing back into the left atrium, it is tethered by a set of muscles – the papillary muscles – which are supplied by small arteries to function properly. These muscles are particularly sensitive to ischemia. If ischemia or a myocardial infarction has occurred, this tethering function can be impaired and the mitral valve can leak – causing blood to damn up back into the left atrium.

† And to a lesser extent the newer volatile anesthetics.

The Cardiac Procedure

Operating on a beating heart is very difficult; open heart surgery to repair a broken valve, or structural heart defect, almost impossible. To do so, circulation to vital organs like the brain would need to be interrupted. If short, say three to five minutes, brain damage is unlikely to occur, but surgery of any longer duration would be unacceptable, unless a means of ensuring continuous oxygenated blood flow to the brain was developed. Consequently, before the development of cardiopulmonary bypass (heart-lung machine), cardiac surgery was in its infancy and limited in scope.[*]

Clarence Walter Lillehei (1918-1999), flamboyant and reckless in his personal life, was a brilliantly courageous surgeon who bucked tradition. Loved by his many patients, he trained innumerable thoracic surgeons at the University of Minnesota. Known as the "father of open heart surgery" he championed surgical approaches for maintaining blood circulation to the patient's brain while operating on the opened heart. Cross circulation – attaching a live donor patient so as to maintain circulation of oxygenated blood, not disrupted by the cardiac procedure – was the approach he adopted at first.[†]

Finding this too risky he developed the first functional cardiopulmonary bypass machine: "The Helix Reservoir Pump-Oxygenator System" designed for extracorporeal circulation in 1956.[5, 6] While many advances have been made since, the basic design of this pump made possible the complex cardiac surgical procedures, like heart transplantation, that would follow. At their essence, cardiopulmonary bypass (CPB) machines – sometimes called heart-lung machines – aim to completely exclude the heart and lungs from the body's circulation, allowing the surgeon to perform the operation on a stalled heart. They are designed to drain blue venous blood from the vena cava into a reservoir in order to oxygenate the blood and pump this back into the arterial circulation through a plastic PVC[‡] cannula inserted either into the femoral artery or aorta. This cardiopulmonary bypass system can keep the patient alive, while the heart (and lungs) can be removed from the body.[§]

---

[*] John Gibbon tried his hand at developing a cardiopulmonary bypass apparatus in 1953. The complex heart machine, developed in Philadelphia, with a screen oxygenator and roller pumps, resulted in so many complications that he became discouraged and abandoned the approach.

[†] Dr. Lillehei used this approach in 45 patients, preferring parents as the living oxygenator for the child patients he operated on.

[‡] PVC = polyvinylchloride.

[§] Cardiopulmonary bypass systems are highly complex. Not only do they need to oxygenate the patient, they are

Case Two

In 1967, looking up from the street below, the last thing Denise must have seen was Groote Schuur Hospital, jutting out of Devils Peak, before the car hit her and her mother. Sailing through the air, Denise crashed headfirst into the hubcap of a parked car, coming to rest, blood pouring out her mouth, nose and ears. She lay quite still, blood matting her beautiful dark hair. Her distraught father, Edward Darvall, having heard the screeching tires and the sickening sound of impact, rushed out of their car, parked so that Denise and her mother could go and buy a cake at the Salt River bakery. "Denny! Denny Denny!" he cried as he lifted her up gently, blood streaming on his hands. "Don't move her," yelled Dr. Louis Ehrlich, summoned by the sounds of collision in the street. "She doesn't speak, she doesn't say anything." Darvall whimpered. An ambulance, all lights flashing and siren sounding arrived soon after. Ferrying the now dead mother, but still breathing Denise, and her abject father, up the hill and to the hospital emergency room in three minutes. Denise, a pretty twenty-four-year-old, had suffered greatly from the crash. The doctors diagnosing irreversible coma from a skull fracture – brain tissue oozing from her right ear – and fractures of both legs and her pelvis. Nevertheless resuscitation was quickly started. Denise was intubated through the nose and ventilation-assisted, while intravenous lines were started in her arm, for blood administration, and through the right saphenous vein in the groin, to measure

often used to cool and rewarm the patient and to correct carbon dioxide and acid base levels in the perfused blood. The essential design feature is the "oxygenator" which dissolves oxygen in the blood to bind to hemoglobin. Dr. Lillehei's initial design was to "bubble" a stream of 100% oxygen through a nylon plastic diffusion plate at a rate of 12 liters per minute. Remaining bubbles, not absorbed by the hemoglobin in blood, are a major problem. If present when pumped back into the patient, they can cause gas emboli, leading to strokes. Hence a "debubbling" apparatus is included in the array of PVC tubes, containers and reservoirs which drain blood from the venous side, and then transport this to the arterial side. Propelled using a set of roller pumps with "teeth" tightened, to squeeze the plastic tubing containing blood through the closed system ending back in the cannulated aorta. The rate of rotation of the pumps can be adjusted to meet the blood flow required to sustain life. Another problem, before a patient can be "placed on bypass" is that the disposable plastic system used in the bypass apparatus, can only be connected to a patient when fully primed with blood or other fluid. This to ensure that no air passes to the patient when cardiopulmonary bypass starts. In turn, this requires that the bypass apparatus is primed with donated blood often diluted with a physiological solution lowering the viscosity of the blood. Blood clots when it comes into contact with plastic, which creates another source for emboli. Heparin has to be administered to inhibit this. Antifoam also has to be used in priming the system, which if administered in too large a quantity is another source for emboli. So the bypass period is fraught with potential problems and complications. Quite apart from the fact that with Dr. Lillehei's machine, there was no way of administering an anesthetic vapor like halothane by inhalation; as a result, many patients wakened, during the surgery performed with cardiopulmonary bypass.

central venous pressure. A cathode ray EKG monitored her heart – a beeping yellow dot, bouncing across a circular orange screen above her head. The blood pressure and heart rate, initially very low, was further supported with a slowly dripped isoprenaline* infusion.

Before any next steps could be taken, the neurosurgeon, Dr. Rose-Innes, would have to declare brain death incontrovertibly. And, Edward Darvall, no matter his distressed state, would have to give consent. Consent to use his precious daughter's heart to save a dying man's life – Louis Washkansky – dying of irreversible ischemic heart failure. "Well doctor, if you can't save my daughter, try and save this man [instead]," Darvall said."[7]

Dr. Joseph Ozinsky (1927-2017) was a talented anaesthetist with a penchant for humorous quips, used frequently to allay the anxiety of his patients – and as needed, excitable surgeons. Known as Ozzie to his friends and colleagues, he was born and schooled in Cape Town. Completing his anesthetic registrar training at the University of Cape Town (UCT), he travelled to London for further training and specialist qualifications, before serving as the first cardiac anaesthetist,† establishing the cardiac surgical program in Cape Town with Professor Christiaan Barnard.

Christiaan Neethling Barnard (1922-2001) grew up poor, his father a minister in the Dutch Reformed Church at Beaufort West in the Cape Province.[7] Undaunted, young Chris wanted to study medicine and become a famous doctor. Passionate and charismatic, he completed medical school at UCT. Specializing first in internal medicine, he progressed to training in surgery, developing a mounting interest in animal research to spur surgical innovation. Travelling to the United States to further his research at the University of Minnesota, he learned cardiac surgery from Dr. Clarence Lillehei, achieving both a PhD and Master of Science degree during this remarkable two-year surgical apprenticeship. Returning to South Africa in 1958, Dr. Barnard established the first cardiac surgical unit in the country with a gift of the cardiopulmonary bypass machine that Lillehei had designed,

---

* Isoprenaline, was the only available synthetic drug that could increase heart rate, and contractility of the heart. Pharmacologically it is a B_1 and B_2 sympathetic receptor activator. B_1 stimulation increases heart rate and contractility of the heart allowing the heart to beat both faster and contract better. B_2 stimulation, causes bronchodilation and also causes vasodilation of arterial blood vessels including pulmonary artery vessels.

† I was privileged to have Dr. Ozinsky teach me cardiac anesthesia, which would define most of my anesthetic practice.

having learned to use this under his tutelage.*

But before starting a human cardiac program, Drs. Ozinsky and Barnard first practiced on twenty-five dogs, training to anesthetize, operate, place on, and separate from, the newly developed cardiopulmonary bypass machine successfully. The first few dogs dying as a result of mistakes that were made. Once Dr. Ozinsky and Dr. Barnard had perfected the techniques required, they turned to the first patient, Joan Pick, nevertheless fearful that one of many complications could occur. Fifteen years old, Joan had a simple problem. Stenosis (obstruction) of the pulmonary valve, fortunately requiring only a very short bypass time to repair. Just as well, because after Dr. Ozinsky had anesthetized her and she was connected to the heart-lung machine, the reservoir which was supposed to be filled to the brim with blood, became dangerously low; air embolus a threatening complication.† Surgery was completed hastily and separation from CPB performed. Fearful that air embolus might have damaged her brain, Chris and Ozzie watched her closely for any signs of recovery from anesthesia. Miraculously, she opened her eyes. "Close your eyes," said Dr. Ozinsky. Which she did promptly! Showing that her brain was undamaged and she would recover fully.

Next morning, July 29, 1958, the *Cape Times* newspaper heralded the first successful cardiac surgery in South Africa.

As an innovative, skilled, experimental cardiac surgeon, Barnard was acutely aware of the lethal nature of ischemic heart disease. Coronary artery disease diminishes the blood vessel supply to heart muscle, irreparably damaging the heart, causing resistant cardiac failure. No amount of medication can cure this condition and so a surgical solution needed to be found. The surgical answers to the problem at the time; scoring the pericardium to enhance blood supply or attaching an internal mammary artery from the chest wall directly to the heart muscle, were considered largely ineffective. One day, while preparing for a talk at the University of Pretoria, 1,000 miles north of Cape Town, on the future of cardiac surgery, Barnard imagined a possible approach. He called his assistant in the animal laboratory at the medical school and asked him to

---

* When Dr. Barnard was asked years later by President Lyndon Johnson how it happened that the first heart transplant was performed in South Africa, he attributed this to the support and funding that he had received through Dr. Owen Wagensteen and Dr. Walter Lillehei from the U.S. government in allowing him to develop this cardiopulmonary bypass machine at the University of Cape Town.

† One of the cannulation sites of her groin femoral artery and vein vessels had sprung an undetected leak under the drapes, blood was being lost from the CPB circuit and so the levels were running dangerously low.

anesthetize two dogs. Taking out the heart from one dog, he replaced it with the other's, using cardiopulmonary bypass. Removing the aortic cross clamp from the newly transplanted heart, allowing circulation to resume, it started beating immediately. Barnard had his answer: cardiac transplantation would be the surgical solution to ischemic heart disease.*

Five years later, Denise Darvall's death would make this a human possibility. It took this long to develop and perfect the surgical, anesthetic and medical management techniques to make this a viable option. Drs. Barnard, Ozinsky and their transplant team, including a surgical technician named Hamilton Naki,† would refine their approach by practicing on a further forty-eight dogs‡ at the animal laboratory. There was another important problem to solve however: acute rejection of the transplanted heart. The human body mounts a destructive immune response to any foreign tissue or organ introduced, as a defense mechanism. This is species-specific. Because of this specificity, dogs cannot be used, and so human experience was key.

Human kidney transplantation would become the stepping stone to the heart. Barnard revisiting America for a further three-month training in kidney transplantation surgery and rejection management. Returning to South Africa he led the transplant team to perform the first successful kidney transplant a year later, Mrs. Edith Black§ receiving her new kidney in October 1967. National newspapers had a field day announcing this in apartheid South Africa: *"Mrs Black Gets Black Kidney."*

---

* Concurrently, during the period 1960-68, American, Russian and Argentinian surgeons developed coronary artery bypass grafting (CABG) surgery to address this problem, learning how to attach harvested saphenous veins (from the legs) and the internal mammary artery (from the chest wall) to coronary blood vessels to bypass blocked arteries and re-establish circulation to blood-starved (ischemic) heart muscle. In the heyday period of 1990-2000, CABG surgery became the most common surgical procedure performed in America, numbering around 500,000 cases a year. With the development of percutaneous coronary intervention technique – which stented open coronary arteries without the need for surgery – the number of CABG surgeries declined over the next ten years to around half of this number annually.

† Hamilton Naki, who will recur in this narrative, started work as a gardener at UCT and was asked by Dr. Robert Goetz to help in the animal laboratories to hold down a giraffe he was studying. Impressed by "Hami's" potential, he persuaded him to continue work as a surgical technician in the lab, and so later he helped Dr. Barnard refine animal transplantation techniques in this laboratory. Dr. Robert Goetz was later credited, in 1960, with performing the first CABG surgery in America.

‡ They used the techniques described by Dr. Norman Schumway and Dr. Richard Lower, with whom Dr. Barnard had worked in America, adding to their experience of over 300 dog heart transplantations.

§ Mrs. Edith Black, was classified as a "white" person. Dr. Christiaan Barnard was a passionate anti-apartheid protagonist. He took much of this philosophy from his father, whom he greatly admired, a pastor for the Dutch Reformed Church, who ministered to a "coloured" (mixed race) congregation in Beaufort West.

With this success,* Dr. Barnard and the transplant team were ready. Seeing little sense in the sacrifice of further animals to perfect heart transplantation techniques, Barnard approached Professor Val Schrire, head of cardiology, for a patient at imminent risk of a heart failure death, whose life could be saved.

Louis Washkansky (1913-1967), a boxer with a jocular bent, was knocked out by ischemic heart disease. Almost, but not quite – his ravaged heart had laid him low. So low that despite all the modern medications, he could no longer walk or talk without becoming short of breath. In fact, his lungs were filling up with backed up fluid, which his failing heart could no longer pump out. Cheyne-Stokes breathing was the hallmark of heart failure. Washkansky would lie back in bed, taking ever deeper breaths and then stop breathing altogether. Then, after a dangerously long pause, as he turned blue, he would start breathing again. Ann, his wife, found this terrifying to witness, thinking him dead already. He was dying, but not ready to throw in the towel. Despite his travails, he was still in good spirits. Sitting up in his hospital bed, smoking a cigarette, Washkansky was informed that there might be a surgical solution to the problem. The first ever human heart transplant could be performed – if a donor were to become available. Looking up from the novel he was reading he said, "If that is the only chance… I'll take it."[7]

Barnard, like most cardiac surgeons, reviewed Washkansky's cardiac angiogram films first before interviewing the prospective patient. Demonstrating marked destruction of the muscles of both right and left ventricles, the ruined heart looked like a big dilated bag barely contracting in the chest. The cause, readily apparent – two of the three main coronary blood vessels were blocked and the other hardly open. Excruciatingly high heart pressure measurements explained the pulmonary and peripheral edema that Washkansky was suffering from. Horrified, Chris turned to Professor Schrire, stating that he had never seen so much massive destruction and wondering how Washkansky could still be alive, and, what made him struggle on? Schrire responding that Louis was an amateur boxer who wouldn't give up until he was completely knocked out – cold.

That could happen literally any day. The patient, family and transplant team living in constant fear that the next day would be the patient's last. Attempts at optimizing the patient, often to no avail, while he slowly deteriorates;

* Mrs. Black went on to live for a further twenty-two years.

156

a Klebsiella infection festering in Louis's right leg – that no antibiotics could arrest.

Three weeks later Washkansky had started losing his sense of humor and hope. Every day giving Dr. Barnard the same ultimatum. If they didn't find him a heart he would get up, leave the hospital and go home, despite the fact that he was now coughing up blood and usually too breathless to speak properly.

Reclining at home that Saturday, December 2, in 1967, after a hectic work week, Barnard answered the ringing telephone – his registrar informing him that in all likelihood they had found a suitable donor; a young girl hit by a car. Her name: Denise Darvall.

Louis Washkansky, fifty-four years old, weighed in that evening at 58 kilograms, 1.65 meters.

Chris Barnard visited him on the ward asking him how he felt?

Timorously mentioning that he felt a little shaky, like the way he felt before going into the ring as a boxer, Louis then enquired about his chances. Not sure thought Chris, but didn't say so, as he made his way to theatre to scrub and gown for the operation.

Dr. Ozinsky by his own account "conducted the anesthetic with optimism."[8] Bolstered by the knowledge that since its inception, the cardiac, surgical and anesthesia unit had performed more than 1,000 operations together. Nonetheless, this human heart transplantation was going to be the first and the patient was terminally ill and going downhill fast. This posed a litany of anesthetic problems.

Firstly, Washkansky's heart, liver and kidneys were failing.

Would the anesthetics cause Washkansky's heart to fail completely, flooding his lungs with fluid and decreasing his blood pressure causing ventricular fibrillation, before they could get onto bypass?

Would the liver and kidney failure affect drug metabolism and make impossible the maintenance of acid base and potassium level balance on bypass?[9] Would the detrimental effects of the prolonged bypass time needed, for this unpracticed operation in humans, prove to be insurmountable?*

---

* Cardiopulmonary bypass using the heart-lung machine is of course a completely unnatural state. Lifesaving in allowing the operation to occur, it is fraught with problems of air, fluid, blood clot and tissue embolism. This can cause blood vessel obstruction in the brain, kidneys, bowel, liver and other organs, leading to the steady decline in function of all of these systems. Blood flow is not pulsatile but continuous, which results in changes in blood pressure and perfusion to tissues with increasing acid and potassium levels leaching out into the central circulation. The body also mounts an intense inflammatory response to the insult of CPB which again leads to the

Could the new heart work in this old tired body? Or had it been irreparably damaged by the need to ascertain Denise Darvall's introcontrovertible death, before excising the heart.*

If not irreparably weakened, would the fact that the transplanted heart was not appropriately wired be its downfall? In the new body it could not be connected to the usual nervous sympathetic and parasympathetic conduction systems, driving the heart forward.

Would it still be able to pump effectively?

Would it even start when they came off the heart-lung machine? If it did, could the new heart pump with sufficient pressures to overcome the dangerously high pulmonary artery resistance that Barnard had ascertained from Louis's angiograms?†

Secondly, would there be unforeseen, surgical misadventures leading to major blood loss, lung or heart damage that needed to be contended with by the anesthetist?

Make no mistake, Ozzie taught me, while the surgeon is concentrating on the surgical procedure, the anesthesiologist needs to be able to manage all such matters and shepherd the patient safely through the operation, while reassuring the surgeon that everything is in order.

deterioration in organ function. In an attempt to minimize the damage, patients are cooled – in the Washkansky operation to 21°C – which has secondary problems affecting blood- clotting mechanisms, drug metabolism and resistance to drugs such as insulin used here to treat Washkansky's diabetes. The longer the CPB period the worse the problems, hence surgeons are always in a rush to complete the surgical procedure once the heart-lung machine is connected.

* In the adjacent operating theatre (B), Denise Darvall's chest would be opened by Dr. Marius Barnard, Chris's younger brother, and her aorta and right atrium cannulated, after which her heart could be cut out. But this resection could only start when her heart had stopped completely. She would be disconnected from the ventilator first and the team had to watch her EKG monitor till it was completely flat-line, signifying complete cardiac electric standstill before the first incision, opening her chest for surgical resection could be made. While this was a necessary procedural step at the time, it meant that the donor heart was already dying and its ability to function when transplanted into LW would be significantly compromised. Timing had to be exact between the two operating theatres. Washkansky had been anesthetized and his chest had been opened, the point of no return, but CPB was only started when Darvall's heart arrested at 2.32a.m., December 3, 1967. A further problem compounding the situation was that Darvall's heart was deteriorating fast, her temperature having risen to 39.5°C and she needed a higher isoprenaline infusion rate to keep the heart going.

† This is still the main problem encountered today in heart transplantation. The recipient having very high pulmonary artery resistance which the new heart has to overcome and so the right heart fails, in its ability to pump. However, today, we have multiple drugs, beyond the isoprenaline used in the first heart transplant, to help us with this problem. Nitric oxide can be used to decrease this pulmonary hypertension, while inodilator drugs like dobutamine and milrinone both increase heart contractility and dilate pulmonary arteries.

Louis Washkansky was propped up on pillows gasping for breath in operating theatre A. Dr. Ozinsky had connected two green blood pressure cuffs to his right and left upper arms and the first intravenous line was dripping Plasmalyte B. Blood pressure was monitored by inflating and then deflating the cuff and reading off the pressure on an oscillotonometer – determined by palpating when the brachial pulse reappeared at the elbow. Silver electrodes were strapped on both lower arms and attached to the left calf leading to the small electrograph which displayed the bouncing EKG trace on a green circular screen. Heart rate 90, blood pressure 130. That was all the monitoring there was for induction.

"Auld Lang Syne," said Louis Washkansky as Dr. Barnard walked in to check on his patient before induction of anesthesia. Adding that it felt like new year's eve because the planned surgery would take out the old, and implant the new. Washkansky in very good spirits because the long-awaited transplant operation day had now finally arrived.[7]

12.50a.m. Induction*

Dr. Ozinsky gave Louis some atropine before induction and suggested he needed to recline. "Can't you do it while I am sitting up?" "No," said Ozzie, "you need to recline." "These surgeons are worse than movie stars. They don't like anyone stealing their limelight." – cautiously and very slowly administering thiopentone, 200mg in total.[†10] Onset of anesthesia was slow – slowed to two minutes from the low cardiac output state. Succinylcholine also took a long time to work. Washkansky needing extra oxygen and ventilatory assistance before intubation. Anesthesia was maintained lightly, with halothane and nitrous oxide ventilated into the lungs by a Bird ventilator. Placing a temperature probe in the esophagus and a catheter in the bladder for urine output measurement, Dr. Ozinsky added two further intravenous lines for blood and fluid administration to prepare for incision.

---

* The first heart transplant is beautifully chronicled in the Heart of Cape Museum. This museum is located in the old operating theatres in Groote Schuur Hospital, where the events took place, and was opened December 3, 2007, exactly 40 years later. It is well worth a visit.

† Remarking later that every medical student knows that cardiac disease is a relative contra-indication for this drug, but if given carefully is rarely followed by trouble.

01.30a.m. Incision

Dr. Rodney Hewitson, first assistant surgeon, looked up and said, "Can I, Ozzie?" "Yes." "Incision," and Rod made a right groin incision, cannulating the saphenous vein for central venous pressure measurement and laying open the femoral artery. Just in case. Should a misadventure occur when the surgical team incised to split the chest, this artery could be quickly cannulated to start cardiopulmonary bypass at a moment's notice. Sawing the chest open, while Ozzie stopped ventilation – to avoid laceration of the underlying lungs – a large retractor cranked open the chest, bringing Waskansky's gigantic struggling heart into full view. "One thing is certain" Barnard intoned, "He'll never leave this table without a transplant," walking over to the adjacent theatre to harvest Denise's heart.[7] Rodney proceeding to cannulate the superior and inferior vena cava, which would allow drainage of blood back to the heart-lung machine, primed with six units of heparinized blood and a physiological saline solution – kept cold to allow protective cooling of the patient. "Heparin." Ozzie administered heparin intravenously making absolutely certain that it was given. Critical, as full anticoagulation is needed to avoid deadly clots forming during bypass, and needs to circulate, before Dr. Hewitson inserted an arterial cannula into the ex-boxer's femoral artery. When bypass was started this cannula would feed pumped oxygenated blood back up the femoral artery to the aorta, cross-clamped by the surgeon to exclude the heart; arterial blood propelled to the brain and rest of the body.

02.32a.m. Cardiopulmonary bypass commenced

"Rodney, all set?" He nodded in reply, taciturn as always. "All set Johan?" Barnard called out to the chief perfusionist, who had readied the heart-lung machine. "Yes Professor." "Pump on."[7] The hum of five motors pumping blood to the patient could be heard – but all was not well! The arterial pressure measurements in the system were far too high and climbing. "Line pressure 200!" – It should have been half. – "250"… "What's the pressure, Ozzie?"…"275"… "Johan what's the flow?"… "I'm only on half flow, Prof"… Rodney admitting that the likely cause of the problem was the small femoral artery blood vessel, that he had cannulated, in preparation for bypass. There was only one solution. Bypass could not be achieved at these pressures through the constricted artery. There would be insufficient blood flow to Washkansky's brain and the high pressures could result in one of the plastic connectors breaking loose – exploding blood across the room. Barnard and Ozzie knew there was only one answer: cannulate the patient's aorta directly. Disconnect the femoral artery briefly, and connect the arterial side of the bypass to the aortic cannula. This would require switching off the cardiopulmonary bypass pumps at the critical time, but not yet. Cooling had already started to preserve Washkansky's brain.

"What's the temperature now?" asked Barnard, clearly agitated. "29.5," said Ozzie. "Johan, get him down to 26," Barnard stipulated and proceeded to incise the aorta to place a new cannula in this far larger blood vessel. Now screaming out orders to Sister Jordaan assisting him, because of the extreme pressure of the situation, and forgetting that the bypass pump was still on and churning blood at half throttle, he yelled, "Now clamp the line," – he meant the femoral line, which she did. And the pump was still running! A loud "crack" resounded in the operating room – a connector breaking from the built-up-pressure – exploding blood onto the floor and surrounding walls from the bypass machine. The closed de-aired bypass system now totally disrupted. (To state that this was now a crisis would be to understate the situation entirely, it was a catastrophe in the making). "Turn off the pump!" shrieked Barnard, enquiring whether there was air in the arterial side? "Yes, it is full of air Prof!"[7]

The pump was now off, Washkansky had been cooled, and the only thing that was keeping him alive was what his destroyed heart could still do in pumping blood to his dying body. Completely dependent on his failed heart, as the bypass machine had been stopped and was not safe to use. Louis's heart was barely contracting at thirty beats per minute. The immense fear spreading through theatre was that Washkansky's heart would finally fail and start fibrillating in total collapse. But Louis was a fighter, if his heart would just hold on…before throwing in the towel. Barnard was beside himself, but still in control. He knew just what needed to be done. De-air the heart-lung machine so it could be restarted. He connected the arterial and venous cannulae together and instructed that the pump be switched on again. This would bubble all the entrained air out of the circuit, but could take three to five minutes until Johan, the perfusionist, was satisfied. Ozzie transfused blood and probably started some isoprenaline during this critical period to keep Washkansky's heart going. Just. All that could be heard was the slow beep of the EKG machine, the hum of the pumps circulating the blood, and the sound of Johan thumping the bypass machine's helix and heat exchangers using a rubber hammer to knock out any remaining bubbles. Except for that, the theatre was deathly quiet – quiet with anticipation and dread.

"All right, Professor, all clear."

"Pump on," Barnard said with relief.

Ozzie called out the pressures: "Line pressure 100 – venous eleven. The ventricles are fibrillating." Everyone could see Washkansky's heart finally failing in the opened chest cavity. The deranged heart was collapsing. But fortunately the heart-lung machine could again take over its work, allowing the operation to proceed.

Barnard would later write, that with the death of Louis Washanky's God-given heart now imminent, it was time for him to return to B theatre for the heart of the donor.

For the anesthesiologist, "bypass time," when the patient is safely connected to the heart-lung machine, is usually a time for making sure the patient is anesthetized. Also, as the anesthetist functions as both a caretaker and physiological bookkeeper of this unnatural state, it is a time to assure that biological functions are monitored and optimized. To guard against Washkansky waking up in the middle of surgery,* Dr. Ozinsky turned on the halothane vaporizer attached to the heart-lung machine, knowing full well that this would provide sufficient anesthetic for the purpose, having developed the technique himself.[11] Then, scanning the operating theatre, blood still dripping from the green tiles on the wall from the explosion, he looked at the different monitoring devices at his disposal. Crude by comparison with today's devices, the oscilloscope EKG made no sound but still demonstrated the fibrillatory saw tooth pattern of Washkansky's heart lying in the pericardium. A round circular Bourdon pressure gauge, attached to the bypass machine, indicated the arterial line pressure, a bright red needle quivering at the correct blood pressure reading: 120mmHg.

A gray, half-shoebox-sized device with a perspex curvilinear window demonstrated yet another black needle, hovering over the esophageal temperature of the

---

* Drs. A. Bull, J. Ozinsky and G. Harrison developed the technique of introducing a halothane vaporizer, attached to the gas supply of the DeWall-Lillehei pump oxygenator, demonstrating that 1% halothane administration provided satisfactory arterial blood concentrations and electroencephalographic readings, to assure that the patient would remain unconscious.

patient: 22°C. Ozzie bent down, grabbed the urine collection bag attached to Washkansky's bladder by the slim catheter and positioned it hanging from the operating room table, so he could witness every drop of new urine, a technique I still use today. This was rapidly filling up, a total of 2,200 ml during the bypass period. Yet another Bourdon pressure gauge displayed the venous pressure: 4mmHg. He glanced at the blood coursing through the bypass tubing looking for signs of blood clotting to connectors. Any sign of clotting and more heparin would need to be given. All was in order at this early stage of bypass. However, the patient's physiological state needed to be intermittently monitored by drawing blood samples from the bypass machine. Samples drawn to assess: acid base balance, blood hemoglobin content and potassium levels, using an Astrup machine and hemoglobinometer. Critical to determine whether more blood, potassium or sodium bicarbonate (to treat acidosis) needed to be administered. Crucial not only during bypass, but especially when separating from the heart-lung machine when the new heart needed the best chance to work. For the transplanted heart to work without help, Washkansky's blood's biochemical state would have to be optimal to give it every chance to beat forcefully in its new body.

Barnard returned to Theatre A, having excised Denise Darvall's heart in Theatre B, carrying it in a basin, which he placed on the green toweling covering Washkansky's legs.

"Don't let it fall off."*[7]

He then proceeded to cut out the old to replace it with the new – leaving a yawning pericardial cavity with some tiny pools of blood. This is the strangest sight imaginable, a human without a heart, kept alive by a bypass machine, and is the point of no return. Barnard set about suturing in the new heart.[12] While Ozinsky got ready to restart the transplanted heart and come off bypass – mentally preparing – thinking through the steps that they had practiced so many times in dogs in the animal laboratory. Drawing up the necessary drugs, he readied an isoprenaline infusion to strengthen the heart and a lidocaine infusion to stabilize its rhythm. He made sure the defibrillator was working and that there was enough calcium gluconate to strengthen the heart and counteract the negative effects of protamine that would be needed to reverse the heparin to stop the bleeding after separation from bypass. Nevertheless, further blood was checked and hanging, primed to be given

---

* Fortunately it did not fall off this time, but transplant hearts have been known to be dropped on the floor; everyone in the operating room is so hyped up and nervous during the procedure!

should bleeding after bypass prove to be a problem. Ozzie checked the Astrup readings, administered potassium* and gave hydrocortizone; anticipating the new organ – to minimize the body's rejection response.

05.43a.m. Cardiac transplant completed

"Warm the patient," Barnard called out. Johan turning up the temperature on the heat exchanger of the heart-lung machine and Dr. Ozinsky switching on the thermal pump that would push warm water through the rubber mattress beneath Washkansky's body. The aim was to get him back to 34°C; anything lower could cause cardiac arrhythmias in the new heart.

To fill the heart, Barnard loosened the vena caval venous snares, allowing blood to flow into the right atrium. More trouble: air coursed from the previously open atrium into the pulmonary artery causing an airlock. Barnard stabbed in a scalpel, releasing air which bubbled out and then proceeded to de-air the rest of the heart. Satisfied, he sutured closed the stab wound in the pulmonary artery and released the aortic cross clamp – which had isolated the new heart – propelling oxygenated bypass blood through Darvall's heart now embedded in Washkansky's body. This is the moment of truth – the heart becoming tense as blood coursed into the muscle. Ozzie, looking intensely at the green dot on the EKG oscilloscope thought he saw something, "I'm getting some fibrillation and it looks...yes, it looks like it's becoming more active."[7] This was critical. It showed that Denise Darvall's heart wanted to live in the new body. But fibrillating was not enough. Perhaps it would start to beat on its own or, as had so often happened in the dog lab, fibrillating was all it would do, failing to beat on its own, the new heart refusing to take over. Doing little more than fibrillate briefly, and die.

"Ozzie, get ready to defibrillate" Barnard commanded, as Sister Jordaan passed him the two paddles he would apply to the squirming heart to shock it, and erase all electrical impulses in the hope that coordinated heart contraction would follow. Ozinsky first administered 100mg of succinylcholine to paralyze

---

* Cooling of the patient on bypass for cerebral protection causes kidney urine concentration function to be "paralyzed" resulting in diuresis, hence more than two liters of urine in this case. This causes loss of potassium in the urine which has to be supplemented. This is most important as low potassium levels result in cardiac rhythm instability, in particular ventricular fibrillation. Hence potassium levels must be brought into the normal range (3.5 to 5.3 mEkw/L) before restarting the heart and separating from bypass.

Washkansky completely, so that the defibrillatory shock planned for the new heart would not cause a violent body jerk.

Then said, "Go on – shock it," as he switched on the 20-joule charge on the defibrillator machine. Nonetheless, Washkansky's body arched back from the electrical discharge, stopping the heart completely. It just lay there, not a sign of life. Then…very slowly at first, a contraction of the right atrium, and then, and then, the stalled heart came haltingly back to life.

"What are the pressures now?" Chris asked with mounting excitement.

"Blood Pressure 90, heart rate 120," Ozzie responded, proceeding to give some calcium gluconate and start the isoprenaline infusion to strengthen the new heart's contractions. Already worrying about the next steps ahead. The test whether the new heart could overcome all the problems associated with transplantation and make a go of it on its own – without assistance of the heart-lung machine.

06.06-06.13a.m. Separation from CPB

"Bypass pump off." Immediately the pressure readings were read out as an indicator of how well the heart was beating on its own: "Blood pressure 95…80…75…" – the heart laboring and straining to maintain the pressure –" "75…60…55…"

"Start bypass again." The first solo flight hadn't gone well. Was this just a matter of time for the heart to recover or was it just not possible that it could survive on its own?

"Increase the isoprenaline! Is the potassium normal?"

"Yes."

"Okay Johan, bypass pump off." The tension was evident in Barnard's high-pitched voice.

"Pressure 85…70…60…"

"Restart the pump."* Barnard was worried, extremely so. "This had happened in dogs, you could not get off the pump with the transplanted heart, you could get half-way – but not all the way."[7] Perhaps more time was needed for recovery; they had no other option. Then…

"Pressure is increasing," said Ozzie. "Ninety-five over 65, venous six." The

---

* Today we have learnt that to come off bypass, we do so slowly. Slowly turning down the bypass flow allowing the heart to pick up. Also we have much better cardiac strengthening drugs that can make a major difference in

heart showed it, beating in the chest, displayed for all to behold, it was starting to contract much more vigorously.

"Johan, increase the venous pressure. Okay, let's stop the pump again."

All peered anxiously at the heart, knowing that three times and you are probably out. The heart hesitated as it absorbed the added venous load and then plucking up courage it became more certain of itself: Pressure 80…75…80…90…95…

Overcome with emotion, Barnard said, "Dit lyk of dit gaan werk," in Afrikaans, his mother tongue. "It looks like it is going to work." And it did.[24]

The next day this human triumph was announced to the world.*

The *Cape Times* newspaper read: "World's first heart transplant. Groote Schuur doctors make history. Life beats anew for city man."[†] Showing off a front-page picture with the whole team that made it work;

Ozzie standing just to the right of Barnard.

The Thoracic Procedure & Patient

Remember, that surgeons were loath to breach the thoracic cavity. Fearing fatal circulatory collapse. Recall Ralph Waters' inadvertent placing of a red rubber endotracheal tube too far down the trachea into the right main stem bronchus:[‡] this "isolated" the left lung, while allowing ventilation of the right, sustaining life. Surgery could be performed on the left lung, and thoracic surgery was made possible. However, using this "endobronchial" intubation technique, the anesthesiologist could not control ventilation to the now collapsed left lung, nor suction pus or blood from this lung undergoing an operation. A "double lumen" tube – directing ventilation separately to each lung in turn – would solve the conundrum. Essentially two endotracheal tubes bonded together, the most commonly used Robertshaw left-sided double-lumen tube (DLT) was

---

tenuous transplanted hearts like this one. Often the heart needs time to recover from the ischemic insult and so we will "rest" the heart on the cardiopulmonary bypass machine for a while when we encounter the problems that Dr. Barnard experienced with the first human heart transplant.

* Louis Washkansky would survive for 18 days, with his new heart working perfectly. He developed septicemia from the Klebsiella infection in his leg, his immune response likely impaired by the drugs, cortisone and azathioprine that were needed to suppress the body's rejection response to the transplanted heart. Dr. Philip Blaiberg would be the second heart transplant recipient. He survived for 18 months. Today heart transplant recipients live full new lives.

† Monday, December 4, 1967.

‡ In 1932, Chapter 4.

designed so that the tip of the left tube (angled at 45 degrees) could enter the left main bronchus; while the right-side lumen terminated above the carina,* just at the aperture of the right bronchus below.[13] (Picture your right hand turned up; curl up your ring finger and pinkie, covering this with your right thumb. Extend your other two fingers: your middle finger slightly longer than your index finger represents the left tube, your index finger, the right tube hovering over the right bronchus below).

An attached tracheal cuff surrounds both tubes, while a second cuff is attached around the end of the left tube in the left bronchus. Both cuffs can be inflated after intubation, via pilot tubing molded onto the DLT, that extrudes from the patient's mouth, color coded for ease of identification. Once positioned under anesthesia, the anesthesiologist inflates the left cuff, and using a stethoscope listens for ventilation breath sounds over the left lung. Confirming this, he inflates the tracheal cuff, via the pilot tubing, squeezing the anesthetic bag filled with oxygen, to confirm breath sounds to the right. Sounds simple, if the tube is indeed correctly placed. Not so simple if it is in too far, not far enough, down the wrong side, or if disease in the lungs – filled with pus or blood – is making auscultation increasingly difficult, while the patient is becoming hypoxic; because the tube is in a less than perfect position.†

The thoracic patient, is often less than optimal as well. In developed countries, lung resection surgery, is most usually for cancer; many patients having underlying lung disease caused by smoking. While in less developed countries, infectious disease, particularly tuberculosis, requires surgical intervention. Here the lungs may well be destroyed by bronchiectasis or abscess-filled cavitation, or worse still, complicated by the dreaded bronchopleural fistula. One of the most feared conditions in anesthesiology, a bronchopleural fistula is a connection between the bronchiole in the lung and the pleural cavity outside of the lung. The pleural cavity, which is usually maintained in a negative-pressure

---

* The carina is the apex of the inverted V of the trachea branching off into the left and right bronchus below. These two main stem bronchi then subdivide into further smaller bronchi and then re-divide into the smaller and still smaller bronchioli, which lead to the alveolar sacs where oxygen and carbon dioxide exchange occurs. This is known as the bronchial tree.

† Today we use fiber-optic bronchoscopy, to visualize the trachea and bronchi to ensure that we are in the correct position. At the time of my training, this was an unheard-of luxury, and identifying correct placement of the DLT in a sick patient often exceedingly difficult.

state (expansion of the chest and pleural cavity, when we inhale, ensuring this) is now filled with pus. Pus can freely flow from the pleura through the bronchopleural fistula into the lungs, especially if the patient moves or lies down. Hence bronchopleural fistula patients prefer to sit up, leaning forwards, so they can cough up copious pus and secretions. Initial treatment is with a chest drain connected to an underwater sealed bottle, allowing the pus to drain from the chest and allowing the lung – which may be in a partial state of collapse – to re-expand.

Thoracic surgery on the left lung is usually performed with the patient anesthetized, intubated, and ventilated, lying on their right side. Their left arm spread out at right angles to the chest on an arm board, introduced after turning the patient, so that the surgeon can incise the thorax with a suitably large cut, to get access to the lung beneath. The operation is performed with the left side of the DLT clamped closed to arrest the left lung, allowing the surgery to proceed. However, often, the remaining right lung, which is now compressed by the weight of the heart above, the diaphragm below, and engorged with blood, may not be sufficient to maintain oxygenation of the patient, despite the 100% inspired oxygen we invariably give. So we either continue to ventilate the operated lung, add positive airway pressure, or intermittently inflate the operated lung (if the first two options are not possible) between surgical incisions. Today we monitor this high-risk procedure with an oxygen saturation and end-tidal carbon dioxide monitor. But then, at the University of Cape Town, all we had was the color of the patient's skin and tongue, to guide us as to when hypoxia might be occurring.

Case Three

Dr. Rodney Hewitson did not usually say much, but this time he did. "Berend, let's look at the patient's X-ray. It does not look good and shows a pus-filled lung cavity – I want to resect – with a bronchopleural fistula and an intercostal drain in place." He was referring to the patient's radiograph prominently displayed on the illuminated X-ray box, which was a central feature of every operating theatre of the time. Even in this small operating theatre, off to the side of the two main cardiac theatres, housed in the new cardiac wing at Groote Schuur. "Are you ready to look after him?"

As the anaesthetic registrar on the cardio-thoracic rotation, I was. I had checked the Robertshaw double-lumen tube, inflating its two cuffs carefully to make sure that they did not leak. As we only use one ventilator attached by means of a single hose to the patient, I had made sure that I had the specialized transparent DLT Y-connector that split in two. This would be attached to the two lumens, crowning the red rubber tube, allowing ventilated oxygen to be distributed to both the left and right lung. Most importantly I had the solid stainless steel surgical clamp that would be used to isolate the lungs. Applied to the left or right side of the specialized DLT Y-connector, ventilation would be interrupted to the respective lung instantaneously – oxygen flowing instead to the other lung. I was ready to apply this to the left side when the patient was suitably positioned and Dr. Hewitson was ready to make his incision to resect the pus filled (loculated) empyema the patient was suffering from.

Key to anesthetizing such a sick patient with a loculated empyema and a bronchopleural fistula is that the patient has a working intercostal drain – to drain excess pus – and that he is positioned with his left lung downwards for induction. This is because, as we anesthetize and paralyze the patient and take over his breathing – using positive-pressure ventilation – there is a risk that ventilatory breaths are lost through the bronchopleural fistula, building up pressure in the loculated pleural cavity, causing pus under pressure to spread to, and cross-contaminate, the right lung. Under anesthesia the normal protective airway reflexes guarding against this are lost.* To minimize this potential, after suitable pre-oxygenation, I rapidly administered etomidate and succinylcholine and immediately placed the double-lumen tube appropriately down the left side, before starting anything more than just minimal positive-pressure ventilation. Inflating the two cuffs, the right lung was now suitably protected from cross-contamination and I released a sigh of relief. The patient's color was not optimal, so I continued ventilating both lungs, with good effect.

Positioning a patient on to their right side for thoracic surgery, is always a team sport, often fraught with the potential for complications. This patient was to prove no exception. The anesthesiologist is at the head, assuring that the patient's head and airway are safe during the turn, and usually gives the countdown "One, two, three..." to co-ordinate the turn. The surgeon standing

---

* This is why patients with this problem prefer to sit up, to cough out secretions, in so doing protecting their right lung from being contaminated by pus from the left.

on the left side usually lifts the patient, turning them at the thorax. An assistant catches the patient on the right, while a nurse manages the patient's legs.* Turning is always a high-risk, high-intensity event. Often monitors are displaced and the repositioning can disrupt airway devices and may have unintended cardiovascular effects, causing the blood pressure to drop, and if the patient is not properly anesthetized, the patient to move, again with untoward effects. I was ready to call the countdown for the turn, secure in the knowledge that I had isolated the two lungs so there would be no cross-contamination between the left and right lung from pus leakage, as both of the cuffs had been inflated.

"Ready Dr. Hewitson." I didn't dare call him Rodney as Dr. Chris Barnard had. "One, two, three, turn." The diminutive but strong Dr. Hewitson heaved him over, while I steadied the DLT with my right hand over the patient's mouth, my left supporting his head in the turn. As the patient flipped on his right side and the left was elevated, I looked down at the Y-connector to see that it was still attached to the lumens of the DLT. To my dismay, pus was shooting from the left Y to the right Y and started travelling down the right tube lumen. Possible cross-contamination! A complication we had tried so hard to avoid. How could I not have thought of this possibility; that pus could cross not only at the lung level, but also via the double lumen tube – from the left pus-filled lung, up the left tube under pressure, crossing by means of the Y-connector outside of the patient's body and down the right side. Fortunately, I had a suction catheter at the ready for just such a problem. Disconnecting the Y-connector, from the double-lumen tube quickly, I suctioned the right lumen furiously, hoping to avoid further problems. Then rapidly reconnected to the ventilator, making sure to suction the left lumen and clamp the left connector limb first, before doing so. In thinking back, this is what I should have done first – before turning the patient – a valuable lesson in lung protection during thoracic anesthesia that I have carried over in my teachings since.[14]

---

* If it is a really big patient, someone else will manage the hips. Turning patients prone for surgery, is even more risky as there is always a period of monitoring silence and the risk of dislodgement of airway devices. Fortunately, I have only once had to turn a patient prone who had a double-lumen tube in place for extensive thoracic cancer surgery; he weighed 130kg.

The Pediatric Patient

A neonate, infant, or child, is not just a little adult; they are distinctly different human beings. Different in anatomy, physiology and their pharmacological responses to drugs, more especially anesthetic agents, that progresses from birth to maturity.*[15] Let's start with the neonate, or just born. Exiting the uterus, she takes her first faltering breath, opening up the dormant amniotic-filled alveolar sacs and setting into motion a transitional circulation in her young body. Transitional – to transit from the amniotic fluid-filled uterus to the air medium that we live in. A rude shock indeed. Not surprising that she comes crying into the world helping this transition. The first opening breaths allow the neonate's lungs to expand, drawing blood into the collapsed lungs, lowering the pressure in her pulmonary arteries. The crying, and the cold-air shock on her skin and face, bring up her blood pressure, which had been much lower when she was leashed to her Mom's placenta via the umbilicus. This rise in her systemic blood pressure – and fall in her pulmonary blood pressure – causes a baffle, the foramen ovale, to close shut between her right and left atria.† Her young underdeveloped heart now pumping blood to her fledgling lungs for oxygenation and de-carbonation and passage to the rest of her growing body – struggling to adjust to the outside world. This transitional circulation is at first tenuous; sometimes flip-flopping – if adverse circumstances abound – that the anesthesiologist needs to be mindful of when anesthetizing such young patients. Adverse circumstances like hypoxia, hypercarbia, acidosis, and cold, triggering a sudden reversion to high pulmonary artery pressures, causing the foramen ovale baffle to re-open, setting up a downward spiral of cyanosis in the neonate.‡

The neonatal and infant heart is functioning at the end of its tether. Beating faster, underdeveloped, and stiffer than a more mature heart; it cannot respond to additional stresses very well. While an adult heart can increase its cardiac output threefold, this young heart cannot – mounting a response no

---

* Neonate is birth to five weeks of age, infant to one year, child one to twelve years. A pediatric patient is defined, in the U.S.A., as younger than eighteen years.

† The foramen ovale is held open in utero to allow umbilical blood to flow through the connecting sinus venosus to the right atrium, – through the foramen ovale, – and so to the left atrium and on through the left ventricle and aorta to the body.

‡ In many patients with congenital heart disease, where pulmonary artery pressures may remain high, this remains a permanent problem. In healthy neonates this transitional circulation is usually normalized by two weeks after birth. The foramen ovale is permanently closed by one year of age, except in 10-20% of adults where it remains

greater than a one-third increase, so ten times less. Further compromising the situation, the autonomic nervous system is underdeveloped and so responses to sudden drops in blood pressure cannot easily be adapted for – while the heart and the described baroreceptor response are more sensitive to anesthetic agents than the adult patient.

If that were not enough, while the baby has three times the oxygen consumption of an adult, its lung function is fragile at best. It is not a matter of appropriate size or speed of breathing but of durability and mechanics. The chest being very pliable, babies just don't have the same inspiratory strength and tire quickly because of the substantial work of breathing when under duress.

Getting cold, is another problem. Because of their thin skin, often little body fat, large skin surface area compared to a relative small body size, and inability to shiver like adults, children get cold easily. Very cold. Especially when anesthetized, and so immobilized and their thermoregulatory system is further impaired.

Immature kidney and liver function adversely impacting the excretion and metabolizing of drugs, is another feature affecting the administration of anesthetics. Because of the fact that many medications are administered on a per kilo basis, precise dosing of drugs needs to be performed, to avoid inadvertent overdosing in pediatric patients with little to no reserve. Made even more difficult by the child's increased sensitivity to drugs such as morphine which are not well metabolized in the liver till a later age. Surprisingly, neonates and young children actually need higher concentrations of sevoflurane to assure anesthesia, but because of their increased respiratory rate and cardiac output, onset is more rapid and the opportunity to overdose the child, if the anesthesiologist is not vigilant, has led to a great concern for cardiac depression and cardiac arrest in these young patients.

Last but by no means least, the pediatric airway can be very challenging. Babies are born to suckle at the mother's breast, and breathe at the same time, so children are obligate nasal breathers. Their facial structure at birth is designed to this end. Witness the slightly upturned noses of most newborns.

"probe patent" upon anatomical dissection of cadavers. There is also a duct or connection between the fetal pulmonary artery and aorta, called the ductus arteriosus. This funnels oxygenated blood arriving from the placenta in the heart from the pulmonary artery to the aorta when the fetus is still in utero. As soon as the child is born this starts closing, usually completed by three days after birth. If this remains open, known as a patent ductus arteriosus, this can contribute to the flip-flop transitional circulation described.

Their airways are hence substantially different from the adult situation. Large tongues, a high glottic opening,* angulated vocal cords and voluminous surrounding aryepiglottic folds, in oversized heads – when compared with adults – can make airway management and intubation in babies distinctly difficult. Especially if you're in a hurry and the child is rigid and stiff.

Cases Four and Five

Mary, a sprightly three-year-old, had been plagued by chronic tonsillitis. Born into an Irish-Canadian family, her parents had brought her to the Ottawa hospital for a routine tonsillectomy worried that she would be scared of her first anesthetic.† Never having received an anesthetic themselves, they weren't sure how to allay her anxiety, nor their own. Waving goodbye, the kindly anesthesiologist picked Mary up and carried her in to the operating room, placing her gently on the waiting table readied to perform the brief operation. This being 1960, halothane was the anesthetic of choice for children. After a mask was applied carefully to her face, Mary cried a little in fright as halothane, oxygen and nitrous oxide were administered. Settling down, an assistant placed an IV to administer further anesthetic drugs – when her arm stopped flailing – stilled by the onset of anesthesia. Just forty seconds into the anesthetic, the heart rate started going up – not down – as expected with the extremely potent halothane; Mary becoming completely rigid and stiff. The anesthesiologist, struggling to squeeze oxygen into her chest, administered 20mg of succinylcholine to paralyze her so he could prize open the child's clamped mouth to perform intubation. Her heart rate rising from 100 to 140 and her blood pressure dropping from 110/65 to 60/40 – precipitously. Upon endotracheal tube insertion, Mary suddenly became pulseless. Ashen in color; no heart beat could be detected. Starting cardiac massage, a heart surgeon was called from a nearby theatre to assist the resuscitation. Cutting open Mary's chest he proceeded to massage her heart gently with his gloved hands hoping to restore her heartbeat, trying on and on for half an hour or more. To no purpose. Despite epinephrine, lidocaine, calcium and bicarbonate

---

* In premature neonates (born at less than 37 weeks gestation) the glottis is at the level of the cervical vertebrae (C3); at full term neonates at C4; and in adults at C5 or C6.

† The case histories were provided from the Malignant Hyperthermia Association of North America database by Dr. Sheila Riazi. The names are fictitious.

administration, Mary was pronounced dead. Her pupils fixed and dilated.

Three years later, Caitlin, Mary's sister, needed surgery. Again aged three – her mother had been pregnant at the time of Mary's death – she needed surgery on her forearm for a fresh burn injury. Admitted to a different Ottawa hospital for care, Caitlin was wheeled into the operating room. Halothane again administered and after an IV was in place, succinylcholine 20mg was given for successful intubation. Her heart rate shooting up from 90 to 160 as she again became rigid and stiff like her sister before her. Applying an EKG monitor to her chest rapidly, the doctors diagnosed deadly ventricular fibrillation. Starting chest compressions, multiple shocks were delivered using a defibrillator again without effect. Caitlin pronounced dead, thirty minutes later.

The parents distraught, sought answers. Answers to explain the horrible deaths related to anesthesia that had been visited on their children by halothane and succinylcholine administration. Contacted by Dr. Beverly Britt, a Toronto-based anesthesiologist who had been working on the problem, Mary and Caitlin's parents were asked to undergo a test that might explain the mystery: a caffeine-halothane contracture test, performed on a muscle biopsy taken from their thighs. The father found to be extremely positive for the test. And subsequently – many years later – upon genetic analysis, found to have a deadly genetic mutation associated with a particularly aggressive form of malignant hyperthermia (MH).* Had this been known back then (in 1960) and the life-saving dantrolene therapy already identified† prior to Mary and Caitlin's anesthetic deaths, it is just possible, that their young lives might have been spared.[16, 17] Just possible, but still not assured, because of the particularly explosive nature of the family's propensity to develop MH. Nonetheless, had their genetic susceptibility to MH been known beforehand,

---

* Malignant hyperthermia is a genetically inherited condition. Triggered by volatile anesthetics and succinylcholine administration, it causes extreme muscle contracture and hypermetabolism resulting in a rapid rise of body temperature, blood acidosis and derangement of potassium levels. If not stopped by the drug dantrolene this can lead to cardiac depression, ventricular fibrillation and death. With the sophisticated diagnostic tests that are now applied, patients can be tested for the likelihood of developing this problem under anesthesia. So that a "non-triggering" anesthetic can be administered to safeguard the patient from developing this deadly condition. It appears now that patients inherit variable susceptibility to the intensity of MH that can develop. The family in question having a particularly intense response to triggering anesthetics witnessed by the immediate collapse and cardiac arrest upon anesthesia administration.

† Dantrolene was introduced into clinical practice in 1979. Professor Gaisford Harrison from the University of Cape Town, was the first to demonstrate the life-saving capacity of this drug. Using the experimental "Hot-Pig" model where MH was triggered in Landrace crossed Large White Pigs by halothane administration, he showed this heretofore deadly complication from anesthetics could be effectively treated by dantrolene administration.[18]

Mary and Caitlin would not have been given triggering anesthetic agents (like halothane) and dantrolene would have been readied just in case. This tragic story explaining well how the mortality from MH in patients receiving an anesthetic has declined from 70% in the 1960s to close on 5% today.[18, 19]

The Trauma Patient

Really, anyone can be a trauma patient. Young or old, sickly or in spanking good health, misadventure is indiscriminate. Trauma can take many forms: injuries, falls, road traffic accidents and in South Africa's Western Cape, interpersonal violence. In the late 1980-90s Cape Town was notorious as the "murder capital" of the world.* Not as serene as the pictures of Table Mountain crowning the city might suggest; hidden from view, in the streets and townships, gangsters settled their differences with an age-old weapon, the knife.

Groote Schuur Hospital had been equal to the challenge, developing a Severely Injured Unit as early as the 1960s and in the 1970s a fully-fledged Trauma Unit with two trauma theatres staffed round the clock by a surgical and an anesthetic registrar. Centered at the front of the hospital, ready to receive the wounded ferried up the winding road, from the city below, by all accounts it was a disaster area in the making. Dr. Negin Parbhoo describes the situation aptly:[2] "Weekends were like a miniature Vietnam, with gangsters from the Cape Flats and surrounds providing an endless stream of hair-raising experience." He continues, "Penetrating injuries of the chest, stabbed hearts and cardiac tamponades were a matter of course and left the anaesthetists unfazed." Perhaps unfazed but not untroubled.

Case Six

Ndlabe Nzumi† had spent the better half of Friday evening drinking at the local shebeen in Nyanga Township. Stoked on the local brew, he had got into an argument playing cards. Settled usually with Xhosa expletives, things got ugly when the opponent drew a knife. Revved-up, angry and scared, Ndlabe

---

* In 2000, the Western Cape had the highest homicide rate per capita in the world and the third highest mortality from road traffic deaths globally. Reference: Andre Koopman reporting in "Parliamentary Bureau," Cape Argus newspaper, October 18, 2001.

† Not his real name.

stepped back from the makeshift card table. Three quick stabs to the chest felling him nevertheless. Collapsing to the floor, his girlfriend started wailing for help as he became pale, started sweating, looking like he was going to die – soon. "Get help. Get help. Get him to Groote Schuur."

"Stabbed heart," the surgical registrar announced as I prepared the trauma theatre at the start of my twelve-hour shift in the trauma unit. "We must work quickly! I have called the cardiac surgeon on call." Sure enough, Ndlabe showed all the tell-tale signs: white as a sheet despite being black, thready radial pulse, congested neck veins, and a very low unsustainable blood pressure. Signs of cardiac tamponade – the stab wound had penetrated the heart leaking blood into the surrounding pericardial sack – compressing the heart chambers. Troubling to an anesthetist, because induction and anesthesia maintenance would compromise his condition further; even more so as ventilation of the lungs would be needed. Ventilation through an endotracheal tube increasing the patient's intrathoracic pressure, stopping venous blood from flowing to his already compressed cardiac chambers – further decreasing cardiac output.

"Full, fast and tight" is what the anesthetic registrar is taught to achieve in cardiovascular parameters, in managing the patient. Buying time until the surgeon can open the chest rapidly, decompress the tamponading heart, and suture closed the stab wound. And so I did; administering ketamine, which kept the blood pressure up and the heart fast, succinylcholine for intubation and very careful hand ventilation, and ephedrine to speed up the heart and keep the arterial pressure up.

Dr. John Odell, the cardiac surgeon, relieving the tamponade and suturing closed Ndlabe's torn right ventricle speedily afterwards. All good and well, but we were not out of the woods yet. We needed to transfer our patient to the cardiac ICU for postoperative management. Situated in the new Cardiac Wing, adjacent to Groote Schuur Hospital, this was a long trek down dark dank corridors and up an elevator, before we could safely deposit Ndlabe for ongoing care and monitoring – dangerous ventricular arrhythmias caused by the laceration of his heart, the abiding concern. I called ahead, asking the ICU staff to set up the arterial line pressure monitoring system then used in this unit. Unsophisticated by today's standards, this pressure manometer consisted of a vertical column of thin diameter plastic tubing. Filled with saline colored with methylene blue, the level at which it settled, once connected to the radial arterial artery catheter, indicating precisely, on a taped measuring scale, the patient's level of blood pressure.

Transporting him on a rickety stretcher, I ventilated Ndlabe gently through the endotracheal tube, as John and I entered the elevator that would take us to the second floor and straight into the waiting ICU. No worse moment imaginable – he went into ventricular fibrillation. The next instance would be cardiac arrest! In an elevator? Or in the corridor? Far better if we could get him quickly into the ICU above to resuscitate him. Hesitating only slightly, John and I were of one mind, push on, up the elevator, and into the prepared cardiac ICU. Resuscitating him with intravenous lignocaine, to restore the cardiac rhythm, we arrived somewhat breathless in the ICU.

Connecting Ndlabe to the prepared arterial pressure manometer, I noted from the methylene blue-colored saline level that his blood pressure was still dangerously low. A bolus dose of adrenaline would set matters right, but how much? There is no textbook dose for this situation. I gave my best guess dosage of adrenaline, hoping for the best. Too much. Ndlabe's heart rate increased, and the blood pressure level rocketed up the manometer, spraying methylene blue on to the ceiling above. The blood pressure literally hitting the roof. Now I knew where that famous expression came from: "The blood pressure hit the roof." Looking around in embarrassment, I saw that the ceiling of the ICU was peppered with blue spray marks. "Give it time," a bystander said. He was right, the blood pressure settling down nicely; Ndlabe fully recovering from the traumatic episode in his life.

Writing in his doctoral thesis on the department of anaesthetics at UCT, Negin had stated: "Stabbed hearts and cardiac tamponades were a matter of course and left the anaesthetists unfazed." I am not so sure I was unfazed. I remember indelibly my thoughts on seeing Ndlabe's pale mouth and tongue while intubating his trachea: "Is this man going to die today?" I thought, "A man this pale from blood loss cannot live to tell the tale."

Fortunately, I was wrong.

The ICU Patient

Poliomyelitis had been a killer. Respiratory failure induced by paralysis of the nerves essential to breathing, the culprit. Seeking a solution, Dr. Philip Drinker combatted the inevitable respiratory collapse of his polio patients by encasing them in an "iron lung."[20] Fashioned as an artificial cylindrical respiration tank, his patients lay on a mattress, their head protruding, an airtight rubber collar adjusted tightly around their necks. An electrically driven pump mechanism assured alternating negative and positive pressures in the sealed system, expanding and compressing the enclosed patient's chest and so drawing in and expelling air through their opened mouth and nose. Although widely applied, mortality remained high; nine out of ten patients dying despite the heroic efforts with the iron lung.

In Copenhagen – in 1953 – the polio outbreak was particularly severe. Prompting, Dr. Paul Ibsen, head of the department of anaesthesiology at the local Kommunehopitalet to be consulted to contrive a possible remedy.[21] Applying techniques used in his operating theatres, he administered an anesthetic and placed a red rubber tracheostomy tube through a high cut in the child's neck; Vivi, a twelve-year-old patient, was cyanotic and dying from polio-induced respiratory weakness – despite Drinker's respirator. Ibsen noting an immediate improvement in Vivi's condition as he ventilated her lungs with an anesthesia bag system. Before she had been sweaty and clammy. Now, as the raised carbon dioxide retained by inadequate ventilation in the iron lung was dissipated by the bag system, she became pink and her blood pressure dropped to more normal levels.[22] Wanting to be sure that he had diagnosed the problem and provided a solution, Ibsen placed Vivi back in the iron lung, switching on the electric pump again. Finding that the cyanosis and clamminess returned, he proceeded to ventilate her through the tracheostomy tube demonstrating, once and for all, that the iron lung was inadequate to the task. His technique would prevail instead. Intermittent positive-pressure ventilation improving the chance of survival from respiratory failure for Vivi and other polio patients – mortality reduced from 90% to 26%.*[21]

To manage such patients, Ibsen introduced an observation room at the Kommunehospitalet in Copenhagen. At first an extension of the postoperative recovery room, this would become the first intensive care unit in the world.[23] Staffed around the clock to ensure continued watchful care of critically ill patients with respiratory and circulatory failure – in Ibsen's time, an anesthesiologist, ear nose and throat surgeon and nurses attended the unit. And because

---

* This helped turn the tide and save hundreds of patients' lives. In 1955 Jonas Salk introduced the first polio vaccination which has largely eradicated the threat of poliomyelitis worldwide.

patients needed twenty-four-hour ventilation through the tracheostomy tubes – mechanical ventilators being expensive and in short supply – medical students were drafted to manage the ventilation by hand. Thirty shillings per eight-hour shift, the going rate.

Intensive care units developed from there. Decreasing mortality of critically ill patients, when compared with their care on regular wards – one of the drivers. Another, the increasing complexity of surgical procedures like cardiac and thoracic operations, requiring intensive life support and monitoring to ensure proper recovery. Today, many specialties have dedicated ICUs. There are neonatal, pediatric, neurosurgical, neurology, cardiology, cardiothoracic, general surgical, trauma, medical and respiratory ICUs with many different medical specialists involved in the intensive care and monitoring of patients. An anesthesiologist conceived of the idea in 1953 when respiratory system failure needed to be treated; today, almost any system failure can be managed as a consequence.

We turn now to the respiratory ICU at the University of Cape Town in the late 1950s where an anesthetic therapy to treat another deadly disease, tetanus, was being developed.

Case Seven

Fully blown tetanus is truly horrible to observe. Except for medical textbook pictures showing patients arched back – only their head and heels touching the ground – from the muscle-induced spasms, I have not witnessed this. I have however, been taught to manage these patients to avoid this development; during my three-month rotation on the respiratory ICU at Groote Schuur Hospital.

Brian Sasman grew up in Ottery on a farm in the Cape Flats. So called because it is a particularly flat area of Cape Town's environs. At the age of ten his mother had sent him out to complete a gardening chore. Compost had to be mixed and moved over to the waiting shed. Digging deep, and barefoot, he trod on a nail. Nonplussed, as always, he completed the job and returned home, ready for supper. Explaining, events to his mother, she became increasingly worried when the wound in his foot became infected and he started complaining that his jaw was a little stiff.

"Brian, we must go to GSH to have this seen to. You may be developing lockjaw," she said in Afrikaans, the Cape Coloureds' preferred language. He was admitted immediately. The medical officer in the emergency unit knowing instantly what the problem was. Tetanus. Brian was developing tetanus. If not treated soon, this could degenerate into muscle spasms from the spreading infection in his foot, releasing tetanus toxins into his bloodstream. Spasms so bad that adequate breathing would not be possible and Brian could die a painful, terrible death from asphyxiation.* He must be admitted to the ICU. But first, Brian was taken to the operating room urgently, anesthetized, paralyzed and intubated so that two things could be done without delay. First, the spreading wound in his foot, infected with the bacteria *Clostridium Tetani*, needed to be cut out to stop the process and large doses of anti-tetanic serum needed to be administered. Secondly, a tracheostomy needed to be placed, so that Brian could be ventilated in the ICU. He was in for the long haul and needed intensive care around the clock to survive this ordeal, having a mortality of 90% at the time.

Professor Arthur Bull, the first chair of the department of anaesthetics at UCT (1965-80), described the new anesthetic approach to the treatment of this deadly disease.[24] Brian was anesthetized with a combination of phenobarbitone and diazepam. And paralyzed using curare injected intramuscularly to counteract the muscle spasm that would stop the mechanical ventilator from effectively supporting breathing through the newly placed tracheostomy tube.† Intensive care with artificial ventilation was needed for weeks on end, buying time for the prescribed antibiotic therapy to eradicate the tetanus infection and the harmful toxins that were causing the life-threatening muscular spasms. There were other problems requiring intensive care to address.[25] Problems of artificial nutrition and combatting the ever present threat of another infection, while protecting Brian from the effects of an interminably prolonged anesthetic.

A tube was placed in his stomach for feeding and he was turned carefully every two hours – making sure not to dislodge the ventilator – so that he would not receive pressure sores from lying still. Deadly still from the muscular paralysis induced by curare that allowed him to survive the ordeal. If a ventilator disconnect occurred in the middle of the night, he would be dead.

---

* Textbooks describe this death as due to the tetanus toxins causing muscle spasms, depicted in the facial muscles as "Risus Sardonicus" the mask of death – the face contorted into a grinning mask-type sneer – as the patient dies of hypoxia through inadequate ventilation.

† Curare was given intramuscularly so that it could work longer than if given intravenously.

So he needed to be continually monitored. In addition, vital signs were regularly checked and recorded; any signs of infection evaluated with a chest X-ray, or blood, or urine analysis, in order to identify and treat any other bug that could kill him – all over again. Obstruction of the tracheostomy tube with secretions from his lungs was another major problem. Nurses suctioned the tracheostomy two-hourly, to make sure that this didn't happen.

It is not a wonder that my colleagues often joke that the *intensive* care unit is an *expensive* care unit, underscoring all the resources that need to be diligently applied to keep a patient alive.

Brian was one of the early survivors of this new anesthetic therapy that improved tetanus mortality from 90% to 10%. Ventilated and cared for in an ICU for over two and a half months, he has no memory of the events. He did suffer from a mild weakness in his left hand which improved with physiotherapy. So much so that he became a skilled and valued anesthesia technical assistant in the J. S. Marais Laboratory where I completed my research work – with his help – for a PhD in Pharmacology.[26]

Research Training

In my book, "research" is a four-letter word; it causes one to curse a lot. Frustrating, incredibly difficult to do well, and uncertain in its outcome. Nevertheless, I wanted to pursue an academic career, so I needed to learn how to do research. Having completed my specialist examinations after just three years of registrar training, I had two years of further clinical training to go before I could become a consultant anaesthetist. I had time on my hands and so approached Dr. Ozinsky for advice. Professor Harrison, who had offered to teach me research, was away on sabbatical leave, putting Ozzie in charge of the department in his absence.

"Research time? is usually a waste of time," he retorted. "Most people produce nothing useful." He could see though that I was serious about this. Having noted that I had just published a pediatric research study[27] while serving as a registrar, learning pediatric anesthesia at the Red Cross Children's Hospital, he gave me some slack. "Why don't you go over to the anaesthetic department's research laboratories, where Professor Harrison has his office and ask Dr. David Morell for advice. David has developed a sophisticated assay technique for measuring blood lignocaine concentrations and Professor Rosemary Hickman, a trained surgeon, has an isolated perfused pig-liver system in the J. S. Marais Surgical

Laboratory below. Barnard suggested she develop this system to treat patients in liver failure, but the patients bled too much, and so the apparatus is not being used any more."*

Hamilton Naki (1926-2005) got up early, extra early, because there were rumors of unrest planned nearby and he wanted to be the first to arrive at the J. S. Marais Surgical Laboratory, no later than 6.00a.m. Impeccably dressed in a black suit and tie, a Homburg on his head, he left his tiny room in Langa Township on the Cape Flats, making his way to the bus stop. A deeply religious man, he always carried a bible, newspaper and umbrella. Having grown up in the Transkei where he attended school up to Standard Four, Hami had moved to Cape Town at the age of eighteen, finding work as a gardener at UCT in the 1940s. Summoned to the surgical laboratory by Dr. Robert Goertz, a surgical researcher, to help hold down a giraffe he was anesthetizing, Hami made such a good impression, that he was drafted to assist. Soon learning techniques for animal anesthesia and surgery; Hami became the lab's assistant surgeon. Assisting Professor Christiaan Barnard in developing the experimental dog heart transplant program, Hami and Chris worked side by side in the animal laboratory for years,[†] Barnard remarking, "Hamilton Naki had better surgical skills than I did. He was a better craftsman than me especially when it came to stitching." Serving the animal laboratory for close to fifty years, Hami became an expert in pig liver transplantation, attempting to teach me the necessary surgical techniques so that I could isolate the liver in preparation for the planned

---

* Professor Hickman injured her hand while training as a surgeon and so instead dedicated her career to surgical transplantation research, chiefly in pigs. She had developed the isolated perfused pig liver model and achieved the Master of Surgery Degree for this work. This model, which kept alive resected pig livers, was developed to provide temporary relief for patients in liver failure by using the connected pig liver to clean their blood of toxins that their own liver could no longer process. An idea that Prof Christiaan Barnard had thought of while in America, unfortunately did not work in practice. A number of patients were treated in this way to buy time for eventual liver transplantation. They did in fact "wake up" from the liver-induced failure coma state, but soon relapsed, developing worsening bleeding problems, limiting the device's practical application. Rosemary, an outstanding scientist, served as one of the two supervisors, with Professor Peter Folb, for my PhD in Pharmacology, conferred by UCT in 1992. In addition, she performed much of the surgeries required for this complex research. My father, Dr. J. T. Mets, having himself completed a doctoral dissertation and serving as a senior lecturer at UCT, was allowed to "cap me," placing the red hood signifying achievement of the PhD degree, at the annual graduation ceremony held in the University of Cape Town's Jamieson Hall.

† Chris Barron: Obituary, *Cape Times*, May 2005: "Not the least of Naki's contributions to medical history was his ability to get on with Barnard, whom many people found impossibly highly strung and temperamental. Naki's temperament, one of infinite tolerance and patience, complemented the explosive heart surgeon's perfectly and the

isolated pig liver perfusion experiments. I never became good enough at the complicated surgery required, so Hami performed this surgery for me. I asked him once, after he had yet again given me a perfect liver for the metabolic perfusion experiments, "Hami how did you learn all these surgical techniques?" He looked at me, paused, smiling in his inimitable way, his broad mouth opening on large perfect white teeth, "I steal with my eyes," he responded.

Today, he would perform the liver resection and cannulate the hepatic artery and portal vein, after Brian Sasman had anesthetized the identified pig, earmarked (literally) for the morning's planned experiment.

The pig is a particularly good animal model for research. Its gastrointestinal tract, blood groups, heart and lungs are very similar to that of humans. (Quite apart from the usual analogies made.) Hence, I was trying to answer the question whether the pig liver could also be a good model for the metabolism and breakdown of lignocaine, a commonly used local anesthetic. And if so, then could lignocaine metabolism be used as a marker or indicator of hepatic ischemic damage, often occurring during liver transplantation in humans?[28] To study this we needed to take the liver out of the pig's body and keep it alive for around two and a half hours. Professor Hickman had created a specialized perfusion apparatus to do this. Much like the bypass equipment used by Barnard to keep patients alive during cardiac surgery, this apparatus featured a disposable plastic bubble oxygenator and two Sarns roller pumps,* which squeezed oxygenated pig's blood through two plastic cannulae attached to the hepatic artery and portal vein by Hami. The rate of perfusion set comparable to that previously determined in separate experiments in the live pig. Oxygenated blood would thus be delivered to the pig liver keeping it alive, the cyanotic blood draining out through its hepatic veins, fed back to the oxygenator, setting up a continuous circular loop of blood. Similarly the temperature and acid base status of the liver perfusion was monitored and controlled. Once the perfusion was stable, lignocaine was infused at a standard rate to achieve concentrations similar to

two were able to work shoulder to shoulder for years." For his work with Dr. Barnard and the many other surgeons and physicians he assisted, Hamilton Naki received an Honorary Master's Degree from the University of Cape Town, as well as a National Presidential Award: The Order of Mapungubwe, one of South Africa's highest awards for contributions to science, in 2002.

* It is indeed possible that these were the very Sarns roller pumps used during the first heart transplant, as most of the equipment in the laboratory was handed down from the GSH operating rooms. This was never confirmed though. But is a nice thought.

that found in humans, and then multiple blood samplings of the hepatic artery, portal vein, and liver venous drainage were taken for later analysis of lignocaine levels, as well as its four major metabolites – the most important having the unpronounceable name of methyl-ethyl-glycine-xylidide, MEGX for short.*

Brian Sasman was held back for a year of school. Understandable as he had missed at least two months while unconscious, anesthetized and paralyzed to treat him for tetanus. Still bearing the scar from the tracheostomy in his neck, he completed Standard Six, leaving school at sixteen to help supplement his family's meager income – finding part-time work as a cleaner at the anaesthetic laboratory and orthopedic workshops. Five years on, Professor Bull, while working in the laboratory, inquired as to the origin of Brian's scarred neck. To his amazement, Brian related his story. Bull recognizing immediately that Brian Sasman had been one of his early successful tetani patients, offered him a job as an anesthesia technician on the spot. Brian having already shown himself to be unusually adept at lending a hand – in between his cleaning duties – was soon put to work anesthetizing animals and helping with all manner of research projects in the department.

Today he would start by anesthetizing the pig for Hami's liver resection and then finalize preparation of the perfusion apparatus – awaiting my arrival from the abbatoir with the all-important fresh heparinized pig's blood, that was needed to prime the perfusion circuit and start the experiment. Hami's, Brian's and my preparations, intersecting at 8.30a.m. sharp to complete the experiment at a standardized time of day, in order to minimize any potential variations in diurnal liver metabolism.

Anesthetizing a pig is one thing; you have to catch it first. Brian had developed an ingenious technique. He would corner the pig in its pen, grab it around its waist, and then hoist it on to a trellised cage. Momentarily immobilized by the fact that its trotters were hanging through the trellises, he grabbed its ear, identified a vein, and injected thiopentone quickly. Deeply anesthetized, he turned the porcine on its back for intubation. Now breathing spontaneously, through the placed endo tracheal tube, he placed the pig on a cart, covered it with a green cloth and transported the twenty-five-kilogram animal rapidly from the swine pens, across to the surgical laboratory. Nitrous oxide and

* Using an HPLC analysis developed by Dr. Rosemary Allin in the Anaesthetic Laboratory.

oxygen was then administered – using a Bird ventilator – once the pig had been positioned on its back on the surgical table situated in the laboratory directly opposite the prepared perfusion equipment, where Hami sat quietly waiting. Dressed in a green gown, he had readied the surgical equipment and could now start the porcine hepatic resection.

The slaughterhouse pigs were really squealing now. A cacophony of fear as they were chased from pen to ever narrower pen by men with sticks egging them on at the Elsie's River abattoir. A Muslim slaughterhouse, strict Halal protocol needed to be observed. The enormous chief slaughterer stood center stage, bedecked in a giant yellow southwester covered in fresh blood. Standing in large rubber boots, the tools of his trade were all around him. Up above, a giant bicycle chain, with massive inverted hooks attached, whirred round and round, ready to ferry the dead pigs into the refrigerated section of the building. Below, in this outside area of the abattoir, white tiles were being sluiced by assistants diluting the gallons of blood on the floor. Surrounding this slaughter pen was a four-foot concrete wall so that frightened pigs could not escape. To the slaughterman's left a narrow gate was closed, keeping the terrified pigs from entering the enclosure, squeezing, snorting, screeching and bouncing around, they had the fear of death in their eyes. The next step was always too ghastly to contemplate, but I needed three liters of fresh pig's blood for the planned experiment. I had brought my plastic container primed with sufficient heparin. The chief slaughterer had two assistants; together they had perfected the process. One carried an electrocution device that he clamped around the swine's head, while the other pulled down the first hook from its pulley attached to the circling bicycle chain above. Giving a sign, the gate was opened ajar and a pig shot out. Deftly clamping its head, a shock was applied; a grunted squeal resounding, as its whole body spasmed. The second assistant, gaffing a hook through a hind leg, hauled the pig – head down and stunned – up towards the circling cycle chain, its head hanging level with the slaughterer. "Bismillah," he murmured, as he swiftly drew his sharpened knife in one deep incision, precisely severing the pig's throat, carotid artery, trachea and jugular veins, as prescribed. The pig's blood draining out in seconds as he held up my container to capture as much blood as he could. Mercifully, four or five swine was all it usually took to garner sufficient blood. His assistant wiping off the container and handing it to me with a slight bow and smile; they knew I would be back soon.

*

Isolated pig liver perfusion, sounds easy but really isn't. Many things can go wrong and ruin the day's experiment. The problem is much like keeping alive a patient on cardiopulmonary bypass. Except here the 700-gram pig's liver is the patient.

Meticulous hepatic resection surgery must be performed to avoid damaging the liver in the process of taking it out for the perfusion. Cannulation of the hepatic artery and portal vein must occur expeditiously as severing the vessels interrupts the liver's blood supply, and it starts becoming ischemic immediately. Timing must be perfect, the bypass equipment primed with just the right amount of fresh blood ready to connect the resected liver; literally where seconds count. Delays or errors will cause deterioration in liver function which is the primary subject of study in the first place. Then there is the problem of the oxygenator. Setting the perfusion flows wrong or inadvertent blood loss could empty the oxygenator causing air embolism. Too long a study period and the limited life of the oxygenator becomes a factor as the antifoam protective surface wears off. Too high a line pressure will result in liver damage or worse still dislodgement of a plastic connector. In short, there are many factors that needed to be attended to. Consequently, I found research like this more stressful than patient care, and prepared for this with the greatest attention to detail.

Today was no different. Hami had completed the liver mobilization which would allow rapid resection and cannulation when the bypass circuit was primed and ready at the right temperature. "Good morning, Hami, good morning, Brian, everything all right?" I carried in the fresh, still frothing pig's blood, and decanted this slowly into the reservoir of the bypass machine, starting the roller pumps to allow recirculation to bring it to the right temperature. Arterial blood gas samples were drawn and measured in the lab and the blood perfusate acid-base status was adjusted and monitored using a pH meter to ensure that the perfusate constituents would be optimal.

"Brian, everything all right? Have you taken the baseline samples?"

"Yes, Doctor."

"Okay, Hami, let's go," I said, turning to him. As always, he was resting on his chair, gowned and gloved and ready for the final, critical step, rapid cannulation and release of the liver. He started and handed me the liver in close to three minutes.

"Brian! Pump off," I said, as I walked the two steps from the operation table to the waiting perfusion apparatus. Stopping the perfusate circulation would allow me to separate the connectors, which would then be re-connected quickly to the cannulae that Hami had placed in the liver, now warm in my gloved hands. I placed the liver on the waiting gauze "diaphragm" that was central to the functioning of the perfusion apparatus. Created to resemble the function of the pig's own diaphragm, which the liver usually abuts – this could be activated by a spin wheel to move up and down slowly – simulating respiration.

Stationery now, I de-aired the cannulae, and connected the hepatic artery and portal vein rapidly, ensuring that the venous drainage cannula could drain blood from the liver, through a hole in the diaphragm, into the galvanized iron receptacle over which the diaphragm was suspended. This conical receptacle, eighteen inches square, caught the venous blood for drainage back to the oxygenator, completing the perfusion circuit, now with the liver interposed.

"Pump on!" I slowly dialed up the two Sarns roller pump flows to the preset limits, making sure that the hepatic arterial pressure did not rise too much, and kept a watchful eye on the bile flowing through a plastic cannula connected to the bile duct for that purpose. Looking at the liver hopefully, after many failed perfusions, I was gratified that this one was perfect; the liver pinking up nicely and showing no dead edges. I settled down to the liver biopsy and blood sampling protocol, the focus of the next two and a half hours' work; always watchful that the perfusion parameters remained correct.

But this day was to be different, historical even. I had never met Professor Christiaan Barnard, despite knowing so much about him.

Imagine the scenario in the J. S. Marais Surgical Lab. A laboratory created by Dr. Barnard where he had practiced animal surgery for innumerable years before today. With Hami and many others he had worked here tirelessly to perfect techniques for cardiac surgery and transplantation.

The lab was large, with six animal surgical tables, three on each side like a classroom, various studies ongoing, today. In the back corner was the isolated perfusion equipment where I was conducting my experiment. Right across from me, facing me and the back wall, Hami was closing the pig we had just taken the liver from.

At the far end, the entrance, a commotion! Someone is talking rather loudly, with a recognizable piercing nasal twang. Quite tall, but stooped, in casual working clothes, Chris Barnard was in Cape Town from his farm at

Beaufort West. Picking up provisions in his "bakkie" parked just outside the laboratories' front door, he decided to come in to have a look around.

"I started this lab," he intoned loudly for all to hear, and carried on in the same vein, pointing out in his high-pitched voice where various animal experiments had been performed.

Hami, unfazed, his back to Barnard at the entrance, but hearing it all nonetheless, looked up at me catching my eye, his face creasing into a wide smile.

"Skollie [scoundrel]," was all he said, quietly to me.*

---

* Skollie is an Afrikaans word used on the Cape Flats which can be loosely translated as "scoundrel." Probably used here by Hami as a term of endearment with mild disapproval. "Skollie" is a word used to describe the gangsters that infest the surrounding townships of the Cape Flats. Hami, a man of great religiosity, probably said this to convey both admiration and mild disdain of Chris Barnard's personal life; at the time separated from his third wife.

8

Outcomes – APGAR Scores & Other Stratagems

The roles of risk assessment, guidelines, standardization and checklists in improving safety

Crashed Boeing B17 "Flying Fortress" Prototype. October 30, 1935: the impetus for checklists in aviation.

Too much airplane for one man to fly.

– Newspaper reporter

If you're young or old or frail and sick, outcomes from anesthesia and surgery may not always be good, especially if you are "sensitive" to anesthetics.[1]

In fact, recent global studies of outcomes from elective* surgery demonstrate that operations are downright dangerous; one in two hundred patients dying after surgery, while around two out of every ten patients have postoperative complications.[2]

No wonder many heed the age-old adage, "Avoid the surgeon's knife!" whenever possible.

The problem is that medicine in general, and surgery and anesthesia more specifically, have become the art and science of managing extreme complexity, with a lasting question; can humans in fact master this properly and safely?[3]

It is the hope (and subject of this chapter) that through appropriate risk assessment and mitigation strategies, evidence-based guidelines and standardizing of practice, using checklists as a communication tool and aide-memoire, anesthesiologists will be able to manage this increasing complexity, with improved patient outcomes, the result.

Nevertheless, anesthesiologists, like pilots, are ever ready to use their clinical experience and training to face situations for which there are no adequate protocols, guidelines, or a checklist to accomplish the task; much as Captain Chesley Sullenberger faced in crash-landing Flight 1549 on the Hudson River, January 15, 2009.

Scores & Risk Assessments

Virginia Apgar (1909-1974) a pilot† and a virtuoso violinist was appointed the first director of the division of anesthesia at Columbia University's Presbyterian Hospital in 1938. Possessed of enormous energy, Dr. Allen Whipple the then chairman of surgery, suggested that she change direction from surgery to anesthesia, knowing that four previous female surgical

---

* Prescheduled surgery that is not emergent.

† Dr. Apgar wanted to fly under the George Washington Bridge that Captain Sullenberger flew over to crash-land in the Hudson River.

residents had been unable to establish surgical practices in New York City; patients of the time expecting male surgeons. "Even women won't go to a woman surgeon."

Further motivating Dr. Whipple was his belief that innovations and improvements were needed in the rudimentary practice of anesthesia to advance the surgical care in his department. Virginia having "the energy, intelligence, and ability needed to make significant contributions in this area." With her characteristic brilliance and optimism Apgar set out to do so.* Her training in anesthesia typical of the time. First she spent a year with the nurse anesthetists at Columbia Presbyterian Hospital and then joined Professor Ralph Waters, completing six months in the first residency training program in the country he had started in Madison, Wisconsin. Returning to Columbia, Dr. Apgar became the division director for anesthesia. A division with only one member – herself, until 1945; recruiting exceedingly difficult as anesthetics was not respected by surgeons and the pay commensurately low.

Nevertheless, by 1949, Virginia was appointed as the first female professor at the College of Physicians and Surgeons of Columbia University. That year too, Dr. Emmanuel Papper was appointed as the first Chairman of the newly created Department of Anesthesiology and so Virginia decided to focus on obstetric anesthesia, practicing at the Sloane Hospital for Women, adjacent to the Presbyterian Hospital on 168th Street.

Here, most important to improving outcomes of care, Virginia created a scoring system used to assess a newborn baby's viability and need for resuscitation. Later known as the APGAR score. A score that is now used world-wide to predict and improve neonatal survival.

Early one morning in the cafeteria, after a particularly harrowing evening on obstetric anesthesia call, one of the medical students sharing breakfast asked Dr. Apgar how a newborn might be easily evaluated. "That's easy, you'd do it like this." Virginia picked up a paper napkin from a tray and jotted it down. "Five points – *heart rate, respiratory effort, muscle tone, reflex response*, and *color* – are observed and given zero, one, or two points." "The points are then totaled to arrive at the baby's score." A total of nine or ten was optimal. Then she rushed off to try it for herself, her white coat flapping behind as she made her way upstairs to the obstetric unit.

---

* She avoided women's organizations and causes, though she sometimes privately expressed her frustrations with gender inequalities and was known to say "women are liberated from the time they leave the womb."

Studying more than a thousand newborns in the Sloane Hospital obstetric unit, Dr. Apgar reported on the new scoring system at the International Anesthesia Research Society meeting in 1952.[4] Demonstrating, in this first report of its kind – assessing outcomes from anesthetic care – that babies born by Cesarean section under general anesthesia* had far lower scores (5/10) than those whose mothers had received a spinal anesthetic (8/10) – prompting adaptations of anesthetic and resuscitative techniques to improve outcome.

Despite initial resistance, the then known "Apgar" score became more widely accepted; not only did it reflect the immediate status of the newborn, and so need for assistance – but also the prognosis.

Notwithstanding its obvious utility, the Apgar scoring system was difficult for medical personnel to remember. Hence a practical epigram: APGAR, was proposed for the scoring system:

Appearance (color)
Pulse (heart rate)
Grimace (response to flicking the sole of the baby's foot)
Activity (muscle tone)
Respiration

(Effort: absent – scoring 0, slow irregular breaths – 1, and crying – 2)
(Scored and documented at one, five and ten minutes after delivery)[5]

Henceforth called the APGAR scoring system – many young medical students, including myself, never knowing that the APGAR epigram had its origin in a Doctor's actual name: Dr. Virginia Apgar.

The 1950s represented a watershed into research directed at improving the well-being of mothers and their babies; an enterprise supported by the National Institute of Health entitled the Collaborative Perinatal Project.[6] Central to this endeavor was the newly developed APGAR score assessment that each newborn was subjected to by a legion of willing medical students and nurses who documented data at the time of birth. Low APGAR scores handily predicting

---

* Cyclopropane.

not only immediate outcomes – a very low sustained score often associated with the demise of the child – but also foretelling long-term decrements in neurological outcome; babies with low APGARs often demonstrating neurological impairment in later life.[7] The score was found to be especially useful in attempts to mitigate the risk of poor outcomes by indicating clearly when enhanced resuscitative measures, like assisting the newborn's breathing while suppling extra oxygen, was needed.[8] Paving the way for better perinatal care of the babies and also the mothers; maternal mortality being a major problem to contend with in the obstetric anesthetic care of the time.[9]

While the APGAR score was the first score used to predict outcomes, it was by no means the last. The American Society of Anesthesiologists introducing the New Classification of Physical Status, better known as the ASA Score, in 1964.[10]

Surgical patients would from then on be classified as ASA 1 through 5, based on their physical condition preoperatively: Class 1 – "a normally healthy patient" up to Class 5 – "a moribund patient not expected to survive for 24 hours *with* or *without* an operation." The ASA Score was never meant to be a risk assessment score, merely a classification of physical state, nevertheless early investigators studying the "Role of Anesthesia in Surgical Mortality" soon recognized that when anesthetic administration contributed to a patient's death, this was closely related to the ASA physical status classification of the patient before surgery.[11]

Still today, fifty years on, every patient before surgery receives an ASA classification; mandated by both the Joint Commission* as well as by Medicare in the U.S.A., as a condition for receiving re-imbursement for the anesthetic care provided.

Nonetheless, there has been widespread criticism of the ASA score. The score does not reliably provide an actionable, objective, risk assessment of the patient's condition with respect to the planned surgical procedure – able to predict mortality from the operation or major perioperative complications like a heart attack. Nor does it provide guidance on what might be done preoperatively to medically optimize the patient to mitigate potential poor outcomes – the holy grail of preoperative risk assessments.

*

---

* The Joint Commission, is a Healthcare Accreditation Organization, that upon regular inspection, certifies the quality of hospitals and medical practices in the U.S.A. and now internationally.

One score, the Preoperative Score to Predict Postoperative Mortality – POSPOM for ease of remembering – uses seventeen factors such as: age, chronic alcohol abuse, diabetes and type of surgery; predicting outcomes using only preoperative data.[12] While useful in informing patients about potential risk of the surgical procedure – helping them decide whether or not to "avoid the surgeon's knife," it does not guide preoperative optimization.

Another, the Surgical Apgar Score looks at three potentially modifiable intra-operative measures: low blood pressure, low heart rate and estimated blood loss, using a derived score to predict poor outcomes like death and stroke.[13] Unsophisticated, nevertheless useful, the Surgical Apgar Score suggests that low blood pressure needs to be avoided during surgery. Now borne out by multiple studies – it is now well recognized that *any* low blood pressure below a mean of 50mmHg – for as short as one minute – increases the likelihood of poor outcome from heart or kidney injury postoperatively.[14] Such outcome studies providing useful guidance on how anesthesiologists should manage their patients intra-operatively; being sure to treat hypotension aggressively to protect their patients from harm.[15]

Another strategy to improve outcomes from surgery is to visit an Anesthesia Preoperative Evaluation Clinic. Investigators in New York City demonstrating that patients who visited their anesthesiologist-run* clinic fared better after elective surgery than those who did not.[16] Fewer deaths occurred postoperatively despite the group of patients visiting the clinic being older, sicker and having higher ASA scores while undergoing more complex procedures.

Explanations abound as to why this might be so. Chief of which; a risk assessment could be performed, allowing the patient to decide whether surgery was in their best interests – and if so, mitigation strategies could be put in place to optimize their preoperative medical status before scheduling surgery. Mitigation strategies like: stopping smoking, losing weight, optimizing blood pressure, heart failure or diabetic therapy, and making sure the patient is taking medications preoperatively as directed by clinic staff. Another explanation offered for an anesthesiologist's role in decreasing mortality; their ability to improve the entire continuum of a patient's surgical care through their role in the co-ordination

---

* Interestingly, but unexplained, a preoperative evaluation by a physician not specifically trained in perioperative medicine has been associated with increased post-operative mortality.

of events peri-operatively[*] – possible because of their in-depth knowledge of the surgical procedures, anesthetic and post-operative pain requirements and management.[†]

Guidelines & Standardization

Henrik Kehlet (1942), a Danish surgeon – perhaps the most well-known surgeon among anesthesiologists around the world – liked to ask simple questions that challenged lingering surgical dogmas.[17]

"Why is this patient still in hospital, today?!" he asked in his nasal Scandinavian twang. "Is it pain or is it nausea and vomiting?" Proceeding to, "Dissect down, get the answers and change care." In so doing establishing simple surgical and anesthesia guidelines to enhance patient surgical care outcomes – now known as Enhanced Recovery After Surgery or ERAS protocols.

Based on a full understanding of the detrimental pathophysiological effects that the stress of surgery and anesthesia visits on a patient, Professor Kehlet proposed multiple different approaches to develop fast-track surgery.[18] Recognizing that many surgical and anesthesia practices were far from standardized nor had a basis in evidence – "because we always do it that way" – he challenged conventional wisdom, bringing evidence-based practice to bear on developing guidelines to improve perioperative care.[19] In so doing he called for minimally invasive operations – ever smaller surgical incisions – to minimize the stress response.

Kehlet also railed against wound drains being left at the surgical incision site – a standard practice – because this limited patient mobility and so slowed recovery. Urinary catheters too should be abandoned, if unnecessary, so that early mobilization of the patient could occur; minimizing the risk of

---

[*] The perioperative period, encompassing the developing discipline of Perioperative Medicine, is a medical management period increasingly overseen by anesthesiologists. It starts with medical preparation of the patient preoperatively, continues with medical management intra-operatively and concludes with medical management of the patient postoperatively; particularly with respect to pain, recovery room therapy and intensive care medicine when needed.

[†] Plans are underway in many anesthesiology departments to develop ever more sophisticated Preoperative Medical Optimization Centers that patients can visit, to for example, provide iron therapy to increase their blood hemoglobin levels – so avoiding the need for blood transfusion intra-operatively. Or to address patient frailty, especially for patients over 65 years of age; providing strength training, dietary supplementation, as well as optimization of medical conditions. Thus, ensuring that patients are in an optimal state before the insult of elective surgery is visited on them.

muscle wasting from lack of activity and the chances of pulmonary embolism occurring from a clot having formed in unused calf muscles. Advocating further for the prescription of blood-thinning drugs to combat this lethal complication.

Recognizing the damaging effect of the surgical stress response on patient recovery, Henrik championed the use of epidural anesthesia for surgery to interrupt the vicious surgical cycle with pre-emptive analgesia.* Multimodal pain therapy; multiple different approaches to providing perioperative pain management – avoiding the detrimental effects of perioperative opioid use – was another component of his ERAS protocols. Consequently, non-steroidal analgesics, acetaminophen and wound infiltrations with local anesthetic compounds were suggested.

Early feeding of the surgical patient was also needed. It interrupted the catabolic response that surgery produced, minimizing further muscle wasting which slowed convalescence. Because surgery damps down immune responses, increasing the chance for infection, he suggested prophylactic antibiotic administration.

Kehlet, a true pioneer, challenged anesthesiologists to develop anesthetic techniques, intra-operative fluid therapy and pain management modalities that would promote rapid recovery, minimize post-operative nausea and vomiting, allowing early ambulation while minimizing post-operative confusion and sleep disturbance – monitoring the outcomes of the therapeutic experiment using simple computer systems to assess postoperative walking and sleep patterns as well as infections and other complication rates.

Recognizing early that to improve outcomes after surgery a multidisciplinary

---

* To provide epidural anesthesia, a thoracic epidural catheter is placed through a Tuohy needle before the start of general anesthesia for the planned bowel surgery. The patient is usually asked to sit up bending their back towards the anesthesiologist. She will then identify the correct place for the catheter insertion and after properly sterile cleaning and draping the area, will identify the thoracic level, usually between two spinous processes of the thoracic vertebrae from T6 to T12. Pre-injecting a small dose of local anesthetic along the planned pathway of the Tuohy needle, the anesthesiologist will then advance the Tuohy needle slowly, to reach the epidural space, just outside the spinal cord between the vertebrae. Injecting further local anesthetic once a catheter has been cited in the epidural space, this local anesthetic can then be infused continuously during and after surgery. The epidural anesthetic provides not only pain relief from surgery but also interrupts the spinal reflex response that surgery initiates. In so doing decreasing the spinal mediated stress response that triggers a systemic neuro-hormone reaction which causes catabolism, (muscle breakdown) organ dysfunction and increased clotting of the blood as well as autonomic reactivity, to name but a few of the detrimental effects of surgery. This technique is not at all new, having been introduced in the 1940s, but Henrik Kehlet was one of the first surgeons to champion its use in a multimodal pain therapy approach to minimize the need for opioid analgesics during surgery.

approach was needed, Kehlet engaged anesthesiologists, surgeons, nurses and even physiotherapists – championing perioperative care as a team sport; each member invested in optimizing the patient's outcomes together.

A colo-rectal surgeon by training, Professor Kehlet focused first on his own area of surgical expertise; demonstrating that using the ERAS protocol-driven fast-track approach, the need for staying in the hospital for recovery could be cut in half – at least. From between eight to eleven days, to just two or three days; with far less complications besides.

Kehlet's siren call for surgery-specific standardization of anesthetic and peri-operative medical care was answered by the American Society of Anesthesiologists in launching the Perioperative Surgical Home concept of perioperative medical management. The ASA charging anesthesiologists (as specialists in medical perioperative care) to help drive the process across different surgical specialties in their hospitals – creating the Perioperative Surgical Collaborative to assess the outcomes from these actions in hospitals throughout the United States.

Improved surgical and anesthesia outcomes the unquestionable result of a surgeon asking the right questions: "Why is this patient still in hospital, today?"

Checklists

Boeing was going for broke.[20] In 1934 the War Department Air Corps had circulated a tender for a new long-range bomber. The aircraft needed to be multi-engined, carry a massive bomb load, reach a flying speed exceeding 200mph and have a range of at least 1,000 miles, preferably twice that. Working in total secrecy, given the competitive nature of the air industry, the B-17 prototype was ready for its maiden flight by July 1935. Highly sophisticated for the time, the plane sported not just two or three, but four massive cowled engines, enclosed cockpits and retractable landing gear. Wing flaps and electric trim tabs assured better performance and maneuverability, while the four hydraulically operated constant-speed propellers optimized speed, but required individual careful adjustments of fuel-mixing to assure maximum thrust – adding immensely to the complexity of flying the machine. Dubbed the Flying Fortress because of the many gun turrets protruding from the airplane, data from practice flights leaked to the press suggested that the plane would proficiently out-perform the competitors. Two other aircraft manufacturers, Martin and Douglas, planning to tender only marginally modified planes at a flight competition scheduled on October 30, 1935 at the Wright Field, Dayton, Ohio.

Hence, as the competition for the tender was regarded as a mere formality and all but won by the Flying Fortress, the Air Corps' chief test pilot, Major P. Hill, strapped himself into the cockpit with confidence. Applying full thrust to all four engines, the plane roared down the runway and took off. Climbing steeply – far too steeply – it rose to around three hundred feet, stalled, rolled on its side, crashed back on the airfield and exploded – killing two of the five crew members – Major Hill included.

Investigators later established that the elevators and rudder were locked – Hill forgetting to disengage this before take-off – causing the plane to go into a death-stall and the contract for the new bomber awarded to Douglas: their DB-1 bomber declared the competition winner. The War Department Air Corps concluding that because the Boeing had crashed, it was too complex to fly safely – a news reporter underscoring the thought by headlining an article on the unfortunate crash: "Too much airplane for one man to fly."

The result: Boeing lost the contract to Douglas and almost went bankrupt, but not quite. A few test pilots in the Air Corps were convinced that the B-17 was flyable; so the Army purchased a small number as test planes.

Before the advent of the complex Boeing B-17, flying a plane may have been scary but it was a relatively simple task to perform – like berthing a sailboat in a fitful wind. Now it was far too complicated to rely on a pilot's mere memory to execute. In a quandary, the test pilots came up with a solution: they developed a checklist. Simple in format, it could fit on an index card. Step by step the cards described what needed to be checked on the list to taxi, take-off, fly and land a plane. With this pilot's checklist in their cockpits, Flying Fortress aviators flew more than 1.8 million accident-free miles; the army eventually buying more than 13,000 of the leviathans – tipping the balance in favor of the Allies against Germany in the Second World War.[3]

Think of a checklist like your shopping list. You know what you need to buy, but faced with the bewildering choices in front of you in the crowded shopping aisle – distracted by someone pushing their cart in your way – you just can't remember in the heat of the moment what you need to purchase. Unless you refer back to the list – crumpled in your hand – prompting you to select the right course of action. A checklist is just that: a reminder; an aide-memoire. It is *not* a substitute for experience, or a decision-making tool. *You* have to decide whether the wilted salad that presents itself in the refrigerator display will do your planned supper justice, based on your experience of such matters. The shopping checklist just has "salad" written on it, reminding you to buy one.

Checklists in medicine have not been used much until the last fifteen years or so – and then sparingly. Contrast this with the seven decades in aviation instigated by the Flying Fortress disaster – the realization dawning that to fly complex airplanes safely, too many steps for a pilot to memorize were required.

One reason why checklists have not been adopted much in medicine is that patients and their diseases are far more various than airplanes. The surgeon, Dr. Atul Gawande outlining the problem in his book *The Checklist Manifesto* thus: "A study of forty-one thousand trauma patients in the state of Pennsylvania – just trauma patients – found that they had 1,244 different injury-related diagnoses in 32,261 unique combinations. That's like having 32,361 kinds of airplane to land."

With this kind of variability in the patients they will encounter, physicians have been largely unwilling to believe that a simple checklist could improve the situation.

Fortunately, Dr. Peter Pronovost, an anesthesiologist, thought differently. Practicing intensive care at Johns Hopkins University, he attempted to stand-ardize and improve the outcomes of just one task: placing a central line in the intensive care unit (ICU). Central lines are placed in a patient's neck to cannu-late the internal jugular vein emptying into the heart. In 2001, in his hospital, central-line infections, a result of this procedure, were seriously sickening – and sometimes killing – one in ten patients. Using a checklist for fellow doctors, he standardized each step in the procedure – the hospital mandating each be veri-fied and checked off by an observing nurse. Steps like: washing the hands with soap; cleaning the patient's skin with antiseptic; covering the patient with sterile drapes from head to toe; wearing sterile gloves and a gown, hat and mask; and covering the insertion site with sterile dressing at the conclusion of the procedure. These steps – which were nothing new but sometimes forgotten – now had to be performed; the checklist serving as both a reminder and confirmation that these essential actions to minimize infection had been taken.

The outcome spectacular: no central-line infections in the following year. The checklist had improved the level of performance of the physicians by forcing good behaviors in the management of their patients.*

In the operating room, like the ICU, we are beset by failure.

Failure to identify the right patient or procedure; the patient getting the wrong operation.

Failure to follow important safety steps ensuring that necessary drugs have been administered and equipment is in place.

Failure to communicate with our colleagues as we are distracted by an immediate crisis.

Failure of technique and apparatus.

Failure to call for help in an emergency – failure upon failure – in this highly complex, emotionally-charged environment. Our patients suffering from our failures.

To try and address this problem on an international scale the WHO Surgical Safety Checklist was developed.

In 2006, Dr. Atul Gawande, an international surgical safety expert based in Boston, received a telephone call from Geneva. A woman with a British accent was calling on behalf of the World Health Organization. They wanted help with a problem. The WHO had established that worldwide surgery and anesthesia was exploding. But was so unsafe that it constituted a public danger; in fact, a crisis.† Could Dr. Gawande provide a solution? Could he develop a global program that would decrease the surgical death rate of a million patients a year? The problem was understandable. Surgery and especially essential surgery that saves life and limb – or the unborn child by Cesarean section – had burgeoned to over 230 million cases a year. But the necessary skill sets to perform them, had not kept pace. Faced with a surgical emergency, doctors and nurses did what they could with limited resources and training. The result: seven million patients a year were left seriously disabled. A crisis, indeed.[3]

When you're not sure what to do about a problem, you hold a meeting.

---

* The approach of standardizing and documenting each step for patient care and procedures would eventually be called "care bundles." This standardization of practice could then be used to assess the outcomes of care.

† There is another crisis: mortality associated with lack of surgery and anesthesia worldwide far exceeds mortality from the major infectious diseases: malaria, HIV and tuberculosis. The Lancet Commission reported that in 2010 there were an estimated 16.9 million deaths from lack of essential surgery and anesthesia, while the deaths reported for malaria, (1.17 million), HIV-AIDS (1.46 million) and tuberculosis (1.2 million) were fourfold less.

Dr. Gawande did; bringing together interested surgeons, anesthesiologists, nurses, safety experts and even patients, from all over the world, at the WHO headquarters in Geneva. Participants invited first to provide oral testimony – based on research and personal experience – and then to offer suggestions on how to resolve the problem. A few suggestions were abandoned;

- An incentive payment scheme for surgical success: too complex;

- A set of officially published standards or guidelines forcing co-operation in operating rooms: the resulting two-hundred-page tome would likely gather dust on a shelf, unused.

Other suggestions drew on previous experiences garnered in different institutions. Experiences like the pre-incision *"Cleared for Take Off"* checklist, which verified right patient/right procedure and ensured that protective antibiotics had been given. Developed by a pediatric surgeon* to combat infection because only one in three children undergoing appendectomy in his institution received their antibiotics on time before the checklist; improving to 100% ten months later upon checklist implementation.

And experiences like the *"Team Briefing"* where the surgeons, anesthesiologists and nurses in the operating room stopped briefly to talk with each other before surgical incision – Was there likely to be significant blood loss? Were there any risks or concerns that the team should know about? In so doing getting everyone on the same page before surgery started.

Still others recounted experience with a *"Surgery Preflight"* checklist – all with a similar design and intent – to remind and verify that important steps had been taken. But this one had thirty items; far too many for routine use.

Surgeon Gawande distills the WHO crisis to its essence: "Surgery has, essentially, four big killers wherever it is done in the world: infection, bleeding, unsafe anesthesia, and what can only be called the unexpected."[3]

The unexpected, a completely different potential failure, is what one must prepare for when the perilous journey of surgery is embarked on. A human body was not meant to be sliced open from stem to stern by a surgeon to excise strangulated bowel that has perforated – leaking infected feces. All manner of

---

* Another pilot.

unexpected, unanticipated problems may be encountered that no checklist can comprehensively prepare for.

Consider surgery in the past. The surgeon captain of the ship, dominating the operating room, believing that he and only he can determine the fate of his patient.

When a simple amputation was the planned operation this may have been the case. Not today. The surgical environment is far too complex. There is multidisciplinary division of tasks, labor and expertise requiring a team effort – much like an orchestra creating a symphony. To be effective the team needs to be cohesive with each executing their expected roles and all invested in a common outcome: surgical success and full recovery of the patient.

Independently, recounting their experiences at the WHO meeting, participants realized that no one checklist could do this complexity justice by anticipating all the failures the team must be prepared for. The most promising approach was to stop and talk briefly before surgery – getting on the same page – about the patient's unique issues and critical dangers they might face together. Further, to foster communication throughout the case, one of the described checklists called for each team member to identify themselves by name and role: "I'm Berend Mets, the anesthesiologist," setting up the opportunity to accurately and clearly communicate individual or common concerns that might arise throughout the case. People talk to each other when they know each other's names.

While the WHO participants allowed that the described approaches likely had merit; improving perceptions of teamwork, guarding against wrong procedures, and assuring timeous antibiotic administration – none so far provided conclusive evidence that a surgical safety checklist could provide what the WHO was seeking; a measureable inexpensive solution to the problem: safe surgery and anesthesia.

Nonetheless, by the end of the WHO Geneva conference, meeting attendees agreed that a well thought-out Surgical Safety Checklist should be designed and tested on a large scale. A working group subsequently extracting key components from the checklists that had been provided, and so, informed by aviation design and implementation theory – gleaned from seventy years of checklist preparation – the Surgical Safety Checklist was created in 2008.*

---

* WHO Surgical Safety Checklist can be found at www.who.int/patientsafety/safesurgery/tools_resources/SSSL_Checklist_finalJun08.pdf?ua=1.

It had three "pause points" central to its design. Three pause points, indicating when a system of checks needed to be performed:

- Pause point 1: Prior to anesthesia (Is the anesthesia machine and medication complete? Is the pulse oximeter on the patient and functioning? Difficult airway and aspiration risk? [7 check boxes in total])

- Pause point 2: Prior to incision (Confirm introduction of team members; confirm the patient's name, procedure, and where the incision will be made. Have antibiotics been given? Is essential imaging, like X-rays, displayed? [7 check boxes in total])

- Pause Point 3: Before being wheeled out of the OR (Completion of instrument, sponge and needle counts; To the surgeon, anesthetist and nurse: what are the key concerns for recovery and management of the patient? [5 check boxes in total])

Incorporated into a visually appealing, laminated A4-sized card, the checklist displays three vertical columns, one for each pause point, colored in different shades of green.* Each green column housing the respective checklist questions with a check box for verification next to it. Entitled the WHO Surgical Safety Checklist – the World Health Organization committed to providing funding for a pilot study to assess its effectiveness.

Launched that same year, eight pilot hospitals around the world (from high and low income countries) started implementing and studying the utility of the checklist in their operating rooms; hoping to study 500 consecutive patients at each site.[13]

The study results impressive: rate of death was decreased by 47% and major complications by 36%.† Just exactly what the WHO had hoped for in seeking Dr. Gawande's help in addressing the crisis.

But was it just the simple checklist that helped to solve this problem or was there something else at work? The investigators themselves and many others

---

* In many operating theatres, surgical scrubs and drapes are green in color because this is nature's most calming color, that of most trees and plants.

† The rate of death was 1.5% before the checklist was introduced and declined to 0.8% afterwards (p=0.003). Inpatient complications occurred in 11.0% of patients at baseline and in 7.0% after introduction of the checklist (P<0.001).

have asked this vexing question.[21] The likely answer: the checklist fostered better communication and enhanced teamwork and system improvements while timely reminders helped identify patients properly and assured that antibiotics were administered on time. Rather than just the mechanics of ticking off boxes on a check list these many intangibles helped to improve the safety of care.

Tellingly, when operating room staff were asked, "If you were having an operation, would you want the checklist to be used?" Nine out of ten said, "Yes."

Just like when you are a passenger in an airplane. Would you want the pilot to use the checklist? My guess is your answer will be, "Yes," too.

To be clear, checklists are not how-to guides, they are not protocols, they are just simple tools allowing experts to conduct their practice safely, be that flying an airplane or operating on or anesthetizing a patient. They are not substitutes for experience or expertise. A key question of safety is when to follow judgement rather than protocol, especially when abject failure brought on by the complexity and novelty of the situation, is staring you in the face.

The Airbus A320, its twin engines howling, lifted up gracefully from La Guardia airport, turning out towards Manhattan on a cold, clear, January afternoon. First officer Jeffrey Skiles easing back the yoke as he assured full thrust of the powerful jet engines. Sitting on his left, Captain "Sully" Sullenberger and he had spent a few short minutes before takeoff engaged in a pre-flight briefing; introducing themselves,* running through checklists, flight plans and any concerns they had about the trip ahead. In so doing, getting on the same page – morphing from individuals to a highly-trained team – ready to deal with any problems that might lie ahead. In the back, 155 passengers and crew were tightly strapped in their seats as they climbed through 3000 feet – flying headlong into a pack of Canada geese. Bird strike! the birds collided with the plane; thudding on the fuselage clearly heard on the cockpit voice recorders. Double bird strike; both engines whined to a halt† – loosing thrust completely 90 seconds into the flight – the smell of burnt chicken suffusing the cockpit. "What just happened?" Sully calmly asked.

---

* They had never flown together before, both highly experienced pilots.

† Jet engines are able to deal with small birds but are designed to shut down when a large bird is ingested, to avoid

"Bird strike. I have lost thrust from both engines."

Recognizing the crisis, the pilots then followed standard procedure, like well-oiled machines. "My aircraft," came the reply as Sully took over controls. He was the senior pilot and had a direct view of the Hudson River flowing along the west side of Manhattan Island to the left of the airplane.

"Your aircraft" Skiles retorted, immediately busying himself with the "Engine Failure" checklist on the cockpit monitor to see if he could restart the engines.

Imagine this. Pilots are trained to look for places to land as they take off. Always fearing that engines might fail, they develop back-up plans computing from experience what might be the safest alternative based on altitude, engine thrust, estimated glide distance, airspeed and landing location. The options for U.S. Airways Flight 1549 were stark: either return to La Guardia or try to reach Teterboro Airport in New Jersey – they had no more than three and a half minutes of glide time.

"When did you decide that you would land in the Hudson?" I asked Captain Sullenberger, at an Anesthesia Safety Conference where he was the guest speaker.

"Thirty-five seconds after the bird strike. I knew that we could not safely reach the other two alternatives,"* he replied.

Banking the plane to the left, the massive George Washington Bridge spanning the Hudson River between Manhattan and New Jersey came into view. The cockpit eerily quiet as the plane lost altitude, both men calmly executing emergency procedures. FLY THE AIRPLANE: step one on the checklist for "Engine Failure" was Sully's prime responsibility, while Skiles ran through the checklists trying to start the failed jet engines and readied the plane for landing – there was no checklist for a water landing.

"Pull up...pull up...pull up," the computerized voice of the low altitude warning system called mechanically as they descended even further, clearing the George Washington Bridge, and lining up the plane to attempt the first ever recorded water landing on the Hudson river.

"Flaps out?"

---

them exploding. Normally an Airbus can fly with one engine when the other is temporarily incapacitated.

* Flight computer simulations constructed by the National Transportation Safety Board, taking into account this 35-second delay that Capt. Sullenberger called the human factor, bore him out. The plane would not have made either of the two offered runways and would have crashed before reaching them.

"Got flaps out." New York skyscrapers dwarfing the plane as it descended further towards the ice-cold water.

Sully turned to his fellow pilot, "Got any ideas?"

"Actually not," came the reply. Now, on final approach, there was nothing more to do but use their hard-won experience and skill to land this highly sophisticated plane.

Pilots, crew and passengers all bracing for impact; the plane ploughed into the frigid water, a bow wave engulfing the cockpit, the windscreen wipers furiously cleaning the windshields, as the plane settled down gracefully like a wounded bird in the Hudson.

A New York Waterway ferry speedily arriving to help save all 155 people on board for another day.

Not too much airplane for *two* men to fly – as a team!

9

Perfecting Practice – Assistant Professor, Columbia University

Running Residency Trainig – Developing Anesthetic Techniques
for New Surgical Procedures

New York Presbyterian Medical Center, Columbia University, Manhattan, circa 1995.

Practice makes perfect.
– A proverb used to improve performance since 1550

"From the frying pan into the fire," remarked Nolan Weight Esq., the immigration attorney I had stumbled on in the New York City Yellow Pages. Enlisted to help me get a Green Card upon being offered a job as an assistant professor of anesthesiology at Columbia University, Nolan was referring to my move from Cape Town to New York City. Probably not far from the truth in 1992, considering the location of New York Presbyterian Hospital in Washington Heights right next to the George Washington Bridge,* spanning the Hudson river.

Created in 1928 at the upper reaches of Manhattan Island, Columbia Presbyterian Medical Center was the first of its kind, incorporating a number of different institutions such as Sloane Hospital for Women, at one site. Affiliated with Columbia University College of Physicians and Surgeons – the second oldest medical school† – Columbia Presbyterian was one of the prime training sites for residents in anesthesiology in the United States.

My start at Columbia was not particularly auspicious.

As a brand new attending anesthesiologist in a new country practicing in a world-renowned center, I had to find my feet while teaching residents at the same time. A set up for failure.

Joining in July, the first month of three years of training for new residents, made the opportunity for mishaps legion.

Labelled a regional anesthesiologist‡ practicing regional and general anesthesia,

---

* The same bridge that Dr. Virginia Apgar (first division head of anesthesiology at Columbia University) wanted to fly under, and Capt. Sullenberger flew over, many years later.

† The first medical school in the United States was established at the University of Pennsylvania in Philadelphia.

‡ Regional anesthesia is practiced as a supplement to or instead of general anesthesia. So named because the techniques employed use injected local anesthetics placed close to bundles of nerves in the body, blocking sensation in regions of the body. Most commonly used in orthopedic anesthesia to allow surgery to be performed painlessly on a limb, these techniques can also be employed for general surgery, like a hernia repair. The nerve bundles can be identified using different techniques. Direct needling and asking the patient if it "hurts" in the nerve distribution area – a time tested approach – is little used today. An alternative, which we were newly employing at Columbia at the time, was to use an electric "nerve stimulator" attached to a sharp needle. The needle would be placed through the patient's skin and advanced in the general direction of the nerve bundle in question – from a knowledge of the underlying anatomy. Sometimes called a "Muscle Twitch Monitor" because when the needle was in the right place this fact was confirmed by watching for movement (or twitching) of the muscle groups innervated by the nerve bundle in question. This identified the right place to inject local anesthetic which would transiently "block" the nerve supply to the affected limb; ablating sensation and often all muscle activity for the duration of the local

because a colleague from South Africa, Dr. Robin Brown, was an expert on the subject, I did not wish to disappoint. Far from adept, I experienced three complications in the first month.

Complications I had not encountered in Cape Town.

The first – a patient who had prolonged numbness in her arm from the automatic blood pressure cuff we had used.

The second – a patient who suffered a spinal tap and headache after an epidural anesthetic I had placed.

The third was potentially far more serious – eloquently demonstrating advances in equipment design that have made anesthesia safer; you cannot do this with modern equipment today!

Assigned a first-year resident, we were fumbling through a "mask" anesthetic. So called, because after intravenous induction with propofol, we maintained the anesthetic only by clamping a mask to the patient's face and administering isoflurane though it. A relatively new anesthetic agent at the time that I was not altogether familiar with. Manipulation under anesthesia was the innocuously sounding, very painful, procedure we were performing – the orthopedic surgeon wanted to set straight the patient's seventy-year-old knee. Sounds easy enough, but isn't. It's a fine balance of depth of anesthesia for a short but painful procedure. If the patient was too light, she could go into laryngospasm – closure of the airway – when the surgeon reset the knee. To deal with the pain we add nitrous oxide to the oxygen we administer – turning the nitrous oxide gas flow on the blue rotameter knob to read four liters and dialing down the oxygen flow on the white colored knob to two liters – standard operating procedure, providing a mixture of 70% nitrous oxide and 30% oxygen. Sufficient oxygen to keep the patient oxygenated and the saturation monitor reading 100% and beeping happily.

Tightly clamping the mask to the patient's face, my resident peered intently at the orthopedic surgeon, anticipating his every move. Equally intently I watched the anesthesia bag – mirroring the patient's inhalations and exhalations – for signs of sudden hesitancy; indicating lightness and possible laryngospasm.

anesthetic. Usually two to three hours, but much longer if required, depending on the amount and type of local anesthetic like lidocaine or bupivacaine deposited. Today we make use of ultrasound imaging to identify the nerve bundles, nevertheless sometimes still using a Twitch Monitor to be doubly sure. In the U.S.A., there is now a Regional Anesthesia Fellowship; an extra voluntary year of training, after completion of the residency. Regional Anesthesia is also a component of residency training, usually incorporated in the requirement for a total of three months of acute and chronic pain management experience.

Sure enough; the surgeon pulled – her inhalation stopped – then stuttered on. Taking over the mask from the resident to be sure that it was well applied to the face with my left hand – I applied gentle positive pressure – by squeezing the bag with my right.

"Dial up the isoflurane to 3% please." I endeavored to deepen the anesthetic to counter the painful stimulus. Not quick enough. She went into full blown laryngospasm; her saturation dropping slightly to 98%, the pulse ox[*] tone starting to deepen. "Give 100% oxygen," I countered, now trying to squeeze gas into her lungs by clamping the mask harder on her face. The saturation was plummeting – 80% – the pulse ox sounding ever lower intonations. I couldn't believe it. I had never seen the SAT[†] drop so fast. "Give SUX quickly." The resident bumbled – but did. I was hoping to break the laryngospasm, allowing me to better force 100% oxygen into her dying body. Saturation 50% and sinking. I intubated her and called wildly, "Get Dr. Brown." Connecting the endotracheal tube to the anesthesia tubing, I squeezed the anesthesia bag and listened to the lungs – tube in the right place – still the SAT was dropping. I was at wit's end. How could this be? She was intubated and gas was flowing into her lungs and still the saturation was not coming up – in fact it continued going down.

Dr. Brown rushed into the OR to save the day. He sized up the problem immediately. Extreme hypoxia; we were administering 100% nitrous oxide and no oxygen at all. The blue rotameter knob turned *up* instead of *down*. We righted course immediately; 100% oxygen flooding her lungs, and not a minute too soon as the heart was already in downward spiral – slowing down from lack of oxygen.

I had nightmares about this case fearing that the patient might suffer a stroke or a heart attack. Fortunately, we were all lucky and she left the hospital unscathed.

The resident and I much the wiser and equipment manufacturers adapting anesthesia machines to make sure that 100% nitrous oxide (devoid of oxygen) can never be administered to patients again – bleeding in oxygen automatically to ensure at least a 21-30% oxygen concentration – avoiding the extreme hypoxia we encountered.

---

[*] Pulse oximeter, this is the "slang" used in the OR by anesthesiologists.

[†] Saturation, again the "slang" used in the OR.

Despite these travails, I must have done something right because two things happened in my first year at Columbia. One I asked for, the other I didn't.

Running Residency Training

I can never understand why Americans like to put their feet up on tables!

Edward D. Miller Jr (1943-), a genial, charismatic giant of a man, is larger than life. Characterized by some as a hail-fellow-well-met, Ed, as chair of anesthesiology at Columbia, created opportunities for others. A catalyzer by nature, he would eventually become the dean of Johns Hopkins Medicine.

Today he had his feet up on the center table in my office, coming to see how his new attending anesthesiologist, freshly recruited from South Africa, was doing. "Fine Dr. Miller, I am very happy to be here."

"Berend, do you want to run the residency program?"

"Yes – Dr. Miller." (I could never call him Ed, until years later). "Can I speak to my wife and get back to you tomorrow?" This had not really been part of my plan. I wanted to start a research lab and practice cardiac anesthesia and generally get ahead so that one day I would have the skill sets and academic record to serve as a chairman of anesthesiology, probably back in South Africa. This was however an immense opportunity, offered nine months after my arrival, to learn about academic anesthesiology on the fast track – running one of the most respected residency programs in the country. The problem was, it was not in the great shape it might have been – residents in training were deserting the program. Morale was down and structured training often lacking; no organized curriculum an example.

I said yes, thinking I could fix this in three years or so, and then get on with my research in earnest, having just completed my PhD in pharmacology at the University of Cape Town. Little knowing that together with the newly appointed Dr. Wendy Silverstein as co-director, we would run the program together for the next nine years; bringing it back to its former glory.

You win some you lose some. Not every aspirant anesthesia resident is cut out to be an anesthesiologist. Just like not everyone is meant to be a pilot. The proof of the pudding is often in the eating. Hoping to be a pilot myself, I took flying lessons. The take-offs and landings were great fun and I could do them quite well; it was the flying that was the problem. I became so disorientated in the air, that I would never be able to find the airfield to land safely. I abandoned the idea. So too in anesthesia training. Residents have to actually practice anesthesia to know whether they are suited. Do they have the physical dexterity, multitasking ability, reaction times and mental fortitude to administer anesthesia competently in a constant high-stress environment? And do they want to? And most importantly, does the residency training program, in their ongoing assessment of the resident's performance, believe that the graduate will be a competent, safe, anesthesiologist in the future? This is where the rubber meets the road. The Residency Clinical Competency Committee has to determine whether the trainee is competent to continue, needs remediation, or failing this, should be terminated from the program – guided to choose a different specialty which might better suit his skill set, temperament and aptitudes. A most difficult determination to make, often against the individual's wishes, but made in the interest of graduating safe competent anesthesiologists.

The unsuspecting public would want no less from Pilot School!

A further absolutely key consideration in clinical training is that the patient must be held safe, at all times, despite the fact that residents are learning, especially in a procedural specialty like anesthesiology. This is managed in anesthesia training by an initially intensive "one on one" period – faculty being paired with a resident for a month's training – and then close supervision by a specialist of all "critical events" like intubation, extubation or the placement of regional anesthetics. Day and night, weekend or not.

In the United States the Accreditation Council for Graduate Medical Education governs all residency training. Running to thirty-four pages in length* the *ACGME Program Requirements for Graduate Medical Education in Anesthesiology* stipulates exactly what residency training programs need to incorporate in order to assure appropriate training and be certified by the ACGME. Considering this the basis for running a good program at Columbia, we annually reviewed the requirements and made sure that we addressed each newly brought stipulation in our program. Beyond this, running a good residency training program is really quite simple. There are but five key considerations:

- A good clinical patient base for experience and a well-organized, structured and delivered education curriculum is essential.

* Accessed Feb, 2017 at www.acgme.org/Portals/0/PFAssets/ProgramRequirements/040_anesthesiology_2016.pdf.

- Anesthesiology faculty must be inspired and engaged to teach and supported with positive feedback for their endeavors.

- A fair evaluation system of the residents must be established which provides constructive feedback to ensure their appropriate development.

- Should remediation be required this must be provided with as its goal the outcome of an outstanding specialist in the discipline of anesthesiology.

- A safe nurturing environment for education needs to be assured for the resident learner throughout their training experience.

During their training and upon graduation from an ACGME approved program, anesthesiology residents are subject to examination by the American Board of Anesthesiology (ABA). Success conferring specialty certification as a diplomat of the ABA. Having already been trained in England and South Africa, the ABA kindly "grandfathered" me in to the system and upon examination I became a proud diplomat in 1996 – a goal I had set out to achieve many years before – never thinking that one day I would be practicing anesthesia at one of the top medical centers in the world.

Developing Anesthetic Techniques for New Surgical Procedures

Surgery and anesthesia is a team effort; improvements in surgical and anesthesia practice closely intertwined. Surgeon Atul Gawande states it well: anesthesiologists are like co-pilots, integral to the success of an operation.

Mehmet and I were having a disagreement!

Better known as Dr. Oz,* Mehmet had just completed his cardiac surgical fellowship at Columbia in 1993 and was a newly minted assistant professor of surgery.

I had been granted my wish and recently transferred to the cardiac anesthesia team. An assistant professor myself, Mehmet and I carried the same rank. I was having none of it.

---

* Dr. Mehmet Oz is the host of the TV program *The Dr. Oz Show.*

Our first meeting ever – at nine at night – we were sorting out our differences on how to manage a critically ill emergent cardiac patient, already on the operating room table, next door. Admitted to the theater without my agreement – I thought he wasn't ready yet – we were heatedly debating the situation in the traditional place, the scrub anteroom well out of earshot of the OR. Upon settling our differences and coming to an agreement to proceed (after a heated alpha-male debate), Mehmet said, "Turn around," then grabbed me around the chest pinning my arms to my side. "One, two three, scream," and we did, together, as he lifted me off my feet – our united yell echoing in the aluminum-clad scrub room. Then we went off and did the case together. Much like Dr. Christiaan Barnard and Dr. Joseph Ozinsky before us; that is how we started becoming a team.

Minimally Invasive Direct Coronary Artery Bypass Graft (MID-CAB) Surgery

"Mehmet what do you have in your hand?"

"A newly designed retractor. I need to have it sterilized so we can stabilize the heart."

Scheduled in Room 20, the thoracic room where we only occasionally did heart surgery, I had seen the patient's name listed on the Operative Schedule. Surprisingly, next to his name was, 'CABG – Tietz Thoracotomy.' Surprising because in 1994 we were performing all coronary artery bypass grafting surgery using cardiopulmonary bypass. Routinely performed via median sternotomy; cardiac surgeons sawing open the chest and placing foot-long retractors to crank open the sternum to gain access to the heart. In contrast, a Tietz thoracotomy was a tiny – maybe three-inch – incision in the anterior chest wall; keyhole surgery at best.

With so little access to the heart, how would we manage to place all the cannulae necessary for cardiopulmonary bypass – commonly used so that the heart could be stopped completely; critical to this precision blood-vessel surgery? Cardiac surgeons needing a completely stilled heart to do the microscopic suture attachments of the left internal mammary artery – previously dissected free off of the chest wall – to the LAD.* In so doing bypassing the stricture that had caused the ischemic heart disease the patient suffered from.

---

* LAD: Left anterior descending artery.

Using special telescopic magnifying glasses (loupes) – allowing the surgeon to see in painstaking detail – to do this precise work; any heart movement critically disturbing their ability to perform the surgery concisely.

"Berend, we're not using bypass, I am just going to make a small incision, take down the internal mammary artery and then suture it to the LAD. We're not stopping the heart, we're going to keep it beating. I am going to use my retractor to hold down the heart muscle. Will you give some drugs to slow the heart and decrease its beating bounce, so I can see what I am doing?"

This was ground breaking: a first attempt at keyhole cardiac surgery without cardiopulmonary bypass – a technique that would later be popularized as "off-pump CABG surgery," or OPCAB.*

I prepared the patient for cardiothoracic surgery using every monitoring device I could find. Placing a double-lumen tube so that I could stop ventilation of the left lung when Mehmet needed a quiescent surgical field, and testing the Swan Ganz catheter to determine the patient's baseline cardiac output: around five liters a minute – just fine. To guard against the two complications that would force us to abandon this new approach – emergently – and crash onto life-saving cardiopulmonary bypass; namely, coronary vessel spasm – I started a nitroglycerine infusion; and for ventricular fibrillation – a lidocaine infusion.

"Give heparin." Mehmet had freed the internal mammary artery and was ready to start the critical part of the procedure suturing the clamped IMA to the LAD just past the stricture that was clearly visible on the patient's cardiac angiogram, performed to plan for the operation.

---

* In addition to Columbia, there were a few other centers in the U.S. and Europe that were developing "minimally (less) invasive" techniques to perform CABG surgery (MID-CAB surgery). Chiefly motivated by a wish to allow earlier recovery of patients (not subjected to large surgical access incisions and the detrimental effects of cardiopulmonary bypass) and the need for blood transfusion. The key problems to address with this technique was that it might not be as secure during the procedure as the then standard approach and whether the surgical outcomes – the patency of the grafted blood vessels – were as good, given that the surgery was performed under adverse circumstances on a beating bouncing heart. Hence the need to find an approach to still the heart locally around the site of suturing the IMA to the LAD, that Dr. Oz was developing, using his new retractor. The two prongs of the sterilized retractor pressed down on each side of the LAD allowing him to better suture the IMA to it. Possibly not as secure for the patient during surgery, because the small incision did not afford the surgeon the opportunity of quickly converting to cardiopulmonary bypass should the heart start fibrillating or fail – the chest would need to be opened emergently to cannulate the aorta for bypass. (Cardiopulmonary bypass is far from innocuous so avoiding using this would be beneficial for the patient in question). These two facts eventually drove OPCABs to be performed through large sternotomy incisions and the development of expensive and complicated cardiac stabilizers and suction devices that could help lift or draw the heart partially out of the mediastinum facilitating this precision surgery.

Consider this: a tiny hole in the chest, two small retractors pulling it open. Below this the heart is sliding in all its fatty redness as it beats and with each contraction bounces into view. Mehmet adjusts his loupes and peering down, places the retractor; two prongs on each side of the LAD just past the stricture. "It's beating too much. Do something, Berend." He wanted me to slow the heart and stop it contracting vigorously so he could see properly what he was doing and start the meticulous surgery.

Blood pressure and cardiac output were already down from the retractor pressing on the heart – not good in this "beating heart" surgery because we needed enough blood pressure to keep the rest of the coronary blood flow intact; in turn to keep the heart from failing to pump enough blood to sustain itself. Like operating on a leg calf muscle while a runner is sprinting, only worse. If the heart fails, it's over, and we would have to crash on bypass. I gave a bolus of phenylephrine (a vasoconstrictor drug which contracts blood vessels in the body) hoping to bring up the blood pressure – stimulating the baroreceptors in the aorta – which in turn causes a reflex parasympathetic nervous system response; decreasing the heart rate and lessening its contractility. Seemed to work; Dr. Oz and his assistant busying themselves with the anastomosis. For a brief while only though.

"It's beating too much."

I glanced at the cardiac output: around four liters, okay, BP 100 systolic, okay. I gave some verapamil* and dialed up the sevoflurane concentration – both designed to decrease cardiac contractility – and administered a further double dose of phenylephrine for good measure, knowing full well that hypotension would be the consequence of the verapamil and sevoflurane administration.

"It's still moving too much – very difficult to suture. Give Inderal."

Inderal† is the most potent beta-blocker we have. Designed to decrease heart rate and contractility profoundly, we are all a little scared of this drug, as administration can cause acute cardiac failure. Glancing at the cardiac output, now at a low three liters, I drew some up from a readied vial, and injected 1mg of propranolol hesitantly.

---

* Verapamil is known as a calcium channel blocking drug and is used to treat hypertension. It has as a side effect decreased cardiac contractility, which would decrease the bounce that Dr. Oz was experiencing, making the suturing exceedingly difficult. Sevoflurane, the anesthetic agent, also decreases cardiac contractility through inhibition of calcium-induced myocardial contraction coupling.

† Inderal is the trade name for the generic drug propranolol.

"Good, much better. Give more!"

I looked at the cardiac output: it was 2.4 liters, about the same as Louis Washkansky's, the first heart transplant recipient's. "Mehmet, I can't. We cannot decrease the cardiac output further."

"Okay, almost done" as he straightened up and looked over the ether screen at me.* "Thanks, I'm reperfusing, see any ischemia on the EKG?"

"No," I replied, "and no fibrillation either. Well done." And it was, very well done; the patient recovering fully and leaving the hospital much sooner than usual.

And my, yet to come, small contributions to developing anesthetic techniques in the tried and true tradition of enabling advances in surgery?

Mehmet ran a course on MID-CAB surgery for visiting cardiac surgery and anesthesia teams hoping to learn the techniques developed at Columbia University. And I? I gave the "how to" cardiac anesthesia lectures, going on to help develop anesthetic techniques for left ventricular assist device placement,[†1] thoracic lung volume reduction surgery[2] and eventually publishing the first case report on two patients receiving cardiac anesthesia for robotic surgery.[3]

---

* The "Ether screen" is often called the Blood Brain Barrier – the anesthesiologist's side being the "brain" side – are the dividing drapes that are erected – sterile on the surgeon's side – allowing anesthesiologists access to the patient's head and neck while the surgeon operates on the "blood" side of the barrier.

† An artificial heart placed to support left ventricular failure. This device was being developed and studied at Columbia University. Battery powered, patients with this left ventricular assist device, could walk or even cycle. Developed as a transition step to eventual heart transplantation, newer devices, which are smaller, are now so called "destination therapy," with heart transplantation no longer necessary.

10

Complications – Things Don't Always Go Well

A deadly complication and how a pilot spearheads efforts to improve anesthetic safety, using human factors design

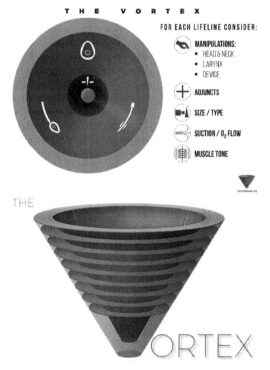

The Vortex Approach to airway management, depicting a mask, LMA and ET tube, and central (blade) prompt for a tracheostomy when needed.

So that others may learn and even more may live.
– *Martin Bromiley*

Complication

Definition: a difficult factor or issue often appearing unexpectedly and changing existing plans, methods, or attitudes.
– *Merriam/Webster Dictionary*

Victoria and Adam – the young Bromiley children – were thrilled by their first plane trip as a family. Returning from a brief vacation five days before their mother, Elaine's, planned nose surgery on March 29, 2005, they excitedly dropped her off at the hospital early in the morning. Going on to shop for cookies with their father, Martin, ready for her return home after the operation. Elaine, an elegant thirty-seven-year-old, who had worked in the travel industry before becoming a full-time mom, had had trouble with her sinuses requiring surgery to remedy. Quite relaxed about the surgery she waved bye to the children, reassured by her ENT surgeon that it was a routine operation – nothing to worry about.[1]

Elaine's anaesthetist, Dr. Alderman,* a diligent and caring man, reassuring her further by his calm presence, examined her briefly before transfer to the operating theatre, noting in the anesthetic record a separate assessment of her airway: 'mouth opening OK'; 'Mallampati II'†; 'neck movements slightly restricted'.[2] To start the anesthetic Dr. Alderman's assistant placed an intravenous cannula in Elaine's left hand and attached routine blood pressure, EKG and pulse oximeter monitors prior to anesthetic induction. The SAT‡ registering 98% without any added oxygen administration when Alderman induced anesthesia with

---

* This and the other doctors mentioned are not their real names. The events are reconstructed based on the referenced Independent Review and from video reconstructions of the events available at: http://simpact.net.au/index.html.

† The Mallampati Score airway assessment is standard operating procedure in anesthetic airway evaluation. Introduced by Dr. Sesahagiri Mallampati, the score is determined by asking the patient to open their mouth wide and to protrude their tongue out as far as possible. Peering into the mouth, the anesthesiologist performs a visual assessment of the relationship of the back of the tongue to the roof of the mouth. Although not faultless, the score is widely used to predict the likely difficulty of intubation. A Score of I or II – usually easy, and of III or IV – often difficult and sometimes indicating that the patient may be impossible to intubate using conventional laryngoscopic devices.

‡ SAT, a term for oxygen saturation monitored with the pulse-oximeter.

propofol and started a continuous infusion of a very potent narcotic: remifentanil, through her IV at 8.30a.m. That's when the trouble started. Planning the placement of a laryngeal mask airway (LMA) via her mouth and over the larynx to maintain her airway, the situation deteriorated fast because Elaine's muscles had stiffened markedly and Dr. Alderman could not open her mouth. SAT 75%* within two minutes, and dropping, despite further propofol administration to release her clenched jaw; Alderman could not place a second smaller LMA to rescue the situation. Belatedly applying a facemask to try and push added oxygen into her lungs – nothing was working. Elaine turning blue as her SAT dropped to 40% – the pulse oximeter growling its dreadful groan to match the deadly drop in oxygen levels. Monitor alarms activating and ringing as the situation in the OR deteriorated. Elaine's airway collapsing, and her heart rate slowing from 81 to 69 to conserve scarce oxygen supplies – panic was palpable in the theatre. Three nurses present trying to help the awful situation, well aware that a crisis was developing. One running out to get a tracheostomy tray which could be used to make a neck hole in Elaine's airway, saving her life. Another calling the ICU to get a bed for Elaine. Now eight minutes into the case, with Elaine totally bereft of oxygen, Dr. Alderman decided to change tack to try and manage the collapsed airway. Trusting that intubation of the trachea would help, he administered SUX† to paralyze her, hoping to introduce a laryngoscope into her clamped mouth. Succeeding, he introduced the laryngoscope only to find that he could barely see the glottic opening of the larynx. Nevertheless, attempting to insert a tube – unsuccessfully. Responding to the pandemonium in the room, a second anesthesiologist, Dr. Brand, came in to assist. He too tried intubation, multiple times – both doctors fixated on performing this procedure – trying over and over again. Twelve minutes into the case, Elaine's oxygen SAT no higher than 40%; her heart rate slowed further starting the now imminent death spiral. Her ENT surgeon who had just come into the OR also attempting intubation, while the nurse announced timidly – far too softly for the din in the OR – that she had brought the lifesaving tracheostomy tray into the theatre. Twenty minutes into the case, Elaine's SAT never budging from 40%, her heart rate started climbing to 140. Completely blue from unrelenting cyanosis, she was making jerky movements of her limbs, a sign of brain irritation.

---

* Any saturation less than 90% is significantly low.

† SUX, a term for succinylcholine.

Martin Bromiley, a trim crew-cut pilot, had flown commercial jets for more than twenty years. An aviation safety expert, he had frequently lectured on the subject. Returning to their North Marston home from the weekly shop with Victoria and Adam he began preparations for Elaine's return. Reflecting later on the critical situation playing out in the theatre before us Martin aired, "We have a breakdown of leadership, of situation awareness, of prioritization, of decision making, of communication, and of assertiveness – and these same human factors are ironically present in 75% of aviation accidents."[3]

Martin was of course absolutely right. The clinicians in their focus on establishing Elaine's airway from above had lost all sense of time and could not see the big picture. The solution to help her and the skills to do so were present in the room. Staring them in the face. The ENT surgeon and the tracheostomy set could still save the day if they approached the airway from below. Cutting a hole in Elaine's trachea to place a tracheostomy tube would permit oxygen to flow to her lungs (despite the collapsed airway) and so avoid imminent brain death. The outcome possibly altogether different if aviation safety practices had been incorporated in Elaine's anesthetic care today.

Finally, twenty-five minutes after induction, an intubating laryngeal mask airway was successfully placed. Elaine's SAT slowly rising to 90% while a tracheal intubation was attempted through the device without success. Her blood pressure rocketing up to 192/126 after the remifentanil infusion was switched off – twenty minutes later – upon which Elaine started breathing again by herself; SATs still fluctuating dangerously low at times and never reaching higher than 95%.

Dr. Alderman, believing Elaine was showing signs of recovery and that breathing was of a normal pattern, transported her to the post-anesthesia care unit of the hospital. Here, her blood pressure and oxygen saturation levels continued swinging erratically and showing no further signs of recovery, Elaine was transferred to an intensive care unit at the adjacent National Health Service hospital, not far from London.

Answering the telephone ringing in the Bromiley home at 11a.m. that morning, Martin spoke to the ENT surgeon. "Elaine is not waking up properly from the anesthetic. Can you come back in?" Visibly alarmed he hurried to the hospital, the ENT surgeon describing that there had been a problem in keeping Elaine's airway open. Had they attempted a tracheostomy? Martin asked. "No," the ENT surgeon replied, explaining that the safer option was used – letting her wake up naturally.[4]

"It was one of those things. Accidents sometime happen. We don't know why. The anaesthetists did their very best, but it just didn't work out. It was a one-off. I am so sorry."[1] Then allowed into the ICU to see Elaine, he was met by Dr. Alderman. Saying nothing at all, Alderman hugged Martin forlornly before leaving him to see Elaine. "She didn't look any different." But she was. Elaine was in irreversible coma; brain scans performed earlier, already showing that devastating brain damage and bleeding had occurred. There she lay, near dead, when she had been so beautifully, vibrantly, alive that morning.

Thirteen days later, her brain ravaged by the complication of not being able to establish an airway, Elaine died. Martin, who had been sitting vigil with her daily in the ICU, was summoned back urgently, finding her still warm to the touch. Bending over, he kissed her good night and goodbye; fifteen years of happy marriage concluding in tragedy.

But the anesthetic story does not end here. In fact, it only really begins.

Martin, assuming that a similar approach would be taken to that of the aviation industry, asked if there would be an investigation – an accident investigation of Elaine's death. "You get an independent team in. You investigate. You learn."

"No," answered the head of the intensive care unit where Elaine had died. "That's not how we do things in the health service. Not unless somebody complains or sues." Dismayed that others might not be able to learn from the obvious failures that had occurred and upon overhearing a night nurse's comment, "It's terrible, I can't believe what happened," Martin persisted. In aviation, failures are prized opportunities for pilots, airlines, manufacturers and regulators to learn from – not to be missed! – in attempts to enhance safety.[1, 4]

Witness the results of an accident investigation of the B-17 Flying Fortress bomber in the 1940s. Pilots were crashing the plane into the runway on final approach – especially after long flights when they were exhausted. Dr. Alphonse Chapanis, a psychologist with a PhD from Yale, asked to investigate. Reviewing crash case histories; their timing and circumstances, as well as the human psychological factors involved, he found a simple solution to the identified source of human error: the two cockpit levers to retract the wheels and set the landing flaps were right next to each other. The tired pilot mistaking the one for the other. Recommending affixing a wheel (undercarriage) and a triangle (flaps) to the appropriate lever so as to remind weary pilots of their intended function – in so doing improving cockpit system design and the source of crashes disappearing overnight. In turn, Dr. Chapanis was considered one of the founders of the discipline of ergonomics – more recently named "human factors" design. Accident investigations having provided learning opportunities that have advanced aviation safety immeasurably over the intervening years.[1, 4]

Martin Bromiley's doggedness in seeking an investigation paid off. By May 2005 an expert, Dr. Michael Harmer* was engaged to conduct an inquiry. Providing an independent review that read much like an anesthetic version of a National Transportation Aviation Safety Board's report of an airplane crash investigation; citing multiple human factors that might have contributed to the failure to save Elaine from harm.[2] Human factors like fixation on intubation; failure of communication; failure to raise the alarm early in a "can't intubate, can't ventilate" crisis; failure to recognize the passage of time and the deteriorating situation in the room; and failure of situational awareness to address the main problem: lack of oxygen delivery to Elaine's brain. Sucked into the vortex of deterioration, clinicians could not see the big picture, nor recognize the self-evident solution to the problem: performing a tracheostomy early enough to save her life.

Recommendations in the Harmer Report abounded:

- Ensure an atmosphere of good communication in the operating theatre such that any member of staff feels comfortable to make suggestions on treatment.

- Ensure that the necessary equipment is available.

- Ensure that there is a time and record keeper in the room. Given the problem that time passing was not registered and anesthetic record keeping was not performed.

- Ensure that Airway Management Guidelines are prominently displayed in the theatre and that the protocol is followed.

- Ensure that the "Difficult Airway" is rehearsed; the report suggesting that a study day on difficult airway management be held for all staff.[2]

---

* At that time the President of the Association of Anaesthetists of Great Britain and Ireland.

Called in to the hospital, Martin Bromiley sat down to read the report. Shock and recognition fighting equally to gain the upper hand in his mind. Shock that Elaine had died despite the obvious expertise and necessary equipment being available in the operating room that day. And recognition that he had read such reports before. "I thought, this is classic human factors stuff. Fixation error, time perception, hierarchy." And further, that there was a "signature" to the events that unfolded in the operating room that day. Had they been recognized and rehearsed for, the complication of Elaine's airway collapse might have been averted.

Seeking to understand how the healthcare industry responded to such investigations, he first made the Harmer Report public, "so that others may learn, and even more may live." Just like an Aviation Accident Report is widely publicized. And then started asking questions of all he could find. Phone-calling around the National Health Service to ask them. Soon determining that:

> The state of healthcare isn't the result of carefully planned and focused efforts driven by a need to maintain or improve safety; it's the result of hundreds, even thousands of years of inertia, denial and vested interest which have created an organization more akin to the teaching professions of old or the church," adding, "All the learning about ergonomics/human factors in aviation and other industries seemed to have reached the hospital gate and gone no further.[5]

Finding common cause with many individuals he phone-called, but no organizational structure to drive a human factors approach to healthcare, Martin booked a hotel room for a meeting. Inviting like-minded individuals, and experts from other industries and academics like Dr. James Reason and Dr. Ken Catchpole. Dr. Reason, a cognitive psychologist, had championed the Swiss Cheese Model for accidents occurring in industry in the 1990s. Positing that in structured safety-conscious environments, factors had to line up in unpredictable ways (like the holes in a Swiss Cheese) for accidents to happen. Catchpole, a human factors expert, defining the science thus: "Enhancing clinical performance through an understanding of the effects of teamwork, tasks, equipment, workspace, culture, [and] organization on human behavior and abilities, and application of the knowledge in human settings."[5]

Together with these two psychologists and many others who attended this first hotel meeting, Martin started the Clinical Human Factors Group (CHFG) in 2007. Its goal: to accelerate the impact of human factors adoption in healthcare. Inspired by the Royal Aeronautical Society Human Factors Group – CHFG has grown massively in influencing safety in the healthcare industry since.[5] Especially in the high-risk endeavor that started it all: anesthesia and the difficult airway. Producing a video, *Just A Routine Operation*, a documentary recreation of Elaine Bromiley's case history, in early 2008, and making this widely available on the CHFG website for all to learn from.

Dr. Nicholas Chrimes (1967), an Australian anaesthetist, got it – early.

Drawing on the *Just a Routine Operation* video to teach human factors in many of the simulation courses he was conducting at the time at Monash Medical Center in Melbourne; Nic – a resourceful type – recognized early that the Difficult Airway Guidelines that might have been available to Dr. Alderman in managing Elaine Bromiley's crisis, were not really up to the task. They documented merely "what needed to be done" rather than reminding the anesthesiologist of the options for airway management and prompting action in the time-pressured emergency situation. "Under stress, cognitive capacity is the same as a hamster," Martin Bromiley has said, and so Nic sought to conceive an "implementation tool" for airway management that recognized and visualized clearly the 3 + 1 options available to assure oxygenation of the patient: there really being only three "non-surgical techniques" (Mask, LMA, ET tube) plus one surgical action (a tracheostomy) to save the day.

Nic was struck also by the fact that clinicians often made the status quo worse by poor decision-making and fixation, "responsible for turning a *can* oxygenate situation into a *can't* oxygenate situation" through repetitive attempts, damaging the airway. Another problem to be addressed was that there was really no shared understanding or common language that the whole team (anesthesia, nursing, surgeons) were familiar with in the OR that would indicate where in the crisis they were – in a vortex cone circulating down the drain, or rising up above the top in a safer "Green Zone," where the patient is being well oxygenated. The Green Zone allowing the team time to regroup – see the big picture – and plan the next critical management steps for the patient.

These ideas had been percolating in the back of Nic's mind for some time. "The idea for the vortex struck me one day. It was instantaneous! It popped into my head as a complete concept. I literally drew it within a minute of it having occurred to me and declared (as a joke), 'It's a vortex!' The name stuck."

The Vortex can best be described as an emergency airway cognitive implementation tool.*[6] Meant to be prominently displayed in the OR, it is conceptually visualized – horizontally and vertically – as a cone; the outer Green Zone ring depicting the safe zone where the patient's pulse oximeter monitor registers good saturation levels (90-100%). The spiraling, narrowing, deepening blue-colored cone indicating ever-decreasing saturation levels as time passes – and life drains away – during attempts to manage the airway using any, or all of the three, depicted airway devices: Mask, LMA, ET tube – in any order judged to be the best approach, for the clinical situation, by expert anesthesiologists. Alongside the horizontal cone diagram are a list of pictorial cues prompting interventions that might be used to optimize the situation. While at the cone's very center, spiraling deep down beyond the darkest blue, is a green patch. Another safe zone, hoped for should other methods fail and a tracheostomy is performed – triggered by a prompt depicting a knife blade cutting through skin. The clinician ever aware that this life-saving Vortex approach needs to be rehearsed and practiced – using simulation – to assure the best outcome in the OR.

Nic consulted Martin Bromiley, "a result of the miracle of the internet." Requesting whether Nic had permission to create two videos to be used as simulated teaching tools using Elaine's case history as a basis? A before Vortex video and an after Vortex implementation video; a "What If" video?[7] Could Nic demonstrate the use of the Vortex approach in a simulated environment to help anesthesiologists learn how to use this life-saving approach?

Yes, said Martin. Nic should do whatever he thought best.

"What If?"

Elaine Bromiley is wheeled into the OR having been previously evaluated by Dr. Alderman and attached to the waiting monitoring devices: BP 128/83, HR† 77 and SAT 100%. The potent opioid remifentanil is again started through the placed IV and propofol is administered, the anesthesiologist again struggling to place the LMA because Elaine has gone stiff, her jaws clenched

---

* Pictured at the start of this chapter.
† BP = Blood pressure, HR = Heart rate.

tight as her SAT starts dropping. Deciding to start facemask ventilation, Dr. Alderman asks the assistant to draw up more propofol, placing an oral airway and starting bag mask ventilation. Referring to the Vortex diagram affixed prominently to the wall, he declares, "We are being sucked into the vortex here." The assistant reading out loud from the list of pictorial cues – prompting interventions that could be used to optimize the situation – they decide that increased muscle tone is a problem that needs to be addressed. Switching off the remifentanil (which can cause muscle stiffness), they administer more propofol hoping to rescue the problem. Nevertheless, they still cannot place an LMA as the SAT reaches 89% (blue zone, spiraling down) and so call for help immediately. Again, clearly announcing steps to optimize bag mask ventilation, read off from the Vortex diagram, (manipulation of device, two-handed mask ventilation) – the SAT plunges to 77%. Nothing is working! Dr. Brand arrives with two nurses, one dispatched to get the Difficult Airway trolley. "How can I help?"

"We are stuck in the Vortex, can you draw up some SUX?" Dr. Alderman asks. "Can I help co-ordinate things?" Dr. Brand taking the lead as the ENT surgeon approaches from another theatre, also offering help.

"Have you been in the Green Zone at any point?"

"No."

"Have you had an optimal attempt of any of the non-surgical techniques?"

"No, we have not yet inserted an LMA and have not had successful mask ventilation with the patient paralyzed."

"Okay, 100mg SUX administered." Turning to the ENT surgeon, Dr. Brand asks him to prepare the tracheostomy kit as the SAT continues to spiral downwards, plunging to critical depths, alarms ringing in the background. The SAT tones growling as Elaine's heart rate starts to increase.

Dr. Alderman changes tack and attempts intubation, while Dr. Brand plucks the Vortex diagram off the wall – the better to read it – visibly pulling everyone onto the same page in implementing the approach. SAT 57%, HR 122.

Noting that two attempts at intubation have been unsuccessful, while the SATs continue dropping, Dr. Brand announces that the ENT surgeon should get ready to "cut the neck." Palpating Elaine's neck to determine the correct position for placement, as the tracheostomy equipment is pulled rapidly from its sterilized packs.

"Critical desaturation two minutes," the recording nurse announces, time-stamping events, as anxiety mounts palpably in the room. Dr. Alderman declaring that because an optimal attempt at intubation has failed, he must revert to trying LMA placement now that Elaine is fully paralyzed. Placing an LMA, Dr. Alderman attaches the breathing system and starts squeezing the anesthetic bag, hoping to see an end-tidal carbon dioxide ($ETCO_2$) trace on the monitor, indicating that oxygen exchange and ventilation of Elaine's lungs is secure.

Dr. Brand announcing, "This will be an optimal attempt at LMA insertion," implying that the next step – should this fail – will be to "cut the neck." Hoping so to enter the Green Zone at the very center of the vortex – the last means of saving Elaine's life. The whole room quiet – save for the deteriorating SAT tone and ringing alarms – all eyes fixed worriedly on the $ETCO_2$ monitor, hoping against hope to see the slightest blip of the monitor trace, indicating success.

Dr. Brand: "Okay we have got some CO_2." True enough, there is a slight deflection displayed on the monitor, tentative at first and then rising steadily indicating better and better ventilation. The SAT delayed in rising – but nevertheless improving – 40, 43, 46, 48 and on to 90. "Okay, we are in the Green Zone now, Dr. Alderman, what do you want to do?" Discussing the options and the precarious nature of the airway situation, they decide to allow Elaine to wake up from the anesthetic rather than proceed...

Concluding the *What If?* video.

Given the competent anaesthetist and ENT surgeon in the room that fateful day in 2005, there is no way of knowing whether the Vortex Approach – using human factors-informed anesthetic techniques – would have saved Elaine Bromiley's life that day.

What is known however, is that Dr. Nic Chrimes was asked to present the Vortex Approach at the Society for Airway Management Annual Meeting in Seattle in 2014. Branded the 'Battle in Seattle,' it was held as a debate among anesthesiologists, as to the best airway resource for difficult airway management: the American Guidelines, the Canadian Guidelines or the Vortex Approach. Showing Elaine Bromiley's case video first at the start of the session, as an example of the sort of situation which such airway resources were designed to address – participants attending the meeting instantly recognized that, "there have been days when that could have been me."

Audience polling at the end of the debate confirming the Vortex Approach, the overwhelming winner – garnering 90% of the vote, and spearheading its widespread implementation around the world. Martin Bromiley receiving a medal from the Difficulty Airway Society, that same year, in recognition of his contributions.

Martin went on to bring up his two children and has married again; still living in the quiet rustic village of North Marston. Receiving the Order of the British Empire in 2016 for his work enhancing healthcare safety through the Clinical Human Factors Group, he continues to chair the organization while serving as a captain for a major British airline.

Asked whether he wanted an official position in the National Health Service, he responded: "I am not an expert on medical practice. I am just a guy who flies planes."[4]

11

Flying the Anesthesia Machine – The Professor, Pennsylvania State University

Coordinating an Operating Theater – Valentine's Day

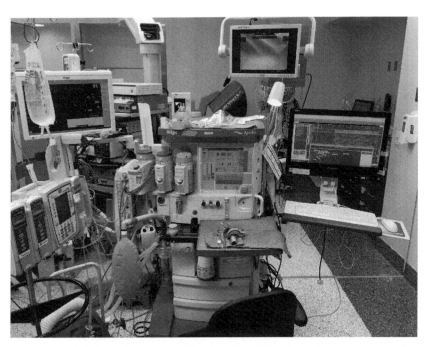

Operating Room 20. Electronic anesthesia machine. Checklist and emergency manual attached on the right. Robotic surgical console and video screen in the background.

The Full Catastrophe of Life.
– *John Cougar Mellenkamp, 1996*

Operating theater 20 is ready, or at least the necessary surgical and anesthesia equipment is, at this early hour: 6.00a.m.

So too are the other thirty-four operating rooms, and ten alternate site anesthesia locations* at the Penn State University College of Medicine, Hershey Medical Center.

After ten years at Columbia University, I moved here to serve as the Professor and Chairman of the Department of Anesthesiology – doing so for the past fifteen years.

As the Chief Supervising Anesthesiologist on Valentine's Day, I am coordinating all anesthesia services and together with the OR charge nurse, running the Operating Room Tracking Board. The Tracking Board, four massive electronic tracking monitors, stretching a full six-meter length across the entrance wall leading into the operating theaters, displays the planned cases by anesthetizing location for the day. Much like air traffic control at an airport, the Tracking Board allows us to track progress of the patient through the perioperative process, using a series of symbols electronically exhibited. The symbols indicating patient status and disposition: in preoperative holding; already in the OR and anesthetized; surgical incision has been made; the wound is being closed – the appearance of a red telephone symbol indicating that the estimated time of arrival of the patient in the recovery room, is one hour on.

To ensure that I can stay in immediate contact with the one hundred or so anesthesiologists, residents and nurse anesthetists assigned to the respective locations, I carry two pagers and two in-house ASCOM phones. Each clinician mandated to carry one of each, so we can stay in ready contact for emergencies and reassignment to different locations, as needed, and at a moment's notice. As a level one high intensity trauma center, with emergency victims brought in by helicopter, this is an all too common occurrence.

Back to the elective OR Schedule:[†]

---

* Alternate site anesthesia locations where pediatric and adult diagnostic or therapeutic procedures will be performed under general anesthesia.

† This is not the patient's real name. A few details have been changed to ensure anonymity of the patient.

OR 20	METS/BEZSYLKO	Robotic Hysterectomy
JONES, JILL	HARKINS G	Robot-da-Vinci-Si
07.30	Outpatient extended recovery	Table-Regular-OR
09.23	ACE	Cystoscope Rigid Set
	General Anesthetic	

Generated in its final form midday – the day prior to surgery – it lists the patients for each OR; the anesthesiologist and nurse anesthetist that I assigned; the consultant surgeon (Dr. Gerald Harkins); plans for patient disposition after surgery (outpatient extended recovery); whether the patient visited our Anesthesia Preoperative Clinic for an Evaluation (ACE); the type of anesthetic (general); the planned operation (robot-assisted hysterectomy) and the OR equipment needed in the room by the indexed time (07.30).*

The OR schedule dictating, what and who, needs to intersect in the operating theater at the appointed time to ensure that the technology- and personnel-intensive process of modern-day surgery can take place. Three million dollars' worth of equipment,† coordinated by ten people, to achieve this noble end.

Around 2.00a.m. the aluminum box-shaped case cart is wheeled into Room 20. Brought up from the sterile processing unit three floors below, it is the size of an average refrigerator, filled with sterilized and disposable equipment, dispensed according to Dr. Harkins' Pick Card – outlining every detail of the sterilized equipment and materials he requires to perform the robotic-assisted hysterectomy, planned on the schedule today. Sterilized meticulously to minimize the risk of surgical infection. Take for example the Heaney hysterectomy forceps used for an operation the previous day. Heaped back onto, the now used and contaminated, Rigid Sterilization Tray, as part of a forty-piece surgical set, it finds its way – together with the rest of the possibly infectious surgical instruments – back onto the bar-coded case cart, it came from. Transported from OR 20 back down three floors by willing human

---

* The time allotted for the procedure is based on the historical average surgical duration times for the described operation by this highly competent surgeon.
† Da Vinci robot, anesthesia machine, mechanized OR table, infusion pumps, video towers and screens, imaging equipment, heating and warming devices, surgical equipment etc.

hands, it is deposited in DECON, the Decontamination Unit, below. Here to be processed by a gowned, masked, and completely protected decontaminator, who peers through his glass visor, while breathing through a special filter, wearing what looks much like a HAZMAT suit used by a fire fighter. (Lord knows what infective material could be returned in the case cart for his cleaning). Collected together in big bins, the Heaney forceps and other instruments are first scrubbed and cleaned using an enzymatic process, and then transported to the ultrasound unit; the high frequency ultrasonic treatment breaking down any lasting surgical debris clinging to the instruments. A dishwasher is next. Then, cleaned and dried, the Heaney forceps is inspected and tested for grip and safety (no sharp edges that can tear flesh) under a large magnifying glass – again by human hand – before being returned to the Rigid Sterilization Tray. Color markers placed in the corner of each tray, and atop the final pile of instruments, will indicate to the surgeon that the instruments have been properly steam-sterilized. The Rigid Sterilization Tray finally closed, and then sealed with a plastic indicator tab. The indicator tab displaying, an imprinted white semi-circle, which turns dark when fully autoclaved.

The Hershey Medical Center autoclaves are massive. Each the size of a small car. I counted six of them, all loaded with trays of varying sizes; small on top, large at the bottom, with a pipe to drain water from the condensed steam on the floor. Forty minutes at 270°F, is what it takes to render every instrument sterile – turning the indicators' colors – to verify the fact for Dr. Harkins tomorrow. Four hours for the whole process, about as long as the planned surgery would eventually take.

A hysterectomy – the surgical removal of the uterus – is a relatively simple operation. It can be performed either trans-vaginally – if the uterus is small – or via an incision in the abdomen: an abdominal hysterectomy. Over the last twenty-five years or so, hysterectomies are usually performed laparoscopically instead. Rather than opening the abdomen with a large surgical incision to remove the uterus, a series of small stab incisions can be made using plastic disposable "trocars" through which a laparoscope and other surgical instruments, like scissors and graspers, can be introduced and manipulated. The laparoscope displaying views of the uterus and abdominal contents on two or three video monitors hanging from the operating room ceiling – adjusted for easy viewing by the operating surgeons. In order to allow better visualization and surgical access to perform this keyhole surgery, the abdomen is pre-inflated with carbon dioxide gas; distending the abdomen to look like a balloon.*

Robotic surgery, developed around fifteen years ago, heralded a further advance in surgical technique.[1] Not actually performed by a robot but by surgical tele-manipulation; the Da Vinci Robotic Surgical System consists of three parts. Each a small telephone booth in size.

The first part, the surgeon's console, positioned on the far side of OR 20, allows Dr. Harkins to sit comfortably in a seat looking into a stereo viewer at a 3-D image of the operating field. Resting both arms on the console crossbar, his right- and left-hand fingers and thumbs grip lightly, the EndoWrist instruments that mimic his movements; translating these to electronic computerized signals which are replicated exactly – like his hands – in the surgical movement of two robotic arms attached to the second part: the Da Vinci Robot Patient Side Cart.

At 6.00a.m. this Patient Side Cart stands ready at the foot of the OR table. Its four robotic arms looking somewhat like a giant electro-mechanical spider; ready to be fitted with sterile attachments, from the case cart, and plunged into Jill Jones's abdomen for the planned surgical operation.

Two robotic arms perform the surgery – mirroring Gerald's every hand movement at the console – while the third arm can be used to provide surgical traction or access – a scrubbed and gowned assistant surgeon, at the patient's side, to detach and exchange this task-specific equipment. The fourth arm, a telescopic endoscope, is capable of transmitting dual independent visual images to the console eyepieces for proper binocular 3-D visualization of the surgical field.

The third part of the Da Vinci system is the Optical Tower. Again, the size of a telephone booth, it stands central in the OR, and is the brains behind the robot; housing the complex computer electronics and video screen used by the assistant surgeon to look into the abdomen.

---

* Called a pneumoperitoneum, this abdominal distension has multiple detrimental effects, particularly on respiration, that the anesthesiologist must deal with. All patients require a general anesthetic with intubation and mechanical ventilation to counteract the high intra-peritoneal pressure effects – impeding diaphragmatic function – which would result in respiratory failure. Further, this keyhole surgery often limits the ability of the surgeon to easily visualize abdominal contents, requiring extreme head up or head down positioning on the surgical table to displace intra-abdominal organs to do so. This in turn causes variations in heart rate and blood pressure which must be addressed by the anesthesiologist.

*

Modern anesthesia machines* are completely electronic. Much like a plane, you cannot fly if there is no power. Hence, we always have an ambu-bag attached on the back. Part of our pre-anesthetic checklist, we use this self-inflating ambu-bag to continue ventilating the patient by hand, should the complicated electronics fail.†

Weighing in at two hundred kilograms, the behemoth anesthesia machine, rides on four wheels, allowing it to be positioned at the head of the OR table, so that the anesthesiologist can administer anesthesia, while closely watching the video display monitors, and simultaneously accessing the electronic medical record, to document every aspect of the delivered anesthetic.

Often named after Greek Gods, like Apollo or Perseus, today's anesthesia machines are designed to accurately deliver, and monitor, the administration of anesthetic gases and vapors incorporating sophisticated ventilators to do so. Tethered by color-coded hoses – green, yellow, white and blue – attached into the back of the machine to the central delivered gas supply points overhead, the machines nevertheless also incorporate matching gas cylinders, to ensure that gas supply can be maintained – no matter what.

Switching on the machine provides a satisfying hum of electronic power as the patient monitoring video display attached on the left, the anesthesia machine monitoring display centered in the machine, and the electronic medical record computer screen attached on the right, light up with electricity. Ergonomically designed to provide key patient and equipment information at a glance, alarm settings are preset to warn the anesthesiologist of impending problems. Based on the cockpit design of airplanes, we call delivering an anesthetic: flying the anesthesia machine.

Crucially, the OR schedule also stipulates the operating room table required: "Table Regular OR." Again, completely electronic, different types of tables are required for different surgeries; the correct table essential to success.‡ Controlled

---

* Cleaned, serviced and equipped overnight with disposable or sterilized anesthetic supplies by the anesthesia technicians assigned to the rooms.

† In our ORs we have emergency non-electric equipment in the anesthesia machine drawer for such an eventuality; a torch, battery-powered pulse oximeter and manual blood pressure cuff device, in order to continue the anesthetic with intravenous propofol – as the vaporizers would no longer work in a power failure. All hospitals have emergency backup generators in the event of a power failure, with dedicated service to the operating rooms.

‡ OR tables may have different requirements for different surgeries; viz. orthopedic or neuro surgery. There may be

by the anesthesiologist using a remote control wired to the bed, the patient position during surgery is adjusted. Lateral tilt: left or right – head up or head down – often to extreme angles; the anesthesiologist making absolutely sure that the patient doesn't slide off the table during surgery. For the planned robotic surgery, Ms. Jill Jones will be slid down the table, after induction of anesthesia, her legs placed in stirrups, slightly raised above the bed.*

Consequently and reliably, all the necessary OR equipment is at the ready, prepared overnight for today, by willing unseen hands – waiting for the main players to arrive to complete the planned procedure: robot assisted hysterectomy on Jill Jones.

I could not be absolutely sure. But I thought they had just been holding hands, when I walked into Jill's cubicle. Her husband Jack, sporting a plaid shirt, sat next to her as they waited expectantly for the preoperative assessments to be concluded, on this Valentine's day.

Previously, Ms. Jill Jones had met Dr. Harkins in his office and the same day visited our Anesthesia Preoperative Evaluation Clinic. Brandishing the electronically produced preoperative evaluation record from this clinic in my hand; I ascertained her surgical, anesthetic and medication history. Noting that Jill was on chronic opioid pain therapy – using a fentanyl patch – she would follow our prescribed clinical and anesthetic protocol for such complex patients and be monitored closely, by our Acute Pain Service and Opioid Stewardship Program, post-operatively.

Around sixty years of age, Jill had experienced more than sixteen operations during her life.

"Almost more anesthetics than I have administered," I jokingly told her.

"Yes," she declared "I am a bionic woman."

Seeking to allay their mounting anxiety, I asked them a few stock questions before explaining the anesthetic plan.

---

different load limits depending on the patient's weight. Tables may have differing height, turning, angling and flex capabilities. Some need to be radio-translucent allowing x rays to be taken through the table without moving the patient.

* We never position the patient in stirrups before induction of anesthesia. Because should she vomit, we would need to tilt her rapidly head down and turn her on her side to avoid aspiration; not being able to do this if she was already strapped in the stirrups on her back. A tilting table is thus essential to the practice of anesthesia. Together with a working suction device – an essential checklist item– before induction of anesthesia.

"Did you get any rest last night?" Jack, a sprightly seventy-year-old, with a trim white beard, piped up. "I didn't sleep all night, but she did – intermittently."

"Yes, I didn't sleep well. I am afraid of cancer." Jill stated hesitantly.

"How was your trip in?" "Well she got up at four, and we drove in my big Dodge truck, sitting up high. It was too cold for the motorcycle!"

Jill, a florist by profession, had lost her first husband and moved to the Hershey area from Pittsburgh. Jack had lived in the area all his life, and upon the death of his first wife had been encouraged by his grandson to post on an over-50s dating website. Meeting online, Jack and Jill had been married for the last three years and were looking forward to a life together. Possible cancer – not the operation – their greatest fear.

Dr. Gerald Harkins, a joyous, industrious man, reputedly the largest volume robotic surgeon in the U.S.A., got up as usual, at 4.30a.m. Gulping down his breakfast, he arrived in his office by 5.00a.m. to complete dictations, review surgical notes and print out the history and physicals for today's patients – so he could be well apprised of the surgical problems we might encounter. Meeting up with his surgical fellow and two residents at 6.30a.m., they visited Jill in the preoperative suite, to reassure her, and answer any remaining questions, before seeing a few other patients in extended-stay recovery from the previous day's surgery. Meeting me in the OR corridor – Gerald and I got on the same page – conferring about today's patients before starting our first case together.

Beth Bezsylko, fresh from an invigorating run the day before, woke up as usual at 5.00a.m. An equestrian, who looks the part – slim, trim and poised – she completed her customary stretching exercises, fed the dog, cat and herself (coffee and a fruit granola bar) and launched herself into the waiting, newly purchased, grey Toyota Tundra truck. Arriving early at the medical center, Beth, a highly competent nurse anesthetist would be my co-pilot, anesthetizing with me all the patients booked for surgery in OR 20 today.

As the Chief Supervising Anesthesiologist (CSA) there is a lot to worry about. Not just flying the anesthesia machine in Room 20, but also coordinating all of the anesthesia services from 6.00a.m. to 6.00p.m. across the Institution. Flying the Institutional Anesthesia Machine together with one hundred or so anesthesiology department members, clinically active, this Tuesday. Consequently, I never sleep well. And never have to wait for the alarm to wake me at 5.00 a.m. sharp; I am usually awake much before. No different today. I'm up, showered, and after a quick coffee and granola breakfast – having reviewed the planned day's schedule while I eat – I am surprised to find a box of chocolates – heart-shaped – on my desk. Left for me the previous night by Ulane, while I was sleeping. Perplexed as to the reason for this gift, I put it in my briefcase and head off to the hospital.

Changed into my scrubs, I arrive 6.00a.m., in the nick of time, for the night/day charge nurse, handoff. Held in the windowed nursing station, across the main OR entrance hallway – we can all clearly see the Tracking Board with the day's work displayed before us. Running through the scheduled cases briefly, we plan for the placement of "add-ons," new surgical cases that have been booked overnight.

"Christy, let's put the pediatric surgical add-on cases in Room 1. I have a pediatric anesthesia team there" – matching the case complexity with the skill set of the anesthesia providers. "Christy, can you call the surgeon and let him know, and I will speak to Dr. Iglehart informing her of the plan?" This change in patient location, from the ADD-ON section of the Tracking Board, to OR 1, occurs almost immediately; the OR secretary changing the location in real-time on the computer screens, with a click of a mouse.

The process of scheduling add-ons continuing more or less constantly throughout the day; a surgeon calling to schedule a case with the OR – the call then directed to the CSA phone on my hip, to tell me about the patient's condition. The charge nurse and I conferring which OR we should put the case in – a neurosurgical case in a neuro room, a cardiac case in heart room, a trauma case in the trauma room. But if it is an abject emergency – any available room! Then displaying this on the Tracking Board and communicating with the surgical, anesthesia and nursing teams – so they are aware of the new case planned for their OR.

6:10a.m.

I head off to the OR conference room where the anesthesia night call team: four residents and a nurse anesthetist, have gathered with today's two incoming residents – a recovery room and a perioperative medicine rotation resident

– to discuss the night's add-on cases; planning for the day ahead. Dr. Eileen Micaroni, the call chief for the night, presents the cases. Some of which we have already placed in OR 1. But many not yet placed. Several booked for alternate site locations that need further optimization; to be coordinated by the incoming residents.

"Dr. Rossi, how would you anesthetize the case?" I ask. "What are the anesthetic considerations you are concerned about?" – referring to a pediatric patient with pyloric stenosis.*

"Is it a surgical or medical emergency?"

"A medical emergency." "That's right Dr. Rossi, good work." I thank them for their night's service, direct the day team as to their duties, and head off to OR 20.

6:40a.m. OR 20.

The scrub and circulating nurses are finalizing preparation of the surgical equipment. Drawing from the case cart, disposable and sterile equipment is passed to the scrub nurse already gowned, sterile-gloved, and ready. She will set out sterile trays heaped with forceps, clamps, curettes, scissors and other tools of the surgeon's trade; on the back table, draped and ready for action. The Mayo stand is prepared. Pulled over the patient when surgery starts to hang over the surgical site, it forms a resting place for surgical tools needed immediately.

The robot too must be prepared so that it can be used in the sterile field. And this is quite a performance; the scrub nurse encasing its massive articulated spider arms with sterile plastic. Looking much like a large tentacled mechanical monster – its enveloped plastic arms waiting patiently to pounce on the patient.†

"Hi Beth, good to work with you today," I say, as I walk into the OR, and go to the back of the anesthesia machine to check the emergency oxygen cylinder and ambu-bag before meeting in front.

Here Beth is readying the medications we will use to anesthetize Jill,

---

* Obstruction of the outflow from the stomach that presents more often in boys at or around three months of age.

† We put a sterile drape over this to avoid contaminating the plastic wraps so the patient coming into the room does not often see this fear-afflating device.

in our first case together ever.* Most of these medications are commercially available, prefilled, labelled syringes – ensuring sterility and accuracy of drug administration – dispensed through a computerized electronic cart system.

"What do we have today?" We compare our notes, having previously accessed the patient's electronic medical records and printed out summaries – literally getting on the same page – about the five patients planned for the day. I look up at the anesthesia machine humming faintly. Beth has switched it on and made sure that all the computers are married and working together; the three video monitoring screens – left, middle and right – ready and waiting to present vital signs and other data when our patient is connected. The middle screen displaying the anesthesia machine "self-test results." Instigated by Beth at a press of a button, the internal machine self-checklist demonstrating that: gas delivery and pipeline pressures, electronics, valve systems and sensor checks are in order, and: ventilator electronics, sensors, scavenger and safety mechanisms are working – without any leaks in the high- and low-pressure systems. While the machine monitoring system: electronics, oxygen sensor, gas analyzers and power source are intact – the emergency battery – 100% charged.

Suitably satisfied that the anesthesia machine is ready to fly, Beth busies herself with further anesthesia equipment preparation. I head off to the Tracking Board to co-ordinate another add-on that has just come through on the CSA phone, committing to meet Beth at Jill's bedside to interview the patient together.

7:20a.m.

Beth calls OR 20 from the preoperative holding area to see if they are ready for the patient. Accompanying Jill Jones on her stretcher to the operating room, she administers 1mg of midazolam along the way, to calm her fears, before entering the theater. Like a pit crew at a race, the surgical and anesthesia team are ready to situate her on the operating room table, question and verify that all the safety checks are in place, and attach monitoring and safety devices. "Jill, we are going to help you move from the stretcher to the OR table, and position your head in that yellow doughnut ring at the top of the bed please."

* We have more than 180 anesthesia clinicians: anesthesiologists, nurse anesthetists and residents, in the department.

As she lies down, Gerald, Beth, the circulating nurse and surgical residents move around her; all with specific tasks to get her ready for surgery – attaching the sequential compression device cuffs around her calves,* adding two arm boards to the bed, covering her with a warmed blanket, while attaching the necessary anesthesia monitors and connecting an intravenous line to the previously placed intravenous catheter in the back of her hand.

7:35a.m.

Finally, after all the preparation, we are ready to induce anesthesia and start surgery.

If you were a fly hovering high up in the center of OR 20 this is what you would see.†

Against the back wall, a robotic surgery console, its seat pushed back ready for Dr. Harkins to sit in. At the very center, the OR table – ringed by four video screens, hanging from the ceiling, allowing all in the theater to witness the robotic surgery to be performed. Upon the table, Jill Jones, readied for surgery, brightly illuminated by two umbrella sized surgical lights, suspended by articulated booms; her right side flanked by two electronic towers. One tower attached by a beam to the ceiling containing essential surgical tools: diathermy equipment, suction pumps and the like. The other, the Da Vinci System Optical Tower. At her feet, ready to dock, the telephone box size, tentacled electromechanical structure, that is the business end of the Da Vinci robot. On her left, a little away from the OR table, the gowned scrub nurse, is still preparing the back table and Mayo stand for surgery. And at the head of the bed – the anesthesia machine – its monitors now displaying Jill's vital signs in full color. Check measurements before induction, already electronically downloaded to an anesthesiologist's record of practice.

---

* SCDs or sequential compression devices are now routine. With the onset of anesthesia, venous return from the legs is slowed because of the lack of muscular activity which "pumps" blood back to the heart. This results in a substantial risk for deep venous thrombosis (DVT). To guard against this serious complication from surgery, SCDs are used. Cuffs are placed around each calf and connected by tubing to the electromechanical device placed below the OR table. This inflates sequentially mimicking ambulation and so accelerates venous blood flow velocity in the heart's direction minimizing the potential for DVT formation.

† Flies do occasionally appear in operating rooms and of course are a major potential infectious problem, should they alight in a sterile surgical field. The tried and trusted method of getting them out of the OR is to switch off all of the lights and open the theatre doors. Flies will exit reliably following the direction of the light outside.

Anticipating the induction sequence, I move next to Jill's left side and ready the intravenous line, as Beth places the plastic mask gently on Jill's face from the head of the bed, providing pre-oxygenation. "Smells like my Barbie doll," she says as I administer, lidocaine, fentanyl and some ketamine. Then I pause, as I always do, looking around and running through a mental check list: Suction? Blood pressure? Saturation? Emergency airway equipment? Before take-off. Take off – the administration of the intravenous induction agent propofol – to unconsciousness, is when we commit to the consequences of our anesthetic induction. Much as a pilot does when they deliver full thrust – pulling back the yoke as they near the end of the runway – committing to flight. There is no going back. With Jill, I am not particularly worried because her airway appears easy, and she is not very ill. I am anticipating a smooth flight, but we always have a backup plan. We call it Plan B. Much like pilots are taught to look for a place to land as they take off, so we plan how we will manage an unexpected difficult airway, or severe drops in blood pressure, should they occur.[*]

Everything goes smoothly. Beth intubates easily, after we paralyze Jill with intravenous rocuronium, connecting her to the ventilator to assist breathing for the rest of the case. Then the surgical team gathers closer,[†] as we together position her for surgery, cleaning her abdomen and then completely draping the patient in sterile material; just the surgical site showing.

Before incision we pause for a "Time Out."

Much the same as the WHO Surgical Safety Checklist, Gerald and his two assistants scrubbed and gowned, pause – getting on the same page – with the whole surgical team. Led by the circulator, everyone in the room stops what they are doing to concentrate on the Time Out. We each introduce ourselves. Then reading the electronic medical record from a computer screen, the circulator again identifies that this is the right patient: Jill Jones, for the right procedure: robotic hysterectomy.

---

[*] Beth and my third case this day was such a patient. Anticipating a very difficult airway upon induction of anesthesia, I asked a senior colleague to join us for the induction and we managed the patient safely together using a Glidescope. In such circumstances, we provide the patient with an "airway letter" to take with them describing our findings, so that should they need to go to another facility, this record of practice will be available to the new institution's anesthesiologists. We are starting to incorporate the Vortex Approach to difficult airway management, described in the previous chapter, department wide.

[†] They have been standing around should we need them for an emergency during induction.

Gerald: "The necessary images are displayed and equipment is available for the procedure."

Beth: "This is Jill Jones for a robotic hysterectomy. She has no known allergies, antibiotics have been given, SCDs are connected and working, and heparin has been administered. We do not anticipate the need for a blood transfusion."

Circulator: "Any issues or concerns?"

"No, no, no…" everyone in the room intones as Gerald's assistant introduces the Verres needle into Jill's abdomen to inflate it with carbon dioxide, making it look like a balloon.

Assisting with the placement of four trocars into the abdominal wall, Dr. Harkins helps his surgical resident introduce the robotic telescope, graspers and suction devices. Then they call for the robot to be pushed into place; docking the plastic-covered tentacles to the devices.

Finally, ready for the robotic hysterectomy to proceed, Gerald unscrubs and goes to sit at the robotic console, leaving his resident scrubbed, at the bedside, to reposition and alternate the necessary task-specific devices. His voice booming overhead from the console microphone, Dr. Harkins instructing her what to do, as the surgery proceeds.

The surgery safely underway, I leave Beth in the room to spend time at the Tracking Board – coordinating the anesthesia services for the hospital. Despite its apparent sophistication, the Tracking Board – designed to provide patient location and status – cannot properly, nor timeously, display the often-changing anesthesia teams assigned to the cases. That is for me to do, using a massive whiteboard and colored markers, attached alongside. Here I annotate the team assignments by OR for all to see, allowing me to make adjustments as needed across our forty-four anesthetizing locations.

Busily at work at this whiteboard, I am interrupted by one of our "swing" nurse anesthetists, who provides break and lunch relief in the rooms. "Happy Valentine's Day, Dr. Mets," says she, sticking a bright red tinseled heart on to my green scrubs. About three inches across, it sparkles there, just about in the right place, on my chest. "Thanks, Jody," as it suddenly dawns on me why the heart-shaped box of chocolates was on my desk this morning. I had completely forgotten.

Making a mental note to get some flowers for Ulane, I head off to the preoperative suite to interview and examine the next patient for OR 20, restarting the well-trodden cycle of anesthetic care that my fellow consultant anesthesiologists repeat throughout the day: preoperative suite – OR – recovery room. About thirty in number today, most consultants manage two ORs with either a resident or a CRNA as the primary anesthetist in each room. Consultant anesthesiologists mandated to be present in the room for all critical portions of the anesthetic: induction, recovery, or if anything untoward happens. "Don't get into trouble without me," is how I put it to the primary anesthetists working with me.

The CSA phone buzzes annoyingly on my hip; my pager is going off at the same time. "Dr. Harkins wants to open. He cannot find what he is looking for with the robot," Beth tells me, as I change course and return to the room. Jill having had more than sixteen operations, had developed a great deal of intra-abdominal fibrosis, making it exceedingly difficult to identify scarred and distorted anatomy using robotic laparoscopic surgery. Open abdominal surgery was needed to negotiate this difficulty. Fortunately, everyone is ready for such an eventuality. But because it was a change in status, Beth had correctly called me to inform me of the situation. The robot was removed, the abdomen deflated, and a large midline abdominal incision carefully made; Beth administering more anesthetic to counteract the increased surgical stimulation.

Prolonged, but eventually successful surgery, the result. Realizing that this extensive abdominal incision, in a patient on chronic opioid maintenance therapy, was likely to result in severe postoperative pain,[*] we engaged our Acute Pain Service. Dr. Hillene. Cruz Eng administering a specialized local anesthetic, TAP block, in the recovery room, after surgery, to counter the pain.[†]

10:43a.m.

The surgery finally over, and the planned cystoscopy complete, Beth and I allow Jill to awaken; turning off the desflurane anesthetic that has kept her unconscious of the complicated surgery that has taken place. "How are you

---

[*] Patients who receive long-term opioid therapy for pain (Jill received a fentanyl patch) have altered and enhanced pain sensitivity. To manage this, we provide ketamine and magnesium therapy intra-operatively and postoperatively use varying techniques to manage this major problem caused by the widespread use of opioids for chronic pain therapy. We have developed a clinical pathway for such patients in our institution.

[†] The transversus abdominis plane (TAP) block has been recently popularized – using ultrasound – to guide needle and local anesthetic placement in the abdominal wall between two muscles, the transversus abdominal muscle and the external oblique muscle. Deposition of local anesthetic in this so-called plane, between the muscles, numbs the sensory nerves supplying the abdominal wall, so providing analgesia, at the surgical incision site.

feeling, Jill?" I ask as we move her to the waiting stretcher that will carry her to the recovery room. "Pain," she grimaces slightly. "Where?" "Here" – her hand hovering over her lower abdomen. "I know…we will have the acute pain service help you as soon as you are fully awake"* – Beth pushing her out of OR 20 and on to the recovery room PACU.†

10:47a.m.

Closely on our heels a swarm of environmental aides, anesthesia and surgical techs sweep into the room to turn it over. Exchanging the used case cart and equipment, cleaning exposed surfaces, removing the trash and mopping the floor; readying the OR for the next cycle of anesthetic and surgical care.

Repeated 142 times this Valentine's Day – a far cry from the two surgical cases schedule for the *week,* when William T Morton publically administered the first ether anesthetic, 170 years ago, in Boston.

Today, the institutional anesthesia machine powers the modern day surgical engine, fueling hospital profitability and patient well-being.

6:00p.m.

My CSA responsibilities concluded, I hand over coordination to the two incoming anesthesiology attendings that will run the Board till 6:00a.m. the next day. Just six ORs running, the OB service upstairs, and one alternate site still in action.

No new add-ons listed on the board yet; I have had two pressing Valentine matters to address.

The first already managed: visiting Jill Jones in the recovery room, knowing that the ultimate gift: of life – no cancer – was likely. Jack and Jill able to continue their newly found life together.

The second, a present for Ulane, my partner in life. I rush down to the hospital gift shop, hoping it has not yet closed. Finding a beautiful bunch of cellophane-wrapped flowers, I pluck the sparkling red Valentine's heart from my chest, sticking it carefully on the floral wrapping – and head, happily, home.

---

* The problem is that she is still amnestic immediately after awakening and needs to give informed consent for the planned TAP block procedure. Jill needs to be fully conscious with intact memory to be able to give a valid consent for this pain-relieving procedure.
† PACU: post anesthesia care unit.

Epilogue

First Day and the Future

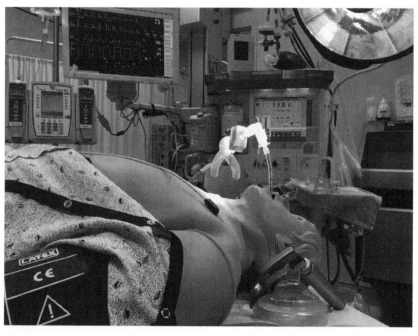

Computerized human mannequin, Pennsylvania State University Simulation Laboratory.

Prime non-nocere: First do no harm.
– *Hippocratic Oath*

Predictions are difficult, especially about the future.
– *Lawrence Peter 'Yogi' Berra*

First Day
July 2016, thirty-four years later.

Eyelashes flick open – closed – open, the human mannequin lies ready in the simulated operating room, replete with a state of the art anesthesia machine (labelled: Only for Simulation Laboratory Use). Overhead, the two surgical lights are on, focused down on the gleaming plastic body below. Wired up to an EKG machine, displaying computer-generated blood pressure, heart rate, and oxygen saturation on electronic monitors similar to those used in the operating room for live patients. Emergency drugs and equipment are at the ready, but no lives are to be saved today. Today – the first day of anesthesia training – the anesthesiology resident will "practice on plastic" in the Penn State University Simulation Center. Learning – without the stress of a patient interaction – how to prepare for and manage an anesthetic. He will learn how to run a pre-flight anesthesia machine check, interpret computerized caution messages, adjust alarm settings, and program infusion pumps. He will practice intubation with differing laryngoscopes, and learn how to start and set the ventilator, suction device and anesthetic vaporizers.

Properly forewarned; after four weeks of clinical practice "One on One" with a consultant anesthesiologist in the operating rooms – he will be back here in the simulation laboratory to be tested. An Observed Standardized Clinical Evaluation lies in his future, success allowing him to continue on to less supervised practice in the operating room. Critical to anesthesia practice, he will also receive training in medicine and pharmacy safety, before going to theater. Having first practiced on plastic, the resident is now well equipped to administer his first anesthetic to a live patient, when his first day of clinical training dawns.

Today is that day. The first day of one on one training. The resident is paired up with an attending anesthesiologist who supervises every step of this first month of clinical training. Teaching anesthetic practice while holding the patient safe, the attending is present at all times during the trainee's care of the patient.*

His first patient – a sign of the times in this age of obesity – a twenty-six-year-old presenting for a plastic surgery operation on the tummy. Having previously undergone successful weight loss surgery; an operation is now planned to remove excess stretched skin remaining after his bulk has shrunk – so reshaping the patient's body. Preparing for this first anesthetic, the resident had accessed the patient's electronic medical record the previous day on the hospital computer systems, printed it out, and annotated carefully, in rehearsal, his planned anesthetic – doses, sequence and timing. Exactly as I had told him to do in an introductory lecture – he had prepared himself mentally for this first clinical encounter, thinking through each step beforehand.

Upon completion of a thorough anesthesia machine check and preparation of anesthetic medications and equipment, his first patient is wheeled into the operating room and helped onto the surgical table. Monitoring is started immediately – attaching a disposable blood pressure cuff and a five lead EKG; displaying three views of the electronic activity of the heart on a large vital sign monitor, attached to the left of the anesthesia machine. A pulse oximeter probe is attached to the patient's finger, and the reassuring pulse tone – confirming 100% oxygen saturation – matches his heart rate precisely. The resident checks to see that all the data is automatically downloaded onto the electronic anesthesia record displayed on yet another touchscreen computer. Feeling a little overwhelmed, "like a firehose of information coming at me" he signals to the attending; I am ready. The gray-haired associate professor of anesthesiology, a nationally recognized badminton player and pilot, looks around – performing a mental check to see that all patient parameters are in order – and starts the induction of anesthesia, quickly administering intravenous lidocaine, midazolam and fentanyl followed by a slow bolus dose of propofol, easily recognizable by its pure white color.

Trying to stay calm, the resident fidgets with the mask that he has applied tentatively to the patient's face, and gently starts the bag/mask sequence, pressing on the disposable anesthesia bag filled with oxygen and sevoflurane

---

* The resident's increasing skills and knowledge base is tested and reviewed regularly and at the end of the one on one period, a decision is made as to their competence to be less stringently supervised. After which, the attending anesthesiologist will be present in the room at any critical events during the anesthetic and operation, but not be expected to be there full-time.

anesthetic, attached by plastic disposable hoses to the anesthesia system. Slowly, we watch the patient's chest rise as the new trainee successfully takes over breathing for the patient, who is becoming increasingly paralyzed from intravenous rocuronium drug administration. Nonetheless, raising his arm in involuntary movement – the patient is still too light – further propofol quickly administered before the resident performs a laryngoscopy and successfully intubates his first patient. I pass him my stethoscope so he can listen to the patient's lungs. The consultant anesthesiologist, obviously relieved by the successful intubation, completes the monitoring, showing our new resident how a temperature probe is placed in the patient's nose and helps attach a modified BIS electroencephalogram sensor to his forehead. An electronic brain wave trace – providing a reading of anesthetic depth – appearing in front of us on the vital signs monitor; all downloaded automatically to the anesthesia electronic medical record. Placing two electrodes on the face – just to the side of the patient's right eye – they assess the extent of muscle paralysis using an attached neuromuscular transmission monitor. The surgery starting, the badminton champion and pilot teaches our new resident quietly – behind the ether screen – talking to him in measured tones so as not to disturb the surgeon with a loud voice.

The tyro resident learning how to adjust the anesthetic depth according to the surgical stimulation and the patient's condition. The consultant, pointing out examples of the patient's monitoring status; the ventilator parameters of volume, pressure and lung distensibility as well as the inhaled and exhaled carbon dioxide and sevoflurane anesthetic concentration levels displayed on the anesthesia machine – situations that cannot be adequately simulated in the laboratory and require patient care to learn. As the successful operation draws to a close, he switches off the sevoflurane vaporizer and IV neostigmine – to reverse residual muscle paralysis – is administered; just as I did thirty-four years before with my first anesthetic. Neostigmine the only agent – administered during this case – that has withstood the test of time.[*] Calling out the patient's name, the resident watches carefully and notices the eyelashes: flick – open – closed – open; the patient is awake and coughing

---

[*] There is a new drug available which may well displace neostigmine as the primary reversal agent of neuromuscular blockade. Sugammadex is a modified gamma cyclodextrin, which acts by enveloping the muscle relaxant drug rocuronium or vecuronium so inactivating their effect in blocking acetylcholine binding to the nicotinic receptor in the neuromuscular junction which causes muscle paralysis.

lightly on the endotracheal tube. Pulling out the endotracheal tube – after a last squeeze of the anesthesia bag – leaving the patient's lungs filled with oxygen – just in case.

The resident's first anesthetic over – visible relief suffuses his face as he places a mask over the patient's mouth and nose with added oxygen, and gets ready to move him from the OR table on to the waiting stretcher.

Safe to say that barring the same neostigmine drug administration and certain time-tested approaches, this anesthetic – with its electronic monitoring and recording – looks very different from my experience over three decades before. At that time, we had only clinical signs of anesthetic depth, and monitored just blood pressure manually and kept a finger on the pulse to assess heart rate, documenting our findings on a paper anesthetic record with a pen or pencil.

Much has changed to enhance anesthetic safety, but what does the future hold for anesthesiology practice for this resident starting out his career in America? And what might that look like if we could look into the next decades?

The Future

The future of anesthesia lies in the developing field of Perioperative Medicine.

While there are certainly gains to be made in further anesthesiology subspecialization; enhanced simulation training; drug design and delivery; artificially intelligent equipment; alarm and monitoring systems; medical care delivery refinements using human factors approaches and system safety developments – similar to those developed in aviation – the biggest problem to address, is ever frailer patients, usually at the fringes of life. The very young* and old – requiring medical management throughout the perioperative period.

Recognizing this, five Anesthesiology Chairs – leading prominent University Departments – put pen to paper authoring: [the] "Future of Anesthesiology is Perioperative Medicine: a Call for Action,"[1] echoing similar sentiments of anaesthetic colleagues around the world.[2]

*

* Fetal surgery, while the baby is still in the mother's uterus, is increasingly being performed. Around 1500 cases a year in the U.S.A.

Perioperative medicine – the medical management of the surgical patient – is conveniently divided into *preoperative, intraoperative* and *postoperative* periods, which provides a useful framework for predicting the future. A perilous task at best.

Preoperative Period: Medical Optimization and Precision Medicine

Frailty – loosely defined as the more a patient has medically wrong with them – is associated with poor post-operative outcomes; increasing morbidity and mortality after surgery. Making intuitive sense, the concept of frailty is only recently driving medical optimization of patients using such approaches as strength training, enhanced calorie and vitamin intake preoperatively, and adjustment of medications and therapy to render patients optimal before elective surgery.[3, 4]

- Expect heightened efforts at establishing Anesthesia Preoperative Optimization Centers.

- Expect the realization of perioperative precision medicine to take much longer than we first thought, as the complexity of the relationship between genomic analysis and its expression in humans becomes better understood.

Perioperative Precision Medicine holds future promise.[5] In its infancy at this time, Precision Medicine seeks to harness the predictive power of genomic medicine into anesthesia practice. A knowledge of the genomic signature of a patient guiding the specific tailoring of drug administration to the patient's requirements to improve outcome from both surgery and anesthesia. The vision: a prospective surgical patient spits into a container. His saliva instantly assessed using Point of Care Testing for targeted genes that are known to affect drug metabolism or postoperative outcomes (like malignant hyperthermia) using a micro-array chip. The anesthesiologist presented with a genomic blueprint for her patient – uploaded into the electronic medical record – guiding perioperative medical therapy precisely according to the patient's profile.

Intra-operative Period: Drugs/Equipment/ Monitoring/System Science Improvements

Drugs

There is an outside chance – predicted before, but not yet realized – that future drug design might put anesthesiologists out of a job. At least the job of managing the complications or side effects associated with the administration of today's anesthetics like propofol and sevoflurane, which are non-specific in their actions. Non-specific in not only providing anesthesia, but having multiple other sites of action in the body. Advances in structural pharmacology and biology holding out the promise – using sophisticated techniques like X-ray crystallography and nuclear magnetic resonance spectroscopy – to define exactly the location of anesthetic action in neural circuits by providing, in exquisite detail, where these agents work (so avoiding side-effects from the anesthetics binding at other sites). Then using the nascent DREADD* approach to target specifically these pathways (and non-other) incorporating future designed biodegradable micro LEDs[†] for optogenic (light) activation. Induction of anesthesia – far in the future – performed simply by the shifting of a light switch: on or off.[6, 7, 8]

Nearer in the future are attempts to reverse the effects of anesthetics by central nervous activation. While in the past we have reversed the effects of benzodiazepine sedatives (with Flumazenil) and narcotics (with Naloxone) working specifically at receptor sites for these drugs in the body, there are now animal and preclinical human studies suggesting that anesthesia can be reversed using methylphenidate (Ritalin). Holding the promise, that in the future, anesthesiologists will be able to far more predictably "wake up" the patient after a deep anesthetic.

Equipment

- Expect the development of standardization and simplification of equipment to decrease the already far too complex care environment.

---

* DREADD: Designer Receptors Exclusively Activated by Designer Drugs.
† LEDs: Light Emitting Diodes.

- Expect artificially intelligent clinical decision support tools to help anesthesiologists make sense of the overwhelming patient information that will be provided in the future.[9]

- Expect 3-D printing, better known as computer-generated "additive manufacturing" to create life-size high fidelity practice models of – for example – an individual patient's airway anatomy – based on preoperative magnetic resonance imaging scans – to prepare the anesthesiologist for the pending "difficult airway," having "practiced on plastic" before meeting the live patient.[10]

- Expect rational, industry-wide, standardized, alarm systems and a human factors design focus enhancing the anesthesiologist's ability to prioritize care – while decreasing distraction – resulting in ergonomically improved anesthesia work environments like cockpits in a Boeing aircraft.

Monitoring

Monitoring will likely shift more intensely from the heart and lungs to the brain. Using electroencephalography, depth of anesthesia will be monitored and target-controlled using computerized algorithms to automatically adjust administration of anesthetic drugs – up or down – to minimize potential damage postoperatively.[11, 12, 13]

Expect a growing focus on the monitoring of brain function to minimize deleterious effects like post-operative delirium – an increasing problem.[14, 15]

- Expect "Analgesia Nociception" monitoring devices, used to decrease opioid administration – a current trend in anesthesia – by assessing parasympathetic/sympathetic body responses to surgical stimulation. The monitored anti-nociception/nociception index balanced to tailor analgesic therapy to the specific needs of the individual patient which varies at different stages of surgery.[16]

- Expect that anesthetic techniques and drug redesign will spur anesthesiologists to cease using opioids during the perioperative period because of their many deleterious effects.

System Science Improvements

The science of medical care delivery will advance with leaps and bounds. Using the developing sciences of human factors design, process redesign, six sigma principles championed in the auto industry, and aviation-inspired safety systems and reporting; anesthetic safety will be continuously enhanced and improved.[17, 18]

- Expect a much safer surgical experience in the future.

Post-operative Period: Medical Management/ Anesthesiologist Outcomes

Medical Management

Frail patients cope poorly with the stress of surgery; experiencing at least a twenty-fold increased risk of death on the third day after surgery.[18] Screening patients for heart damage suffered intra-operatively is a possible tool helping to define those patients needing extra care. Recently an enzyme called troponin, released from the heart into the blood stream, has been associated with poorer outcomes, even though there are no clinical signs of a heart attack.[20]

Expect more deliberate medical care postoperatively attuned to the patient's preoperative condition and monitored biochemically using blood indicators of organ injury.

Anesthesiologist Outcomes

And what of the individual anesthesiologist? Can we measure the effect of their practice on an individual patient's outcomes? We thought we could back in 1985.

In a study performed in cardiac surgery assessing the anesthetic care of nine cardiac anesthesiologists, number *seven* had a higher rate of post-operative heart injury – prompting many departmental anesthesiologists to wear a T-shirt emblazoned with: "I Am Not Anesthesiologist No 7."[21]

But we are much less sure now that we can link an individual anesthesiologist's care to postoperative outcomes, because of the problems of attribution and the very complex statistics involved in the reckoning.[22, 23] Nonetheless, patients can take heart in knowing that anesthesiology is on the right track in figuring this out. A very large data base analysis of outcomes from high-risk surgery, demonstrating that complication rates are at least three-fold lower in anesthesiologists regarded as high performers, when compared to the low performers.[24]

- Expect much more research and computation into factors that can improve patient's outcomes from anesthesia and surgery.

Waking up Safer?

Are patients waking up safer?

Yes – intro-controvertibly – Yes.

But in every case?

No.

Inter-individual genetic variation and disease putting paid to that.

On average a patient will wake up much safer from anesthesia than ever before, and likely will continue to do so incrementally in the future.

Never as safe as flying in a commercial jet-liner, but certainly steadfastly safer than today.

Notes: Chapter References

An Anesthesiologist's Record

1. Beecher H. K., "The first anesthesia records." *Surg Gyn & Obs* 1940; 71:689-93.
2. Archer W. H., "Life and Letters of Horace Wells Discoverer of Anesthesia." *Journal of the American College of Dentists* 1944; 11.
3. Beecher H. K., Todd D. P. "A study of the deaths associated with anesthesia and surgery: based on a study of 599,548 anesthesias in ten institutions 1948-1952, inclusive." *Ann Surg* 1954; 140:2-35.
4. Schiff J. H., Welker A, Fohr B., Henn-Beilharz A., Bothner U., Van Aken H., Schleppers A., Baldering H. J., Heinrichs W., "Major incidents and complications in otherwise healthy patients undergoing elective procedures: results based on 1.37 million anaesthetic procedures." *Br J Anaesth* 2014; 113:109-21.
Image of Cushing Anesthesia Record used with permission from the Massachusetts General Hospital, Archives and Special Collections.

1: Beginnings

1. Cosnett J. E., Edendale Hospital, Pietermaritzburg. "The first twenty-one years." *S Afr Med J* 1975; 49:1486-91.

2: A Brief History of Anesthesia

1. Ellis E. S., *Ancient Anodynes: Primitive Anesthetics and Allied Conditions.* London: W. M. Heineman Medical Bookshops, 1946.
2. Gawande A. "Two hundred years of surgery." *N Engl J Med* 2012; 366:1716-23.
3. Eger E. I., Saidman L. J., Westhorpe R. N. "History to 1978." In: Eger E. I., Saidman L. J., Westhorpe R. N., eds. *The Wondrous Story of Anesthesia.* New York: Springer, 2014:3-10.
4. Keys T., *The History of Surgical Anesthesia.* Huntington, New York: Robert E. Krieger Publishing Company, 1978.
5. Friedman M., Friedland G. W. *Medicine's Greatest Discoveries.* New Haven and London: Yale Nota Bene, 1998.
6. Hunter W., "A Lecture, Introductory to a course on anatomy." *Lancet* 1775; 12:769-73.

7. Bankoff G., *The Conquest of Pain The Story of Anaesthesia*. London: Macdonald & Co LTD, 1941.

8. Robertson H., "Without benefit of Anesthesia: George Wilson's Amputation and Fanny Burney's Mastectomy." *Ann Royal College of Physicians Surg Can* 1989; 22:27-30.

9. Bigelow H. J., "Insensibility during surgical operations produced by inhalation." *Boston Medical and Surgical Journal* 1846:310-16.

10. Smith W., *Under the Influence: The History of Nitrous Oxide and Oxygen Anaesthesia*. London and Basingstoke: Macmillan publishers LTD, 1982.

11. Priestley J., *Experiments and Observations on Different Kinds of Air*. St. John's Church Yard, London: J. Johnson, 1775.

12. Fenster J. M., *Ether Day: The Strange Tale of America's Greatest Discovery and the Haunted Men who made it*. New York: Harper Collinsville, 2001.

13. Archer W. H., "Life and Letters of Horace Wells Discoverer of Anesthesia." *Journal of the American College of Dentists* 1944; 11.

14. Smith G. B., Hirsch N. P., "Gardner Quincy Colton: pioneer of nitrous oxide anesthesia." *Anesth Analg* 1991; 72:382-91.

15. Lord J., Lord A., *Defense of Joseph T. Jackson's Claims of the Discovery of Etherization*. Boston: Office of Littels Living Age, 1848.

16. Vandam L. D., Abbott J. A., "Edward Gilbert Abbott: enigmatic figure of the ether demonstration." *N Engl J Med* 1984; 311:991-4.

17. Long C. W., "An account of the first use of Sulphuric Ether by Inhalation as an Anaesthetic in Surgical Operations." *Southern Medical Journal* 1849; 5:705-1.

18. Atkinson R. S., Rushman R. B., Alfred Lee J., *The History of Anaesthesia. A Synopsis of Anesthesia*. Bristol: The Bath Press, 1987.

19. Snow J., *On Chloroform and Other Anaesthetics*. London: John Churchill, 1858.

20. Zeitlin G. L., *Laughing and Crying about Anesthesia: A memoir of risk and safety*. London: Allandale Publishers, 2011.

21. MacDonald A. G., "A short history of fires and explosions caused by anaesthetic agents." *Br J Anaesth* 1994; 72:710-22.

22. Johnstone M., "The human cardiovascular response to fluothane anaesthesia." *Br J Anaesth* 1956; 28:392-410.

3: Senior House Office – Anesthetics

1. Snow J., *On the Inhalation of the vapor of ether in surgical operations*. London: John Churchill, 1847.

2. Goldsmith D., Trieger N., "Accidental intra-arterial injection: a medical emergency." *Anesth Prog* 1975; 22:180-3.

3. Maltby J., *Notable Names in Anaesthesia*. London: The Choir Press, 2000.

4. Hewitt F., "The Past Present and Future of Anaesthesia." *British Medical Journal* 1896:347-56.

5. Denborough M. A., Forster J. F., Lovell R. R., Maplestone P. A., Villiers J. D., "Anaesthetic deaths in a family." *Br J Anaesth* 1962; 34:395-6.

6. Denborough M., "Malignant hyperthermia." *Lancet* 1998; 352:1131-6.

7. Harrison G. G., Saunders S. J., Biebuyck J. F., Hickman R., Dent D. M., Weaver V., Terblanche J., "Anaesthetic-induced malignant hyperpyrexia and a method for its prediction." *Br J Anaesth* 1969; 41:844-55.

8. Harrison G. G., "Control of the malignant hyperpyrexic syndrome in MHS swine

by dantrolene sodium." *Br J Anaesth* 1975; 47:62-5.

9. Steven R. J., Tovell R. M., Johnson J. C., Delgado E., "Anesthesia for electroconvulsive therapy." *Anesthesiology*. 1954; 15:623-36.

4: Lines of the Parachute to Safety

1. Shephard D., *From Craft to Specialty*. Thunder Bay, Ontario: York Point Publishing, 2009.
2. Beecher H. K., Todd D. P., "A study of the deaths associated with anesthesia and surgery: based on a study of 599,548 anesthesias in ten institutions 1948-1952." *Ann Surg* 1954; 140:2-35.
3. Schiff J. H., Welker A., Fohr B., Henn-Beilharz A., Bothner U., Van Aken H., Schleppers A., Baldering H. J., Heinrichs W., "Major incidents and complications in otherwise healthy patients undergoing elective procedures: results based on 1.37 million anaesthetic procedures." *Br J Anaesth* 2014; 113:109-21.
4. Syed M., *Black Box Thinking*. London: John Murray, 2015.
5. Zeitlin G. L., *Laughing and Crying about Anesthesia: A memoir of risk and safety*. London: Allandale Publishers, 2011.
6. Hewitt F., "The Past Present and Future of Anaesthesia." *British Medical Journal* 1896:347-56.
7. Shrady A., "Plea for Public Anaeshetizers." *Medical Record: A Weekly Journal of Medicine and Surgery* 1894; August 25:239-40.
8. Goldan S., "Anesthetization as a Speciality: Its Present and Future." *American Medicine 1901*; July:1-10.
9. Snow J., *On the Inhalation of the vapor of ether in surgical operations*. London: John Churchill, 1847.
10. Ellis R. H., *On Narcotism by the Inhalation of Vapors by John Snow*. London: Royal Society of Medicine Service Limited, 1991.
11. Thomas K. B., *The Development of Anaesthetic Apparatus*. London: Blackwell Scientific Publications, 1975.
12. Bunker J. P., "Summary of the National Halothane Study. Possible association between halothane anesthesia and postoperative hepatic necrosis." *Journal of the American Medical Association* 1966; 197:775-88.
13. Bunker J. P., "Final Report of the National Halothane Study." *Anesthesiology* 1968; 29:231-2.
14. Cushing H., "On routine determination of arterial tension in operating room and clinic." *Boston Medical and Surgical Journal* 1903; CXLVIII:250-6.
15. Sessler D. I., Sigl J. C., Kelley S. D., Chamoun N. G. , Manberg P. J., Saager L., Kurz A., Greenwald S., "Hospital stay and mortality are increased in patients having a "triple low" of low blood pressure, low bispectral index, and low minimum alveolar concentration of volatile anesthesia." *Anesthesiology* 2012; 116:1195-203.
16. Maltby J., *Notable Names in Anaesthesia*. London: The Choir Press, 2000.
17. Gale J. W., Waters R. M., "Closed endobronchial Anesthesia in Thoracic Surgery." *Anesth Analg* 1932; November-December:283-8.
18. Cooper J. B., Newbower R. S., Long C. D., McPeek B., "Preventable anesthesia mishaps: a study of human factors." *Anesthesiology* 1978; 49:399-406.
19. Stoelting R., Anesthesia Patient Safety Foundation Website. www.apsforg/about_historyphp; accessed June 2016.

5: Magic! The Unfolding Mystery of Anesthesia

1. Purdon P. L., Pierce E. T., Mukamel E. A. , Prerau M. J., Walsh J. L., Wong K. F., Salazar-Gomez A. F., Harrell P. G., Sampson A. L., Cimenser A., Ching S., Kopell N. J., Tavares-Stoeckel C., Habeeb K., Merhar R., Brown E. N., "Electroencephalogram signatures of loss and recovery of consciousness from propofol." *Proc Natl Acad Sci* 2013; 110:E1142-51.
2. Kennedy D., Norman C., "What don't we know?" *Science* 2005; 309:75.
3. Brown E. N., Purdon P. L., Van Dort C. J., "General anesthesia and altered states of arousal: a systems neuroscience analysis." *Annu Rev Neurosci* 2011; 34:601-28.
4. Quasha A. L., Eger E., 2nd, Tinker J. H., "Determination and applications of MAC." *Anesthesiology* 1980; 53:315-34.
5. Franks N. P., Lieb W. R., "Do general anaesthetics act by competitive binding to specific receptors?" *Nature* 1984; 310:599-601.
6. Franks N. P., Lieb W. R., "Seeing the light: protein theories of general anesthesia." 1984. *Anesthesiology* 2004; 101:235-7.
7. Brown E. N., Lydic R., Schiff N. D., "General anesthesia, sleep, and coma." *N Engl J Med* 2010; 363:2638-50.
8. Zeitlin G. L., *Laughing and Crying about Anesthesia: A memoir of risk and safety.* London: Allandale Publishers, 2011.
9. Hudetz A. G., Mashour G. A., "Disconnecting Consciousness: Is There a Common Anesthetic End Point?" *Anesth Analg* 2016.
10. Purdon P. L., Sampson A., Pavone K. J., Brown E. N., "Clinical Electroencephalography for Anesthesiologists: Part I: Background and Basic Signatures." *Anesthesiology* 2015; 123:937-60.
11. Warnaby C. E., Seretny M., Ni Mhuircheartaigh R., Rogers R., Jbabdi S., Sleigh J., Tracey I., "Anesthesia-induced Suppression of Human Dorsal Anterior Insula Responsivity at Loss of Volitional Behavioral Response." *Anesthesiology* 2016; 124:766-78.
12. Mashour G. A,. "Network-level Mechanisms of Ketamine Anesthesia." *Anesthesiology* 2016; 125:830-31.
13. Mashour G. A., "Anesthetizing the Self: The Neurobiology of Humbug." *Anesthesiology* 2016; 124:747-9.
14. Pandit J., Cook T., "Accidental Awareness Under General Anesthesia in the United Kingdom and Ireland." *National Audit Project Five Report.* 2014.
15. Avidan M. S., Jacobsohn E., Glick D., Burnside B. A., Zhang L., Villafranca A., Karl L., Kamal S., Torres B., O'Connor M., Evers A. S., Gradwohl S., Lin N., Palanca B. J., Mashour G. A., Group B-RR., "Prevention of intraoperative awareness in a high-risk surgical population." *N Engl J Med* 2011; 365:591-600.
16. Bedford P. D., "Adverse cerebral effects of anaesthesia on old people." *Lancet* 1955; 269:259-63.
17. Fritz B. A., Kalarickal P. L., Maybrier H. R., Muench M. R., Dearth D., Chen Y., Escallier K. E., Ben Abdallah A., Lin N., Avidan M. S., "Intraoperative Electroencephalogram Suppression Predicts Postoperative Delirium." *Anesth Analg* 2016; 122:234-42.
18. Berger M., Nadler J. W., Browndyke J., Terrando N., Ponnusamy V., Cohen H. J., Whitson H. E., Mathew J. P., "Postoperative Cognitive Dysfunction: Minding the Gaps in Our Knowledge of a Common Postoperative Complication in the Elderly." *Anesthesiol Clin* 2015; 33:517-50.
19. Ballard C., Jones E., Gauge N., Aarsland D., Nilsen O. B., Saxby B. K., Lowery D.,

Corbett A., Wesnes K., Katsaiti E., Arden J., Amoako D., Prophet N., Purushothaman B., Green D., "Optimised anaesthesia to reduce post operative cognitive decline (POCD) in older patients undergoing elective surgery, a randomised controlled trial." *PLoS One* 2012; 7:e37410.

20. Chan M. T., Cheng B. C., Lee T. M., Gin T., Group C. T., "BIS-guided anesthesia decreases postoperative delirium and cognitive decline." *J Neurosurg Anesthesiol* 2013; 25:33-42.

21. Avidan M. S., Evers A. S., "Review of clinical evidence for persistent cognitive decline or incident dementia attributable to surgery or general anesthesia." *J Alzheimers Dis* 2011; 24:201-16.

22. Ikonomidou C., Bosch F., Miksa M., Bittigau P., Vockler J., Dikranian K., Tenkova T. I., Stefovska V., Turski L., Olney J. W., "Blockade of NMDA receptors and apoptotic neurodegeneration in the developing brain." *Science* 1999; 283:70-4.

23. Jevtovic-Todorovic V., Hartman R. E., Izumi Y., Benshoff N. D., Dikranian K., Zorumski C. F., Olney J. W., Wozniak D. F., "Early exposure to common anesthetic agents causes widespread neurodegeneration in the developing rat brain and persistent learning deficits." *J Neurosci* 2003;23:876-82.

24. Mellon R. D., Simone AF, Rappaport BA. "Use of anesthetic agents in neonates and young children." *Anesth Analg* 2007; 104:509-20.

25. Davidson A. J., et. al. "Consortium GAS. Neurodevelopmental outcome at 2 years of age after general anaesthesia and awake-regional anaesthesia in infancy (GAS): an international multicentre, randomised controlled trial." Lancet 2016; 387:239-50.

6: Drugs, Equipment and Monitors – An Alarming Situation

1. Davis D., *The Collapse and Resuscitation of Intravenous Anesthesia.* Philadelphia: F. A. Davis, 1968.

2. Lundy J. S., "Intravenous Anesthesia." *American Journal of Surgery* 1936; December:559-70.

3. Shephard D., *From Craft to Specialty.* Thunder Bay, Ontario: York Point Publishing, 2009.

4. Griffith H., Johnson E., "The use of curare in general anesthesia." *Anesthesiology* 1942; 3:418-20.

5. Stanley T. H., Egan T. D., Van Aken H., "A tribute to Dr. Paul A. J. Janssen: Entrepreneur extraordinaire, innovative scientist, and significant contributor to anesthesiology." *Anesth Analg* 2008; 106:451-62.

6. Mets B., "Management of hypotension associated with angiotensin-axis blockade and general anesthesia administration." *J Cardiothorac Vasc Anesth* 2013; 27:156-67.

7. Mets B., "Should norepineprhine, not phenylephrine be the primary vasopressor in anesthetic practice?" *Anesth Analg* 2016; 122:1707-14.

8. Mets B., "Flumazenil-- a novel benzodiazepine antagonist." *S Afr Med J* 1990; 77:59-60.

9. Snow J., *On the Inhalation of the vapor of ether in surgical operations.* London: John Churchill, 1847.

10. Maltby J., *Notable Names in Anaesthesia.* London: The Choir Press, 2000.

11. Macewen W., "General Observations on the Introduction of Tracheal Tubes by the Mouth, Instead of Performing Tracheotomy or Laryngotomy." *Br Med J* 1880; 2:122-4.

12. Aziz MF, Brambrink A. M., Healy D. W., Willett A. W., Shanks A., Tremper T.,

Jameson L., Ragheb J., Biggs D. A., Paganelli W. C., Rao J., Epps J. L., Colquhoun D. A., Bakke P., Kheterpal S., "Success of Intubation Rescue Techniques after Failed Direct Laryngoscopy in Adults: A Retrospective Comparative Analysis from the Multicenter Perioperative Outcomes Group." *Anesthesiology* 2016; 125:656-66.

13. Nosworthy M. D., "Anaesthesia in Chest Surgery, with Special Reference to Controlled Respiration and Cyclopropane." *Proc R Soc Med* 1941; 34:479-506.

14. McKenzie A. G., "The inventions of John Blease." *Br J Anaesth* 2000; 85:928-35.

15. Swan H. J., Ganz W., Forrester J., Marcus H., Diamond G., Chonette D., "Catheterization of the heart in man with use of a flow-directed balloon-tipped catheter." *N Engl J Med* 1970; 283:447-51.

16. Haynes A. B., Weiser T. G., Berry W. R., Lipsitz S. R., Breizat A. H., Dellinger E. P., Herbosa T., Joseph S., Kibatala P. L., Lapitan M. C., Merry A. F., Moorthy K., Reznick R. K., Taylor B., Gawande A. A., "Safe Surgery Saves Lives Study G. A surgical safety checklist to reduce morbidity and mortality in a global population." *N Engl J Med* 2009; 360:491-9.

17. Alert J. C. S. E., Medical Device Alarm Safety in Hospitals. www.jointcommissionorg/assets/1/6/SEA_50_alarms_4_26_16pdf 2013; April 8.

18. Avidan M. S., Jacobsohn E., Glick D., Burnside B. A., Zhang L., Villafranca A., Karl L., Kamal S., Torres B., O'Connor M., Evers A. S., Gradwohl S., Lin N., Palanca B. J., Mashour G. A., Group B-RR., "Prevention of intraoperative awareness in a high-risk surgical population." *N Engl J Med* 2011; 365:591-600.

19. Murphy G. S., Kopman A. F., "To Reverse or Not To Reverse?: The Answer Is Clear!" *Anesthesiology* 2016; 125:611-4.

Boyles Machine, Image courtesy of Wood Library-Museum of Anesthesiology, Schaumburg, Illinois U.S.A. Lifebox Pulseoximeter, personal image, with permission, Lifebox Foundation U.K.

7: Specialization – Anesthetic Registrar, University of Cape Town

1. Hewitt F., "The Past Present and Future of Anaesthesia." *British Medical Journal* 1896:347-56.

2. Parbhoo N., *"The Department of Anaesthesia – UCT 1920-2000. – A History,"* Doctor of Medicine Thesis, 2002, University of Cape Town.

3. Bateman C., "E. A compelling new specialty." *S Afr Med J* 2001; 91:25-7.

4. Flood P., Rollins M. D., "Anesthesia for Obstetrics." In: Miller R. D., ed. *Miller's Anesthesia.* Eighth ed. Philadelphia, PA: Elsevier, Saunders, 2015:2328-58.

5. Lillehei C. W., Dewall R. A., "Design and clinical application of the Helix reservoir pump-oxygenator system for extracorporeal circulation." *Postgrad Med* 1958; 23:561-73.

6. Dewall R. A., Gott V. L., Lillehei C. W., Read R. C., Varco R. L., Warden H. E., Ziegler N. R., "A simple, expendable, artificial oxygenator for open heart surgery." *Surg Clin North Am* 1956:1025-34.

7. Barnard C. N., Pepper C. B., *One Life.* Toronto, Ontario, Canada: The Macmillan Company, 1969.

8. Ozinsky J., "Cardiac transplantation --the anaesthetist's view: a case report." *S Afr Med J* 1967; 41:1268-70.

9. Mets B., "Cardiac Pharmacology." In: Thys DM, Hillel Z, Schwartz AJ, eds. *TextBook of Cardiothoracic Pharmacology*: McGraw-Hill Companies Inc., 2001:404-32.

10. Gordon P. C., Brink J. G., "Forty years on: the anesthetic for the world's first human-to-human heart transplant remembered." *J Cardiothorac Vasc Anesth* 2008; 22:133-8.

11. Bull A. B., Ozinsky J., Harrison G. G., "The clinical use of halothane anaesthesia during cardiopulmonary bypass for open-heart surgery." *Br J Anaesth* 1960; 32:164-70.

12. Barnard C. N., "The operation. A human cardiac transplant: an interim report of a successful operation performed at Groote Schuur Hospital, Cape Town." *S Afr Med J* 1967; 41:1271-4.

13. Robertshaw F. L., "Low resistance double-lumen endobronchial tubes." *Br J Anaesth* 1962; 34:576-9.

14. Mets B., "Anesthesia for empyema drainage in a patient with a bronchopleural fistula." *American Society of Anesthesiology National Meetings, Dallas & San Francisco 1999, 2000;* Problem Based Learning Discussion.

15. Hall S. C., Suresh S., "Neonatal Anesthesia." In: Barash P. G., ed, *Clinical Anesthesia* Philadelphia: Wolters Kluwer, 2009:1171-205.

16. Harrison G. G., "Control of the malignant hyperpyrexic syndrome in MHS swine by dantrolene sodium." *Br J Anaesth* 1975; 47:62-5.

17. Pollock NA, Machon RG, Rosenberg H. "Early Development, Identification of Mode of Action, and Use of Dantrolene Sodium: The Role of Keith Ellis, Ph.D." *Anesthesiology* 2017; 126:774-9.

18. Denborough M., "Malignant hyperthermia." *Lancet* 1998; 352:1131-6.

19. Denborough M. A., Forster J. F., Lovell R. R., Maplestone P. A., Villiers J. D., "Anaesthetic deaths in a family." *Br J Anaesth* 1962; 34:395-6.

20. Drinker P., McKhann C. F., "The use of a new apparatus for the prolonged administration of artifical respiration." *JAMA* 1929;92:1658-60.

21. Lassen H. C., "A preliminary report on the 1952 epidemic of poliomyelitis in Copenhagen with special reference to the treatment of acute respiratory insufficiency." *Lancet* 1953;1:37-41.

22. Ibsen B., "The anaesthetist's viewpoint on the treatment of respiratory complications in poliomyelitis with special reference to the treatment of respiratory insufficiency." *Proc Roy Soc Med* 1952;47:72-5.

23. Berthelsen P. G., Cronqvist M., "The first intensive care unit in the world: Copenhagen 1953." *Acta Anaesthesiol Scand* 2003; 47:1190-5.

24. Smythe PM, Bull AB. "Treatment of Tetanus." *Br Med J* 1961; 2:732-6.

25. Smythe P. M., Bowie M. D., Voss T. J., "Treatment of tetanus neonatorum with muscle relaxants and intermittent positive-pressure ventilation." *Br Med J* 1974;1:223-6.

26. Mets B., *Lignocaine extraction ratio and clearance as an indicator of hypoxic hepatic injury. A study using the in situ and the isolated perfused pig liver.* PhD Thesis 1992; University of Cape Town.

27. Butt A. D., Mets B., "Cardiovascular and respiratory effects of oral premedication with trimeprazine and droperidol in children." *S Afr Med J* 1988; 73:582-3.

28. Mets B., Hickman R., Allin R., Dyk J. V., Lotz Z., "Effect of hypoxia on the hepatic metabolism of lidocaine in the isolated perfused pig liver." *Hepatology* 1993; 19:668-76.

8: Outcomes – APGAR Scores & Other Stratagems

1. Sessler D. I., Sigl J. C., Kelley S. D., Chamoun N. G., Manberg P. J., Saager L., Kurz A., Greenwald S., "Hospital stay and mortality are increased in patients having a

"triple low" of low blood pressure, low bi-spectral index, and low minimum alveolar concentration of volatile anesthesia." *Anesthesiology* 2012; 116:1195-203.

2. International Surgical Outcomes Study. "Global patient outcomes after elective surgery: prospective cohort study in 27 low-, middle- and high-income countries." *Br J Anaesth* 2016; 117:601-9.

3. Gawande A., *The Checklist Manifesto*. New York: Picador, 2009.

4. Apgar V., "A proposal for a new method of evaluation of the newborn infant." *Curr Res Anesth Analg* 1953; 32:260-7.

5. Butterfield J., Covey M. J., "Practical Epigram of the Apgar Score." *Journal of the American Medical Association* 1961; 181:353.

6. Hardy J. B., "The Collaborative Perinatal Project: lessons and legacy." *Ann Epidemiol* 2003; 13:303-11.

7. Drage J. S., Kennedy C., Berendes H., Schwarz B. K., Weiss W., "The Apgar score as an index of infant morbidity. A report from the collaborative study of cerebral palsy." *Dev Med Child Neurol* 1966; 8:141-8.

8. Apgar V., Holaday D. A., James L. S., Weisbrot I. M., Berrien C., "Evaluation of the newborn infant; second report." *J Am Med Assoc* 1958; 168:1985-8.

9. Guglielminotti J., Wong C. A., Landau R., Li G.,"Temporal Trends in Anesthesia-related Adverse Events in Cesarean Deliveries, New York State, 2003-2012." *Anesthesiology* 2015; 123:1013-23.

10. Owens W. D., Felts J. A., Spitznagel E. L., Jr. "ASA physical status classifications: a study of consistency of ratings." *Anesthesiology* 1978; 49:239-43.

11. Dripps R. D., Lamont A., Eckenhoff J. E., "The role of anesthesia in surgical mortality." *JAMA* 1961; 178:261-6.

12. Le Manach Y., Collins G., Rodseth R., Le Bihan-Benjamin C., Biccard B., Riou B., Devereaux PJ, Landais P. "Preoperative Score to Predict Postoperative Mortality (POSPOM): Derivation and Validation." *Anesthesiology* 2016; 124:570-9.

13. Haynes A. B., Weiser T. G., Berry W. R., Lipsitz S. R., Breizat A. H., Dellinger E. P., Herbosa T., Joseph S., Kibatala P. L., Lapitan M. C., Merry A. F., Moorthy K., Reznick R. K., Taylor B., Gawande A. A., "Safe Surgery Saves Lives Study G. A surgical safety checklist to reduce morbidity and mortality in a global population." *N Engl J Med* 2009; 360:491-9.

14. Salmasi V., Maheshwari K., Yang D., Mascha E. J., Singh A., Sessler D. I., Kurz A., "Relationship between Intraoperative Hypotension, Defined by Either Reduction from Baseline or Absolute Thresholds, and Acute Kidney and Myocardial Injury after Noncardiac Surgery: A Retrospective Cohort Analysis." *Anesthesiology* 2017; 126:47-65.

15. Mets B., "Management of hypotension associated with angiotensin-axis blockade and general anesthesia administration." *J Cardiothorac Vasc Anesth* 2013; 27:156-67.

16. Blitz J. D., Kendale S. M., Jain S. K., Cuff G. E., Kim J. T., Rosenberg A. D., "Preoperative Evaluation Clinic Visit Is Associated with Decreased Risk of In-hospital Postoperative Mortality." *Anesthesiology* 2016; 125:280-94.

17. Carli F., "Henrik Kehlet, M.D., Ph.D., recipient of the 2014 Excellence in Research Award." *Anesthesiology* 2014; 121:690-1.

18. Kehlet H., "Multimodal approach to control postoperative pathophysiology and rehabilitation." *Br J Anaesth* 1997; 78:606-17.

19. Kehlet H., Wilmore D. W., "Multimodal strategies to improve surgical outcome." *Am J Surg* 2002; 183:630-41.

20. Meilinger P. S., "When the Fortress Went Down." *Air Force Magazine* 2004:78-82.

21. Kavanagh B. P., Nurok M., "Standardized Intensive Care. Protocol Misalignment and Impact Misattribution." *Am J Respir Crit Care Med* 2016; 193:17-22.
Image "Crashed Boeing B17 Bomber" National Museum of the U.S. Air Force picture collection. Available to the public for distribution. Downloaded Oct 13, 2017.

9: Perfecting Practice – Assistant Professor, Columbia University

1. Mets B., "Anesthesia for left ventricular assist device placement." *J Cardiothorac Vasc Anesth* 2000; 14:316-26.
2. Mets B., "Current status of lung volume reduction." *Current opinion in anesthesiology* 2000; 13.61-64.
3. Mehta N., Goswami S., Argenziano M., Smith C. R., Mets B., "Anesthesia for robotic repair of the mitral valve: a report of two cases." *Anesth Analg* 2003; 96:7-10.
Image: Columbia Presbyterian Medical Cente:., Archives and Special Collections, Columbia University Health Sciences Library, 701 West 168th St, New York, N.Y. 10032

10: Complications – Things Don't Always Go Well

1. Syed M., *Black Box Thinking.* London: John Murray, 2015.
2. Harmer M.,"Independent Review on the care given to Mrs. Elaine Bromiley on 29 March 2005." www.chfgorg/w-content/uploads/2010/11/ElaineBromileyAnonymousReportpdf 2005:1-18.
3. Bromiley M., Clinical Human Factors Group Website Video: *Just a routine operation.* http://chfgorg/learning-resources/just-a-routine-operation-teaching-video/ 2017.
4. Leslie I., "How mistakes can save lives: one man's mission to revolutionize the NHS." *New Statesman* 2014.
5. Bromiley M., *Clinical Human Factors Group, Strategy and Manifesto Document.* 2011; May 16:1-11.
6. Chrimes N., "The Vortex: a universal 'high-acuity implementation tool' for emergency airway management." *Br J Anaesth* 2016;117 Suppl 1:i20-i7.
7. Bromiley M.,*"What If"* Video. Australian Center of Health Innovation 2014; Society of Airway Management, Seattle Washington. First Public Presentation: http://simpact.net.au/bromiley.html.
The Vortex Diagram: "The Vortex Approach to Airway Managemen" provided with permission by Dr. Nicholas Chrimes, the originator of this new approach to airway management, Melbourne, Australia.

11: Professor – Flying the Anesthesia Machine, Penn State University

1. Goswami S., Kumar P. A., Mets B., "Anesthesia for Robotically Conducted Surgery." In: Miller RD, ed. *Miller's Anesthesia.* 8th ed. Philadelphia: Elsevier, 2015:2581-97.

Epilogue – First Day and the Future

1. Kain Z. N., Fitch J. C., Kirsch J. R., Mets B., Pearl R. G., "Future of anesthesiology is perioperative medicine: a call for action." *Anesthesiology* 2015;122:1192-5.

2. Cannesson M., Ani F., Mythen M. M., Kain Z., "Anaesthesiology and perioperative medicine around the world: different names, same goals." *Br J Anaesth* 2015; 114:8-9.

3. Graham A., Brown Ct., "Frailty, Aging, and Cardiovascular Surgery." *Anesth Analg* 2017; 124:1053-60.

4. Hall D. E., Arya S., Schmid K. K., Carlson M. A., Lavedan P., Bailey T. L., Purviance G., Bockman T., Lynch T. G., Johanning J. M., "Association of a Frailty Screening Initiative With Postoperative Survival at 30, 180, and 365 Days." *JAMA Surg* 2017; 152:233-40.

5. Iravani M., Lee L. K., Cannesson M., "Standardized Care Versus Precision Medicine in the Perioperative Setting: Can Point-of-Care Testing Help Bridge the Gap?" *Anesth Analg* 2017; 124:1347-53.

6. Smith K. S., Bucci D. J., Luikart B. W., Mahler S. V., "DREADDS: Use and application in behavioral neuroscience." *Behav Neurosci* 2016; 130:137-55.

7. LeBard D. N., Henin J., Eckenhoff R. G., Klein M. L., Brannigan G., "General anesthetics predicted to block the GLIC pore with micromolar affinity." *PLoS Comput Biol* 2012; 8:e1002532.

8. Fowler C. D., Lee B., Kenny P. J., "Using Optogenics and Designer Receptors Exclusively Activated by Designer Drugs (DREADDs)." *Dana Alliance* 2014; June.

9. Beam A. L., Kohane I. S., "Translating Artificial Intelligence Into Clinical Care." *JAMA* 2016; 316:2368-9.

10. "Briefing. Additive Manufacturing. The factories of the future." *Economist* 2017. July 1st-7th:19-22.

11. Purdon P. L., Sampson A., Pavone K. J., Brown E. N., "Clinical Electroencephalography for Anesthesiologists: Part I: Background and Basic Signatures." *Anesthesiology* 2015; 123:937-60.

12. Avidan M. S., Mashour G. A., "Mind the gap: attitudes towards intraoperative brain monitoring." *Anesth Analg* 2014; 119:1022-5.

13. Wildes T. S., et. al. "Protocol for the Electroencephalography Guidance of Anesthesia to Alleviate Geriatric Syndromes (ENGAGES) study: a pragmatic, randomised clinical trial." *BMJ Open* 2016; 6:e011505.

14. Mashour G. A., Woodrum D. T., Avidan M. S., "Neurological complications of surgery and anaesthesia." *Br J Anaesth* 2015; 114:194-203.

15. Fritz B. A., Kalarickal P. L., Maybrier H. R., Muench M. R., Dearth D., Chen Y., Escallier K. E., Ben Abdallah A., Lin N., Avidan M. S., "Intraoperative Electroencephalogram Suppression Predicts Postoperative Delirium." *Anesth Analg* 2016; 122:234-42.

16. Daccache G., Jeanne M., Fletcher D., "The Analgesia Nociception Index: Tailoring Opioid Administration." *Anesth Analg* 2017;125:15-7.

17. Rathmell J. P., Sandberg W. S., "Anesthesiologists and Healthcare Redesign: Time to Team Up with Experts." *Anesthesiology* 2016; 125:618-21.

18. Syed M., *Black Box Thinking*. London: John Murray, 2015.

19. McIsaac D. I., Moloo H., Bryson G. L., van Walraven C., "The Association of Frailty With Outcomes and Resource Use After Emergency General Surgery: A Population-Based Cohort Study." *Anesth Analg* 2017; 124:1653-61.

20. Writing Committee for the VSI, Devereaux P. J., et. al. "Association of Postoperative High-Sensitivity Troponin Levels With Myocardial Injury and 30-Day Mortality Among Patients Undergoing Noncardiac Surgery." *JAMA* 2017;317:1642-51.

21. Slogoff S., Keats A. S., "Does perioperative myocardial ischemia lead to postoperative

myocardial infarction?" *Anesthesiology* 1985; 62:107-14.

22. Glance L. G., Kellermann A. L., Hannan E. L., Fleisher L. A., Eaton M. P., Dutton R. P., Lustik S. J., Li Y., Dick A. W., "The impact of anesthesiologists on coronary artery bypass graft surgery outcomes." *Anesth Analg* 2015; 120:526-33.

23. Glance L. G., Hannan E. L., Fleisher L. A., Eaton M. P., Dutton R. P., Lustik S. J., Li Y., Dick A. W., "Feasibility of Report Cards for Measuring Anesthesiologist Quality for Cardiac Surgery." *Anesth Analg* 2016; 122:1603-13.

24. Kheterpal S., Abstract BOC01 "A Study Measuring the Effect of Anesthesiologist Practice on Surgical Outcomes." American Society of Anesthesiology National Meeting Chicago 2016; Reported on in *Anesthesiology News*, March 2017, by Michael Vlesside,:1,30.

Front Cover Picture: Dr. Mets admiring the painting: "Ether Day, 1846" by Lucia and Warren Prosperi, (2000). Used with permission from the Massachusetts General Hospital, Archives and Special Collections. The painting was commissioned by the Massachusetts General Hospital and hangs on the front wall of the Ether Dome Historical Theater. Professor Mets has just delivered a lecture entitled, "A Brief History of Anesthesia – A Balance Between Life and Death," to the Department of Anesthesia, Critical Care and Pain Medicine, Harvard Medical School at the Massachusetts General Hospital. Photographer Dr. Paul Firth. August 31, 2017.

Back Cover: imprint of current day paper anesthesia record.

Praise

I adore your writing style. Very engaging and lots of fun. You really do capture the wild-wild west of our young years.
– *Dr. Mehmet Oz, Cardiac Surgeon, Author, & Dr. Oz Show Host. New York, U.S.A.*

Good stories make history come alive and Dr. Mets' book is full of good stories.
– *Dr. David Wilkinson, Laureate of the Wood Library Museum & Past President of the History of Anaesthesia Society. London, U.K.*

Drawing on his extensive experience, knowledge and ability to tell a good tale, Dr. Mets takes the reader on an entertaining journey describing how anaesthesia came to be the safe and secure foundation of today's effective and complex surgery.
– *Dr. Paul Clyburn, President, Association of Anaesthetists of Great Britain & Ireland. London, U.K.*

83730601R00161

Made in the USA
Middletown, DE
14 August 2018